AUDITING FOR ENVIRONMENTAL QUALITY LEADERSHIP

AUDITING FOR ENVIRONMENTAL QUALITY LEADERSHIP

Beyond Compliance to Environmental Excellence

Edited by John T. Willig

In cooperation with the Environmental
Auditing Roundtable

John Wiley & Sons, Inc.
New York   Chichester   Brisbane   Toronto   Singapore

The following articles were previously published in a slightly different form in *Total Quality Environmental Management*: *Environmental Leadership: EPA's "Beyond Compliance" Pilot Program, Evaluating Management Systems as Part of Environmental Audits; Toward Effective Environmental Auditing at the TVA—Management Audits Versus Compliance Audits; GEMI's Environmental Self-Assessment Program (EASP), Using GEMI's Environmental Self-Assessment; Certification of Environmental Management Systems—for ISO 9000 and Competitive Advantage; The European Eco-label and Audit Scheme: New Environmental Standards for Competing Abroad; Voluntary Standards: Fit or Folly for TQEM?; Environmental Cost Accounting: The Bottom Line for Environmental Quality Management; Council of Great Lakes Industries' Framework and Assessment Tool for Implementing TQEM; Selecting Measures for Corporate Environmental Quality: Examples from TQEM Companies; Quality Metrics in Design for Environment, Benchmarking Environmental Audit Programs: Best Practices and Biggest Challenges; Audit and Root Cause Analysis; Environmental Auditor Qualifications: Meeting New, Rigorous Demands for Quality Audits; Applying TQM to Environmental Site Assessments under the ASTM Standard; Continuous Improvement Through Environmental Auditing at AlliedSignal; Auditing for Environmental Excellence at Union Carbide; Environmental Auditing and Continuous Improvement at Lockheed; Preparing Quality Audit Reports: Ten Steps (and Some Leaps) to Improve Auditing; Evaluating Your Environmental Audit—Moving Beyond Band-Aids in Developing Corrective Actions; Environmental Auditing Roundtable Establishes Formal Standards for Environmental, Health, and Safety Audits; The Power of IT: How Can Information Technology Support TQEM?; and Browning-Ferris Industries' Computerized System for Managing Audit and Environmental Performance.*

The following article was published in the *Federal Facilities Environmental Journal: RCRA Inspections and Enforcement.*

Library of Congress Cataloging-in-Publication Data

Auditing for environmental quality leadership: beyond compliance to environmental excellence/edited
by John T. Willig; in cooperation with the Environmental Auditing Roundtable.
     p.   cm.
  Includes bibliographical references and index.
  ISBN 0-471-11492-8 (acid-free paper)
    1. Industrial management--Environmental aspects--United States.
  2. Environmental audit--United States. 3. Total quality management--United States. I. Willig, John
T. II. Environmental Auditing Roundtable.
  HD30.255.A93 1995
  658.4'08--dc20   94-47037
                                                  CIP

Printed in the United States of America

10 9 8 7 6 5 4 3 2 1

Contents

SECTION ONE

Auditing for Environmental Excellence

CHAPTER 12 121

Council of Great Lakes Industries' Framework and Assessment Tool for Implementing TQEM
Grace H. Wever and George F. Vorhauer

CHAPTER 13 137

Selecting Measures for Corporate Environmental Quality: Examples from TQEM Companies
Chris FitzGerald

Quality Metrics in Design for Environment
Joseph Fiksel

SECTION FOUR

Planning Quality Management Audits

Benchmarking Environmental Audit Programs:
Best Practices and Biggest Challenges
Lawrence B. Cahill

CHAPTER 16   175

Audits and Root Cause Analysis
Randy A. Roig and Peter Schneider

CHAPTER 17   185

Environmental Auditor Qualifications:
Meeting New, Rigorous Demands for Quality Audits
Lawrence B. Cahill

CHAPTER 18   191

Evaluating Auditor Characteristics Essential for Environmental,
Health, and Safety Management Systems Assessments
J. Richard Pooler and Debora L. Jones

SECTION SIX

The Power of Information Technology

CHAPTER 27   **273**

The Power of *IT*: How Can Information Technology Support TQEM?
Lynn Johannson

CHAPTER 28   **281**

Supporting Auditing Programs with Automated Tools
Barbara Jo Ruble

Authors

Howard N. Apsan, Ph.D.,
director of environmental management services,
Clayton Environmental Consultants

Craig A. Barney,
environmental and safety specialist, Lockheed Missiles and Space Company

Lawrence B. Cahill,
senior program director, ERM, Inc.

Paul D. Coulter,
director, Union Carbide Corporation Compliance Audit Program

Gabriel G. Crognale,
environmental consultant

Ira R. Feldman,
vice president, CAPITAL Environmental

Chris FitzGerald,
consultant and editor-in-chief of *Total Quality Environmental Management*

Joseph Fiksel,
principal and vice president, Decision Focus Incorporated

William P. Gulledge,
director, Regulatory Division, Jefferson Group

Gilbert S. Hedstrom,
vice president and managing director, Arthur D. Little,
and secretary, Environmental Auditing Roundtable

Myron L. Iwanski,
lead environmental auditor, TVA Corporate Environmental Audits

Suzan L. Jackson,
consultant and instructor, DuPont Quality Management and Technology Center

Lynn Johannson,
director, E2 Management Corporation

Curtis J. Johnson,
divisional vice president of environmental, health and safety auditing,
Browning-Ferris Industries

Debora L. Jones, RN, MPH,
executive officer, The Darien Group, Ltd.

Rodger A. Jump, PE,
Smith, Barney, Shearson

John J. Kirchenstein,
senior international consultant, Tennessee Associates International

Gail Miller,
associate, Coopers & Lybrand Environmental Services Practice

Robert R. Morton, REM,
corporate director of environmental management services, ATEC Associates, Inc.

J. Richard Pooler, Esq.,
executive officer, The Darien Group, Ltd.

Mark C. Posson,
manager, Lockheed Missiles and Space Company, Inc.,
Environmental Protection Programs

Randy A. Roig, Ph.D., REA,
principal, ERM-West

Barbara Jo Ruble,
senior project manager, ENSR Consulting and Engineering, and co-chair,
Environmental Auditing Roundtable Computer Applications Work Group

William G. Russell,
director, Coopers & Lybrand Environmental Services Practice

Michael C. Schiavo,
policy analayst, EPA Administrator's Pollution Prevention Policy Staff

Peter Schneider,
CEP, principal, ERM-New England

Steven L. Skalak,
partner, Coopers & Lybrand Litigation and Environmental Services Practice

Ann C. Smith,
worldwide consulting, AlliedSignal Environmental Services Inc.,
and chair, Environmental Auditing Roundtable

John R. Thurman,
manager of environmental audits, TVA

Roger W. Voeller,
senior consultant, Arthur D. Little

George F. Vorhauer,
director of corporate quality initiatives, Eastman Kodak Corporate Quality Office

Richard P. Wells,
vice president and director, Abt Associates

Grace H. Wever, Ph.D.,
vice president of environmental affairs, Council of Great Lakes Industries

William A. Yodis,
past president, Environmental Auditing Roundtable and manager of
corporate health, safety, and environmental audit, AlliedSignal Inc.

Preface

At a recent book convention, I was overwhelmed by the number of new and upcoming books on "change." According to management pundits, if you don't "face it and embrace it," change will leave you and your company stranded on the superhighways of the future. Prescriptions for mastering the high-speed forces that threaten your company's competitiveness (read, your paycheck) abound. Today no field of commercial endeavor captures all of this excitement and anxiety more than the environment.

This brings us to *Auditing for Environmental Quality Leadership*. What started as a straightforward revision of a regulatory compliance-driven book quickly became a cross-country and then global chase for topics and tools that auditing pros were using to improve their practices and environmental performance in the face of unprecedented change and, yes, chaos. Each conversation with members of the Environmental Auditing Roundtable brought new insights, questions, and generous offerings to help develop a new handbook for practitioners that focused on the emerging activities of quality management audits. Their willingness to contribute ideas and time and share their experiences to help all environmental managers meet the challenge of change has made this new guidebook possible. Many thanks to Bill Yodis for his encouragement, guidance, and patience.

We hope you will be able to put into immediate practice the ideas and techniques presented here and share them with your colleagues. The payback for implementing just one of the hundreds of ideas and for learning new directions should far exceed the price of this book. Hopefully, our "work in progress" will continue in future editions and reflect the dynamic changes and demands that auditors face everyday. To that end, we welcome hearing from you.

John T. Willig

Introduction

Through the recent years, companies have struggled to define the best ways to manage environmental compliance and obligations. The image that the really good companies go beyond environmental compliance and onto another plane called "environmental excellence" is much the buzz these days. The "old" viewpoint that "we will do what the regulations require" is not seen as being "green" enough for the nineties. For those who have not critically analyzed what it takes to attain and sustain compliance, it is easy to put compliance aside and say it is a "bare minimum." There are those who believe that an audit program that does not examine management's "psyche" and find environmental commitment written on the washroom walls is an artifact generated by antiquated thinking.

I personally see the changes in environmental auditing as an attempt to achieve compliance with the loftier goals of a high-quality environmental management system, with the additional hope that regulatory compliance will be an added side benefit. Only time will tell if these "nouveau" techniques will be effective.

This book focuses on new techniques in environmental auditing and their place in the Total Quality Environmental Management System. There are many ways to increase efficiency and effectiveness in today's operations. The environmental audit has shown itself to be a very cost-effective way of driving the implementation of management programs. In the management sense, it is only a check step in an action process; however, it is often used as a significant driver for improvement within the overall management system.

Environmental auditing techniques developed in the United States during the 1970s and 1980s have been given a significant incentive for improvement by a number of factors with a worldwide basis.

The first is the influence of the Europeans through development of the EcoManagement and Audit Scheme. This scheme was a long time in development, and during this period audit practitioners were given a chance to think about how existing techniques could be improved. The immensely high expectations of the original ECO-AUDIT scheme prompted each audit program and environmental system manager to ask if these requirements might not have some place in their programs. Some did and some did not, but the catalyst of the ECO-AUDIT certainly brought about change. By virtually leap-frogging beyond compliance, the ECO-AUDIT set a new standard to be reckoned with.

The second major influence was the CERES initiatives with the Valdez Principles. Although still not a major player in terms of sign-ups to its principles, CERES started or accelerated a significant number of other initiatives (e.g., GEMI, Responsible Care) which have directed industry in many of the same directions as the CERES Principles. The principles set forth in each set of doctrines provided a new mechanism to reconsider the implications of environmental management and also the role played by auditing.

The third and fourth influences are the poor global economy and Total Quality Management. I have a difficult time separating these because many of the strengths of TQM show up so much brighter in the light of a poor economy. Efforts are being made to "work smarter" and get more for each dollar invested in programs. Total Quality Management methods drive managers to develop programs that are more streamlined, look for root causes, and sort out what adds value from what does not. So many of these activities are also ones that happen naturally in a poor economy. TQM provides a structured method to look for and to make the improvements.

The fifth influence is globalization. The fact that all businesses are becoming aware of the global economy and the inability to separate what goes on in North America from what is happening in Europe and Asia tends to bring more information into the decision-making process. Old paradigms become easier to break when process stakeholders are queried about their expectations. Simply focusing on the requirements of program customers and stakeholders brings a lot of new information and a new slant on how each company will look at its audit program.

All of these influences, combined with the maturing of auditing processes in North America, prepare the way for exciting change. Throughout this book, new techniques and successes will be discussed. Real case studies are used extensively to illustrate how the techniques are used and how they have worked in specific instances.

Several other areas of change are also in evidence.

Metrics are becoming more and more important for measuring the progress of environmental initiatives. As such, information management systems become more complex and so does the auditing and assurance of the data quality. This presents certain challenge for auditors in the nineties.

Also, there is a significant movement toward standardization of environmental auditing principles and practices. Several efforts will be discussed in this book, among them efforts to produce North American and United States national standards, the previously mentioned Eco-Management and Audit scheme, and the International Standards Organization's influence with the ISO 9000 series and the developing worldwide environmental standards which include auditing standards.

And so the journey from compliance to Total Quality to metrics and fact-driven decision making continues within and around environmental auditing. Within auditing, the assembly, review, and reporting of information has become more and more significant. To keep up with these needs, methods of information management technology and automated auditing have been developed and will be discussed in this book.

There are many promises of interesting times in the near future. The pace of change in the recent past portrayed in this book should give a good indication of where the future of environmental auditing is headed. Since continuous improvement has no end, it is a sure thing that the state-of-the-art will continue to change with time. Focus now on how environmental auditing has been integrated into the Total Quality Environmental Leadership culture and the many improvements made recently in the state-of-the-art of environmental auditing. Note that the new systems that work do not completely eschew auditing for compliance, but rather repackage it along with assuring that environmental management systems are in place and functioning.

It has been my pleasure through the recent years to work beside many of the authors who have contributed their considerable talent to this book. They are among those on the cutting edge of environmental auditing practice and have pioneered many of the techniques in use today. I hope you will enjoy their insights on moving environmental auditing beyond compliance.

William A. Yodis is manager of health, safety, and environmental audit at AlliedSignal Inc. in Morristown, NJ, and past president of the Environmental Auditing Roundtable.

AUDITING FOR ENVIRONMENTAL QUALITY LEADERSHIP

Auditing for Environmental Excellence

EPA's Environmental Leadership Pilot Projects

Ira R. Feldman and Michael C. Schiavo

In a June 21, 1994 Federal Register notice (59 F.R. 32062), the U.S. Environmental Protection Agency (EPA) requested proposals for Environmental Leadership Program (ELP) pilot projects and outlines the criteria that facilities must address to be considered for participation. These pilot projects will explore ways that EPA and states might encourage facilities to develop innovative auditing and compliance programs and reduce the risk of noncompliance through pollution prevention practices. In addition, the projects will help EPA design a full-scale leadership program and determine if implementing such a program can help improve environmental compliance.

The pilot project phase of the ELP will be coordinated by the Office of Compliance (OC) within EPA's Office of Enforcement and Compliance Assurance (OECA). In this chapter, the authors show how these voluntary pilot projects will encourage industry to take greater responsibility for self-monitoring, which can lead to improved compliance, pollution prevention, and environmental protection. EPA will recognize facilities for outstanding environmental management practices and give them an opportunity to examine and address barriers to self-monitoring and compliance efforts. Finally, these projects will strengthen federal-state partnerships and allow EPA to gather empirical data on environmental compliance measures and methodologies, which will help inform the Agency's reassessment of its environmental auditing policy.

EPA foresees a number of potential benefits to facilities that are selected for pilot projects. First, EPA will publicly recognize facilities that demonstrate a commitment to compliance through outstanding environmental management practices. Press releases, letters to community groups, local and state agencies, and site visits from EPA are possible forms of recognition. The pilot projects also represent an opportunity for facilities to help EPA design a future, full-scale leadership program.

Pilot project participants will have the opportunity to inform and directly participate in EPA's effort to reassess its environmental auditing policy. As announced in a May 13, 1994, memo from Assistant Administrator Steven A. Herman, EPA is currently reevaluating its environmental auditing policy and will take an empirical approach so that any decision to either reinforce or change that policy is informed by fact. The ELP pilot projects may generate useful data on auditing methodology and measures, and may serve as vehicles for experimenting with policy-driven incentives.

Finally, the pilot projects will allow industry to participate in discussions of other possible policy modifications and incentives that could help facilities overcome barriers to self-monitoring and compliance efforts.

Criteria for Facility Pilot Projects

The following criteria for pilot projects were developed in response to extensive public comment on the original ELP proposal (i.e., the January 15, 1993, Federal Register notice). In this phase of the ELP, EPA is encouraging facilities of all types, including small businesses, municipalities, and federal facilities, to submit proposals for pilot projects that address these criteria. Each criterion must be addressed in some way in the proposal; however, facilities may emphasize criteria that are appropriate to their unique situation in setting specific goals for a pilot project.

1. Compliance History

To be selected for a pilot project, facilities must demonstrate a commitment to compliance. Facilities must describe their local, state, and federal compliance histories, explain how they resolved compliance issues in the past, what they are doing to address any outstanding compliance issues, *and how they are trying to position themselves to go beyond compliance.*

2. Environmental Management and Auditing Systems

Facilities applying to the ELP must describe their existing or proposed environmental management and auditing systems, their systems for resolving issues raised by these programs in a timely manner, and their systems for evaluating and adjusting these programs on a regular basis.

3. Disclosure of Audit Results

As previously mentioned, EPA is currently evaluating its environmental auditing policy and intends to base any decision to reinforce or change existing policy on empirical data. The Agency is particularly interested in examining how disclosure of audit results could improve the public's confidence in and acceptance of industry's self-monitoring efforts, and how disclosure could help facilitate the flow of information to the personnel responsible for implementing audit recommendations.

Facilities applying to the ELP, therefore, must demonstrate a willingness to disclose the results of their audits. *EPA is not requiring disclosure of specific audit results, but would like to experiment with different policy approaches to this issue as part of the pilot projects.* Proposals should indicate the type and extent of information that facilities would be willing to disclose, the means by which they would disclose the information, and the incentives or policy modifications they would seek from regulators in order to make the disclosures. Proposed incentives or policy changes should be limited to approaches based on existing law using administrative authority or policies that lie clearly within the jurisdiction of EPA's Office of Enforcement and Compliance Assurance. Proposals to change statutory deadlines, amend environmental standards, or those that require actions by other agencies are not appropriate for this program.

4. Pollution Prevention

Facilities must describe existing or proposed comprehensive, multimedia pollution prevention programs that are integrated into their overall operations. Facilities should include descriptions of their pollution prevention planning processes, their state pollution prevention plans (if required), their systems for implementing pollution prevention projects, the means of allocating resources to pollution prevention, and how they measure pollution prevention progress.

5. Setting an Example

Facilities must show how they are currently using, or would be willing to use, their auditing, pollution prevention, or environmental management programs as models or benchmarks for other facilities within their company or industry, or for their customers, suppliers, and contractors. Facilities must indicate how they would help others learn from their experience and the type and extent of information they would be willing to share.

6. Performance Measures

Facilities must propose methods of tracking compliance and pollution prevention improvements resulting from their participation in a pilot project. They must also include brief descriptions of additional performance objectives that they are striving to meet and the systems they use to track and monitor progress toward these goals.

7. Employee and Community Involvement

Facilities must demonstrate that their employees and communities are involved in developing and implementing their environmental management programs and suggest means of verifying this involvement.

Proposal Review and Selection Process

EPA plans to select three to five pilot projects. The pilots will be selected from the pool of proposals received based on how completely they address the seven criteria outlined in the Federal Register notice and their potential to demonstrate possible components of a full-scale leadership program. Depending on the level of interest in the projects, the quality of the proposals received, and available resources, EPA may be willing to expand the pilot project phase to include additional projects.

The ELP team will be using an expedited process—in partnership with EPA Regional offices, state environmental agencies, and other OECA offices—to review proposals and to select pilot participants. In response to the Federal Register notice, forty applications for pilot projects were received. Final selections will be announced in early 1995.

Background

On January 15, 1993, EPA published a Federal Register notice (58 F.R. 4802) requesting comment on the possible creation of a national voluntary program to encourage and publicly recognize environmental leadership and to promote pollution prevention in the manufacturing sector. The Agency requested responses to 56 specific questions about the structure of such a program, possible goals and measures, the need for incentives, the role of compliance screening, and other related issues. Two basic components were proposed for the Environmental Leadership Program, a Corporate Statement of Environmental Principles and a Model Facility Program.

EPA received a wide variety of comments on the original proposal from industry, States, environmental groups, and other nongovernmental organizations. In addition, the Agency held a public meeting on May 6, 1993, in Washington, D.C., and received additional comments from 30 groups. Although no true consensus emerged on the best structure or goals for the program, *the comments clearly indicated an interest in a voluntary program to recognize environmental excellence.* These comments are summarized below.

In the January 28, 1994, Federal Register (59 F.R. 4066), the EPA Administrator announced EPA's intent to further develop the ELP concept, initially through a small number of voluntary, facility-based pilot projects. At the same time, EPA opted not to further develop a Corporate Statement of Environmental Principles, but rather to work cooperatively with organizations that have developed their own corporate or industry-specific codes. The Office of Pollution Prevention and Toxics will continue to lead any future Agency involvement in this area.

Summary of Public Comments on Original ELP Proposal[1]

The January, 1993, request for comments in the Federal Register generated over 100 sets of responses from a wide variety of interests, including industry, states, and environmental groups:

Respondent Group	Number of Comments
Corporations	35
Petroleum/natural gas companies	5
Utilities	3
Waste management companies	6
Industrial trade associations	15
Industry councils	3
Professional services/associations	14
Existing "excellence" programs	2
Environmental/public interest groups	6
State agencies	14
Press	1
Miscellaneous/unknown	2
Total	106

More than half of the respondents, primarily representing industry and states, expressed general support for the program concept. Most of these endorsements, however, were contingent on EPA adopting a respondent's suggestion, such as encouraging broad participation, allowing for flexibility, and designing the program to be truly voluntary. Approximately 20 percent of the respondents opposed the idea of a federal program to recognize environmental leadership. There were opponents from all respondent groups, and there were many reasons for their opposition. Environmental and public interest groups, for example, unanimously opposed a voluntary program that did not mandate strict pollution prevention, whereas several industry representatives stated that existing "excellence" programs are sufficient. Both groups also cited resource constraints as a reason for their opposition.

Comments on Specific Issues
Flexibility of Program Goals and Measures

The majority of supporters urged EPA to establish simple and flexible requirements for participation in the ELP. Industry was virtually unanimous in urging EPA to avoid setting uniform standards of environmental excellence, to move away from command and control programs, and to experiment with innovative approaches to environmental protection. Although some respondents endorsed the idea of establishing quantitative, national risk-reduction goals, most also suggested that EPA should consider using qualitative measures of environmental improvement.

Role of Compliance

More than half of the respondents on this issue, primarily representing industry, opposed rigorous compliance screening as a requirement for participation in the ELP. Many stated that full compliance was unrealistic, and that EPA should instead focus on continuous improvement. Most believed that, although compliance history could play a role in the application process, a company should not be barred from participating in some way because of past compliance problems. On the other hand, many states and environmental groups favored some level of baseline compliance as a threshold for participation.

Two-Component Structure

Most respondents, especially from industry, opposed the idea of an EPA-established set of environmental principles, reasoning that they would be difficult to enforce and would duplicate existing private-sector efforts to establish environmental management standards (e.g., CERES, Responsible Care). Many industry respondents stated that companies and facilities should be allowed to develop their own statement of environmental principles instead of being required to adopt a statement developed by EPA.

The comments expressed general support for some type of facility-focused program. Supporters of this idea reasoned that focusing on facilities would be easier than dealing with large, complex corporations. Some respondents warned, however, that some companies might try to "showcase" certain facilities to draw attention away from other facilities with environmental and/or compliance problems.

Incentives

Although a number of respondents stated that public recognition alone would be sufficient motivation to apply for the program, nearly half of the respondents recommended that EPA offer additional incentives. The suggestions included faster permitting, compliance credits, and reduced reporting requirements. Respondents also listed possible disincentives, such as intense public scrutiny, burdensome paperwork, and program application fees.

Single-tier versus Multiple-tier

Many respondents from industry and the states stressed the importance of encouraging broad participation in the ELP. Representatives from these groups recommended a multiple-tier program that would encourage companies of all sizes from all industries to participate in the program. This approach would allow EPA to offer different incentives for different levels of performance. Some of the comments also noted that if the requirements were too strict, only a handful of companies might qualify. Supporters of a single-tier program argued that a multiple-tier structure might compromise the prestige of the program (i.e., because EPA should recognize only the best environmental management efforts), and that a multiple-tier program would be difficult to administer.

Note

1. This section draws on the report entitled "Summary of Public Comments: Environmental Leadership Program Original Proposal," prepared with the assistance of DPRA, Inc. (Arlington, Virginia). Copies of the report and the transcript of the May 6, 1993, public meeting are available from the ELP pilot project team.

Ira R. Feldman is vice president of CAPITAL Environmental, Washington, D.C. **Michael C. Schiavo** is a policy analyst on the Pollution Prevention Policy Staff and a member of the ELP Pilot Project team.

Auditing for Compliance Is Only the Beginning: Lessons from Leading Companies

2

Richard P. Wells

As the constituency concerned with corporate environmental programs has expanded, environmental auditing is extending beyond its traditional compliance focus. This article shows how and why it is one of the tools that companies have to determine whether their environmental management systems are meeting customer expectations and to identify opportunities for continuous environmental improvement.

The most fundamental changes in the field of environmental management have been in the "customers" and their expectations. Five or ten years ago, the customers for corporate environmental programs were fairly well defined. They were the local, state, and federal regulatory agencies that issued permits, monitored compliance, and, if necessary, issued notices of violations and fines. The model of environmental management, subscribed to by both government and industry, was one in which regulatory agencies represented the interests of society and controlled the actions of industry. Industry acted in its own narrowly defined self-interest.

Today, the customers for environmental programs are much more broadly defined. They include, in addition to regulatory agencies, residents of communities where facilities are sited, employees, product customers, stockholders, and boards of directors, as well as national and local environmental organizations. While regulatory agencies remain the ultimate representative of society's interest, corporate environmental performance is seen as a responsibility of the corporation to its customers and stakeholders. Each customer/stakeholder group represents an aspect of society's interest.

With the change in customers has come a change in customer expectations. Regulatory agency interests in compliance with applicable regulatory requirements have been augmented by concerns that go substantially beyond compliance. These expectations encompass the company's overall performance in reducing risks to workers and facility neighbors, in reducing emissions of pollutants that have global or regional effects (e.g., sulfur oxides, greenhouse gases, and ozone depletors), and in preserving material and nonrenewable energy resources for future generations.

As the emerging concept of life cycle thinking suggests, environmental concerns have also extended beyond the organization's boundaries. Corporate environmental management must concern itself not only with the organization's direct impacts, but with those of its suppliers extending back to raw material sourcing, and of its customers extending forward to end customer product use and disposal. Each stage of a product's life cycle has environmental impacts, and to attain success in the environmental arena, companies will find it increasingly necessary to address impacts at each stage, particularly in product and process design.

Another influence that cannot be overlooked is the increasing importance of economics in corporate environmental management. When compliance was the only concern, responsible companies could regard environmental costs as a cost of doing business. Generally, these costs were lumped into overhead and managed centrally. Environmental expenditures were not subject to return-on-investment hurdles because they were regarded as necessary expenditures. In a command-and-control compliance mode, this approach made sense. Central control assured senior management that environmental issues were being addressed responsibly. This freed the rest of the company to get on with the "real" work of making products that met customer expectations.

As environmental performance has itself become a customer expectation, the role of economics in corporate environmental decision making has become more complex. Compliance with regulatory requirements and protection against imminent threats to the environment remain sine qua non elements. If regulatory customers are not satisfied, the company's efforts to address customer environmental needs will be in vain. Many discretionary environmental investments that go beyond minimum requirements are being made, however, and these investments, like other corporate investments, are subject to return on investment hurdles. For this reason, new questions are being asked concerning environmental costs. Can we meet regulatory requirements and improve performance less expensively by modifying products and processes? Do we even know, given corporate accounting systems, how much specific products and processes contribute to our costs?

The answer to the first question is that product and process changes often provide a less costly way of meeting environmental requirements. The answer to the second question is, unfortunately, that corporate accounting systems usually do not tell us how much environmental costs contribute to product costs. Without such information, it is extremely difficult for companies to make product costing decisions.

Environment not only affects the cost side of the profit equation, it also affects the revenue side. As environmental performance improves, product customers recognize the improvement and give preference to a company's products. This is not to say that customers will always select the products of a "greener" company. Far from it. Green products that fail to meet customer expectations for price, quality, performance, and service will fail in the marketplace just as surely as will other products that do not meet customer expectations. Other things being equal, however, true, sustained, and documented improvements in environmental performance will be part of the bundle of attributes that customers consider in making a purchase decision.

An increasingly important focus on the revenue side is industrial products. While much emphasis has been given recently to green consumer products, the more important opportunities may be in industrial products. Industrial products require fewer, larger purchase decisions, and customers can evaluate environmental claims more readily.

The Role of Auditing

What does all this have to do with auditing? A great deal, in fact, if we broaden the definition of auditing. The term "auditing" means different things to different people. (This article clearly takes significant liberties with the definition of audits. It does so deliberately to illustrate the breadth of management system measures.) The most restrictive definition is as a periodic process by which a company documents that it is doing what it says it's doing. When an accountant audits a company's financial statement, he or she asserts that "the financial statement presents fairly, in all material respects, the financial condition of the company...in conformity with generally accepted accounting principles." The "audit" defined in this manner says nothing about the company's financial performance; it only says that the audited report accurately represents the company's condition. The company could be on the verge of bankruptcy, but it would receive a clean bill of health for having accurately represented its financial condition so long as its financial statement said it was on the verge of bankruptcy.

At another level, "compliance audits" ensure that organizations meet the myriad regulatory requirements they are subject to. To paraphrase Abraham Lincoln, some processes are in compliance all of the time and all processes are in compliance some of the time, but all processes are never in compliance all of the time. Compliance audits provide a mechanism for management to get an objective appraisal of an organization's performance in meeting regulatory requirements *before* violations become the subject of regulatory action. Audits are critical as a "leading indicator" because the consequences of discovering a noncompliance situation too late can be severe.

"Risk audits," closely related to compliance audits, focus on early identification of potential problem areas. Even with full compliance, a facility's operations may pose an unacceptable risk of an accidental release that could threaten facility employees, neighbors, or the environment. Management often needs an objective third party to examine its operations to pinpoint potential areas of risk. If an accidental release takes place, it will be small consolation to know it took place legally.

Management Systems Audits

The above are, more or less, the traditional roles of audits in corporate environmental management. "Management systems audits," however, focus on the overall structure of management. To understand the role of these audits, we need to take a step back and place the audits in the broader context of the changes taking place in corporate environmental management.

Particularly in the past five years, starting with the emergence of the concept of pollution prevention and the promotion of Total Quality Environmental Management by the Global Environmental Management Initiative (GEMI), the discipline of corporate environmental management has undergone a fundamental transformation. With this transformation, the role of audits in environmental management has also changed. It is no longer sufficient merely to certify that a company is doing what it says it does to avoid noncompliance and to prevent accidental releases. Rather, it has become necessary to satisfy the expectations of a diverse set of customers whose expectations go considerably beyond compliance. Management systems audits fit in the context of this drive to move beyond compliance with environmental standards. They are a key element of a process of evaluating an organization's environmental performance relative to customer needs.

As shown in **Exhibit 1**, evaluating environmental performance is, at bottom, a process of measuring how well corporate performance satisfies customer expectations. Customer or stakeholder needs can be defined broadly. They include the following:

- Regulatory agency requirements for compliance with applicable regulations and standards
- Customer expectations that products be designed and produced to minimize environmental damage throughout the product's life cycle
- Facility neighbor and employee needs for a safe working and living environment
- Societal needs for the conservation of resources and prevention of ecological damage

Often, it is necessary to translate general customer expectations, evaluating short- and long-term risks to human health and the environment. Scientific knowledge is the filter through which we must interpret customer needs. Frequently, customers, whether product customers or local communities, do not have a complete scientific understanding of environmental performance. Expressed customer

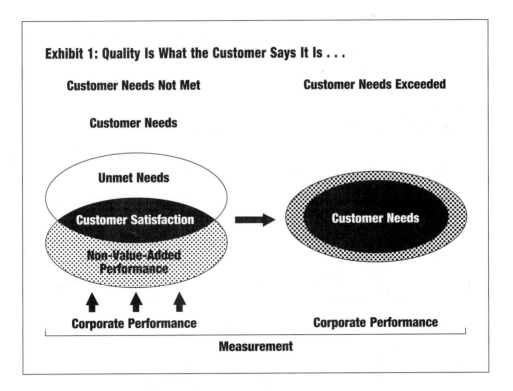

Exhibit 1: Quality Is What the Customer Says It Is . . .

Customer Needs Not Met   Customer Needs Exceeded

Customer Needs

Unmet Needs

Customer Satisfaction

Non-Value-Added Performance

Customer Needs

Corporate Performance   Corporate Performance

Measurement

desires, therefore, may need to be interpreted in the light of scientific knowledge. Science, however, should not become the basis for denying the legitimacy of expressed customer concerns.

Corporate environmental performance, however, does not always overlap fully with customer needs. Most serious are areas of unmet needs—facility emissions may create risks unacceptable to facility neighbors; energy and resources may be inefficiently used; or permit violations may exist. In some cases, organizations also focus on the wrong things, delivering performance that does not add value to customers. Often, substantial expenditures are made to clean up pollution that should not have been created in the first place. Waste treatment and control can fall into this category, adding no value to customers because they mitigate a problem that could have been prevented.

In the right side of Exhibit 1, corporate performance and customer needs overlap, and customer requirements are satisfied or exceeded. While this condition is easy to illustrate, it is much more difficult to achieve. To achieve this condition in practice, two things are necessary: an understanding of customer needs and an ability to shape environmental performance to meet these needs.

Understanding customer needs is an important topic, but it is beyond the scope of this article. Suffice to say that to understand customer needs, it is important to *ask*—through surveys, direct contacts, sales representatives, or alliances with environmental organizations; to *listen* to customer feedback and community response; and to *anticipate* by keeping abreast of scientific developments and examining developments in bellwether regions or countries.

Management Systems Auditing in the Context of Environmental Performance Evaluation

Exhibit 2 illustrates three steps of measurement—processes, results, and customer satisfaction.

- Process measures ask, are we doing the right thing? That is, do we have the processes and procedures in place that will yield the level of environmental performance that our customers and stakeholders expect of us?
- Results measures ask, are we getting the results we want? These results are defined primarily as continuous improvement in environmental performance—decreases in emissions, efficiency improvements in the use of resources and energy, and compliance with regulatory requirements. They can also encompass improvements in financial performance on both the cost and revenue side.
- Customer satisfaction measures ask, are we addressing and meeting customer needs? This is an important question—in some cases, organizations do not communicate their environmental results effectively. Customers and stake-

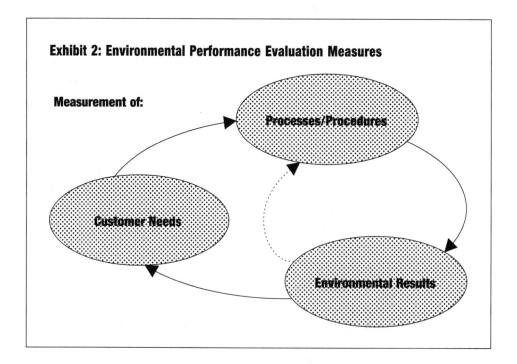

Exhibit 2: Environmental Performance Evaluation Measures

Measurement of:

Processes/Procedures

Customer Needs

Environmental Results

holders may not recognize what the organization has accomplished. In other cases, organizations fail to address key customer needs—the organization may focus on toxics emissions, especially TRI-listed toxics, while facility neighbors may be concerned about particulate matter settling on cars and houses.

Management systems audits address the first of these elements—whether the organization has the appropriate processes and procedures in place. Management process audits have three key uses.

A Leading Indicator of Performance

First, unlike results and customer satisfaction measures, management systems audits are a leading indicator of performance. They allow a company to anticipate performance and to make adjustments, before inadequate processes result in poor environmental performance. As noted above, environmental systems audits are particularly important to prevent sudden and unplanned releases with acute consequences. While chronic process releases can be tracked over time with an eye to continuous improvement in performance, sudden unplanned releases must be prevented before they happen. In the extreme, once the Bhopal incident happened and was reflected as a "result," it was too late.

A Diagnostic Device

A second use of management systems audits is as a diagnostic device. When results or customer satisfaction do not meet our requirements, we must look back to management systems to identify the root causes of sub-par performance. Are there procedures that can be improved? Is follow-up undertaken to ensure that decisions that affect environmental performance are implemented? Do key managers in charge of product and process design and operations decisions see the environment as their responsibility? Is there a system in place to understand and anticipate customer and stakeholder environmental needs? Is the organization communicating its performance adequately? Management systems audits can be effective tools to identify the root causes of gaps in environmental performance.

For example, a major consumer products company found that it was exceeding its internally specified limits for exposure to a potentially toxic substance in an operating area. The company frequently exceeded its standard of 1 mg/m^3, although its average emission was well below that standard (0.50 mg/m^3). The company performed a root cause analysis (which was really a focused management systems audit) of the process in question. The root cause analysis (shown in **Exhibit 3**) focused on four major areas: equipment design, cleaning procedures, maintenance and inspection, and operator training. An in-depth review of management systems identified the root cause of the problem: the equipment was well designed and

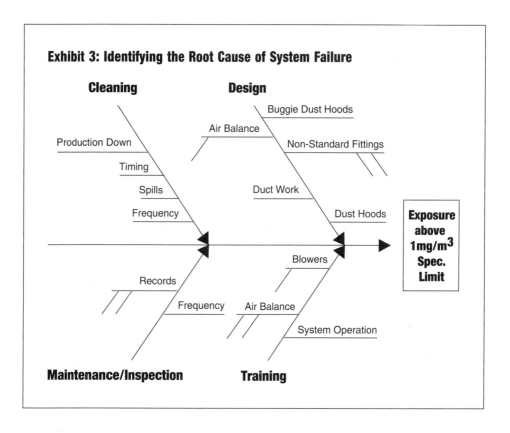

Exhibit 3: Identifying the Root Cause of System Failure

operators were well trained; however, follow-up action was not being taken on problem areas identified through periodic inspections.

As shown in **Exhibit 4**, the results of the root cause analysis improved performance dramatically. Average exposures were reduced from 0.50 mg/m³ to 0.20 mg/m³. More importantly, the instances where the process exceeded the internally specified limit of 1.0 mg/m³ were virtually eliminated (except for a single "special cause," which took place during a process changeover).

The key point to note from this example is that performance improved by changing the management system, *not the technology*. Although a costly technical solution would have worked, it would have resulted in residuals requiring disposal and continued loss of raw materials that could be reintroduced into the process. By focusing on its management systems, the company identified a solution that was both less costly and more effective.

A Benchmark of Management Systems

Third, management systems audits serve as a benchmark of management systems. Given the rapidly changing context of environmental management, organizations frequently seek to ensure that they keep abreast of "best in class" processes.

Structured management systems audits compare an organization's environmental systems against established standards of what an environmental management system should be.

There are numerous models for management systems audits, although these models generally are not referred to as audits. For example, the Environmental Self-Assessment Program (ESAP) developed by GEMI provides a structured format for an organization to compare its management systems to principles for sustainable development established by the International Chamber of Commerce. The Council of Great Lake Industries (CGLI) also has developed a checklist for environmental quality management systems modeled in part on the Malcolm Baldrige Award criteria. Other examples are British Standard 7750, which is meant to establish standards for environmental management systems, and the European Eco-audit scheme, which is meant as a standard for certification.

One note of caution needs to be introduced about management systems audits: systems quality does not necessarily correspond to environmental quality. In a headlong rush to establish the "best" environmental management system or to be certified as meeting international standards, companies may be drawn to elaborate organizational structures that address each of the elements of a best-in-class management system.

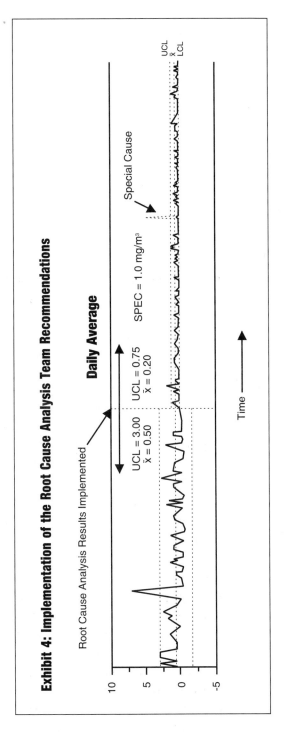

Exhibit 4: Implementation of the Root Cause Analysis Team Recommendations

In fact, the truly best-in-class system would be the one that did not exist at all. Ultimately, a truly effective environmental management system would have elements to handle the following:

- Track and anticipate customer and stakeholder environmental needs
- Measure whether customer and stakeholder needs are being met
- Prevent sudden accidental releases with acute consequences
- Reward performance *in a meaningful manner* for the key product and process designers, line managers, and senior managers who make the fundamental decisions that affect the organization's environmental performance

The environmental staff in an organization would become internal consultants and facilitators to teams sponsored by key managers. Environmental performance would be the responsibility of all staff members, not simply of the corporate environmental affairs department. In a recent speech, Terry DeWitt, Vice President of Environmental Affairs for Honda of North America, summarized this approach, saying that Honda of North America has an environmental staff of 10,000—because environmental performance is every employee's responsibility. A similar attitude was apparent in the comment of a corporate CEO who, when asked, "Who is your company's most senior environmental official?" answered, "I am." Environmental consciousness must be imbued in every aspect of corporate operations; we must avoid letting a fixation on approved systems standards lead us into bureaucratic systems that exist for the system's, rather than the environment's, sake.

Environmental management systems audits do not have to be compared to externally generated criteria for systems quality such as those developed by GEMI and CGLI. For example, Hewlett-Packard (HP) has developed an environmental health and safety audit program that is designed to measure performance and to communicate internal performance metrics among HP's worldwide operations. The system developed by HP looks at both traditional audit areas—e.g., regulatory compliance, emergency preparedness and response, recordkeeping, safety engineering, and regulated waste management—and nontraditional areas that fall into the scope of management systems audits. The latter encompass, for example, management involvement and commitment, including communications and adequacy of resources, internal review procedures, and the effectiveness of site pollution prevention and source reduction plans.

Conclusion

Over the past decade individual organizations and third-party auditors have developed important capabilities to ensure the continued effective operation of environmental management systems. As the requirements placed on environmental managers shift the breadth and scope of audits, their functions must also shift. Environmental managers today are responsible to a much broader constituency both internally and externally, and they must work with a broader range of people than ever before.

Richard P. Wells is vice president and director of Abt Associates' corporate environmental consulting practice in Cambridge, Massachusetts.

Evaluating Management Systems as Part of Environmental Audits

3

Lawrence B. Cahill

Evaluating management systems is a crucial component of any environmental audit. Evolving regulations and directives acknowledge this importance. Remedying management deficiencies can result in long-term, lasting improvements in environmental compliance with external requirements and internal policies. This chapter presents ideas and examples from leading companies on how environmental audits can be designed to enhance TQEM systems.

For the past few years, there has been much discussion in the environmental auditing profession about evaluating management systems as part of a facility audit. Some have gone so far as to say that the management systems evaluation should be the *principal* objective of an environmental audit. It is probably fair to say that many people, though they espouse this approach, are not quite sure what it means.

Within the last two years, there has been considerable legislative and policy activity that needs to be considered in any decision to modify current internal environmental audit programs. Congress has proposed several bills that require audits, or in some way define how they should be carried out. The Department of Justice has provided guidelines on what it would value in deciding if a violation of environmental law should receive prosecutorial leniency. These proposals and guidelines do not focus on auditing for regulatory compliance verification as much as on auditing for the presence of management systems that can assure a high level of compliance. Interest in environmental systems is also expressed in two other efforts; the European Community (EC) Eco Audit regulation and the Environmental Protection Agency's proposed Environmental Excellence program. The EC program contains management standards that an operating site must meet in order to be eligible for an Eco label. The site prepares a public statement on its status with regard to these standards, its targeted level of management, and how long it will take to reach that level. This statement is then certified by an independent auditor for accuracy. The EPA Environmental Excellence program, though not fully developed, is similar in concept. Companies meeting a very high level of environmental program criteria would be invited to join the program and receive the benefit of being recognized by the agency and the public as a facility that goes beyond compliance. In addition, the British Standards Institute has published an Environmental Management Systems Specification that provides guidance on what effective systems should look like and how to evaluate them.[1]

Even with all this activity, one might still ask the question: Does this "management systems" approach add value to an audit? It most assuredly does! Focusing on management systems allows one to identify the underlying causes, as opposed to the symptoms, that are typically at the heart of noncompliance at a site.

For example, if an auditor were to observe something as simple as a label missing from a waste solvent drum, the resultant finding could be described as just that—"a drum had a missing label." Surely the next action would be that the site staff would immediately place a label on the drum, and the matter would be considered closed. However, if that same site were to be audited a year later, it is likely that *at least* one drum would be missing labels. Why?

The auditor failed to address the underlying cause of the problem and, nine times out of ten, this is likely to be the breakdown of a management system. In the case of the problem drum, the label could be missing for a variety of reasons, including:

- The person responsible for drum storage and management has not been trained properly.
- It is unclear as to who maintains responsibility for the drum as it moves to various locations on the site, from accumulation near the point of generation, to a ninety-day accumulation pad, to a permitted storage facility.
- The drum has been sitting around for quite a while and no one is sure of its contents. A sample has been sent out for analysis and the decision has been made to not label the drum until the results are known.
- The purchasing department bought "cheap" labels and they cannot withstand the rigors of outdoor storage. They keep falling off the drums.
- The site inadvertently ran out of labels and the normal purchasing process for resupply takes two weeks.

Now, as we look at the problem, it takes on a different light. Maybe the solution is more complicated than simply placing a label on the drum. Maybe, for example, the site's training programs are not including the right people, or job position responsibilities are unclear, and so on. Thus, the corrective actions can now focus on underlying causes. They might, for instance, state that the site needs to train its operators better, or assign drum management responsibilities more clearly, or do something as simple as incorporating minimum quality specifications into the label purchasing process. By identifying and remedying the true problem, it is more likely that when the next audit takes place a year later, there will be no repeat occurrence. In this way, focusing on management systems can result in long-term environmental compliance improvements, not quick fixes.

What Is a Management System?

One can define an environmental audit as a verification of the existence and use of appropriate on-site management systems. As such, an audit is not meant to substitute for good site environmental management. "Good" management implies that there are systems in place on-site to assure compliance on an ongoing basis. These systems can be defined as "the organizational structure, responsibilities, practices, procedures, processes and resources for implementing environmental management"[2] at an operating site.

"The environmental management system should be designed so that emphasis is placed on the prevention of adverse environmental effects, rather than on detection and amelioration after occurrence. It should:

- Identify and assess the environmental effects arising from the organization's existing or proposed activities, products, or services
- Identify and assess the environmental effects arising from incidents, accidents, and potential emergency situations
- Identify the relevant regulatory requirements
- Enable priorities to be identified and pertinent environmental objectives and targets to be set
- Facilitate planning, control, monitoring, auditing and review activities to ensure both that the policy is complied with, and that it remains relevant
- Be capable of evolution to suit changing circumstances."[3]

Although the above elements should be at the core of a site's environmental management system, they are often difficult to audit against because a site's programs frequently are not structured that way. More typically, the site's environmental management system is the sum total of separate programs, which would include most, if not all, of the following:

- Specific programs designed to address corporate environmental policies and procedures
- Employee training and statements of job accountabilities
- Regulatory tracking system
- Environmental review of new activities
- Waste minimization planning
- Release prevention/emergency response planning
- Environmental auditing, including noncompliance follow-up and reporting

- Community outreach program/complaint management
- Product stewardship
- On-site contractor reviews and evaluations
- Off-site contractor reviews and evaluations

These are the *auditable* program elements of a site's environmental management system.

How Do You Do It?

To conduct an audit of a management system, an auditor needs to select those programs that are to be evaluated and to audit the following components of each of the selected programs:

- Organization
- Administrative procedures
- Staff assignments
- Documentation, reports, and records
- Implementation

These components would be evaluated against the standards set by regulations or corporate policy. For example, if a site is required to have an emergency response plan, it could be because of contingency plan requirements under the Resource Conservation and Recovery Act, spill prevention control and countermeasure requirements under the Clean Water Act, hazardous materials response requirements under OSHA's Hazardous Waste Operations rule, or under a mandated corporate procedure. The auditor would first have to determine which of these requirements apply and then evaluate the program organization, procedures, documentation, and implementation against those requirements.

When a facility falls under more than one set of requirements in one program area, the auditor would have to determine if the site has been responsive to each requirement and if the overall program is workable. For example, in the emergency response area some sites will attempt to develop one site emergency response plan addressing all applicable regulatory requirements. The advantage of this approach is that the site management does not have to determine what kind of incident has occurred before initiating the actions recommended by the plan. On the other hand, having an individual plan developed for each set of requirements simplifies the regulatory response and allows for a more direct assurance to agency inspectors and others that the regulatory requirements have been met. Yet, this approach, though valid, can create response time problems when an incident does occur. In either case, the workability criterion becomes paramount.

Much of the organization and procedural review of management systems can be conducted through interviews and evaluations of the programs' documentation. And if the systems can be identified ahead of time, protocols or checklists can be developed to guide the auditors in their investigations.

One of the most important aspects of the audit, however, is to assure that written procedures are, in fact, carried out effectively. This can best be explained by way of example. Take again, for instance, emergency response planning. One can review the organization and planning documents designed to respond to an emergency and find that they respond well to regulatory requirements. However, the real test of effectiveness is in the implementation. In practice, this effectiveness can be tested either through evaluations of the response to actual emergencies or through drills or simulations. Thus, the auditor can determine that the system is effective only if there are assurances that it is tested or evaluated on a routine basis. In other words, any audit of management systems should include an evaluation of actual practices as well as documented procedures.

Why Is It So Difficult?

Many companies have considerable experience in assessing management systems on environmental audits. Yet, observation of numerous audits suggests that even those with experience have difficulties in applying consistent review techniques. The reasons for this include:

- **Performance Appraisal.** An audit of management systems is truly an indicator of personnel performance, and therefore, it will always have a performance appraisal flavor to it. This means that interviews will have an additional tension that must be dealt with by the auditor.
- **Underlying Causes.** Identifying the root causes of a problem requires extra digging and investigation by the auditor. This will take even a very experienced auditor additional time. Such luxuries may not be available to the team.
- **Lack of Standards.** There will be many requirements placed on an organization (e.g., increased environmental awareness) that will have no standards against which they can be evaluated.
- **Cross-Cutting Programs.** Assessing management systems is difficult because responsibilities typically cut across media, and, therefore, necessary review techniques would be counter to the more traditional approaches.

In addition, developing management systems findings on an audit is just plain difficult. Building the case for a management breakdown requires a certain mindset that has to be learned. For example, an auditor might conclude that the "hazardous waste management system at the site is inadequate." Immediately, staff personnel will justifiably ask the question, "Why do you feel that way?" And the response is all too often, "Well, I'm not sure, but I just wasn't comfortable after looking at the records and talking with a few of the staff." This is an insufficient evaluation.

The above conclusion related to the hazardous waste management system may, in fact, be correct. But the conclusion must be verified and substantiated with evidence. Accordingly, a deficiency statement or conclusion should have the following structure:

"The hazardous waste management program at the site is not completely responsive to Corporative Directive HW-100. Deficiencies include:

1. Five drums at the accumulation point had no labels.
2. Accumulation point inspection logs had not been completed for the past month.
3. Two of the maintenance staff had not received their annual training."

Developing findings in this fashion begins to build a strong case that the system is breaking down and needs rebuilding.

Experience at Work

The following examples illustrate how two leading companies view the auditing process and are working to implement more comprehensive audits of their TQEM programs.

Conoco

Conoco has conducted environmental audits of its operations since 1980 under an Environmental Quality Assurance Program (EQAP). This program was developed to assure compliance with environmental laws, regulations, and corporate policies. Each business focused inwardly to satisfy its own need, and the environmental audits primarily emphasized compliance checking via the traditional "snapshot" approach.

The growing importance of environmental auditing and its impact on the thinking of the regulatory community and public stakeholders has brought a more outward focus on the purpose of all environmental programs at Conoco. As a result, the company is currently restructuring the EQAP by building a stronger process to evaluate environmental management systems. This new approach recognizes that a deeper look into the management systems within operations is needed to complement the more traditional compliance status "snapshots."

These changes have been challenging. Adopting management system evaluations into the traditional compliance-check audits is not a simple process. This is a relatively new concept and Conoco is now beginning to understand what "environmental management systems" really are and how to audit them. Without this understanding, it is sometimes difficult to accept what is perceived as criticism of management performance.

Limited audit staff and time needed to conduct quality compliance-check audits also impede reviews of environmental management systems. These two conditions are self-reinforcing. Compliance checks require more audits to assure that each and every facility is in compliance. This takes more time and drains audit resources. Conversely, the need for numerous compliance checks is reduced when strong management systems are in place to minimize the risk of noncompliance.

The Conoco Environmental Quality Assurance Program is a dynamic process. The company is committed to further improvement by increasing the focus on the management systems as a strong compliment to the compliance checks that are the backbone of the program. Conoco is convinced this focus will bring more assurance that it is meeting its compliance responsibilities in a cost-effective way. Conoco believes that these benefits will be observable, and over time will facilitate implementation throughout the organization.

Rohm and Haas

Using internal audits to measure environmental performance has been a management tool at Rohm and Haas since the late 1970s. In 1986, a revised compliance verification program was implemented. More emphasis is placed on training of internal auditors, providing current protocols, and strengthening the follow-up system to assure audit findings are corrected quickly. This process works well for the company. Operating sites use audit results to raise compliance levels and improve the quality of their management systems.

Alternative Paths

Redefining current audit programs to accommodate measurement of environmental management can take several paths. One is to determine the fault in a management system that caused noncompliance, and then correct it. Although this approach strengthens the system, it is time-consuming and creates inconsistent approaches to managing environmental issues throughout an organization. A second approach would audit against a management standard such as the British Standards Institutes 7750 or the standards developed by the Canadian Standards Institute or the International Standards Organizations environmental management standards currently under development. This latter approach allows the site to install a standard system rather than build one based on failure feedback. It also allows for consistency in management systems throughout an organization.

Regardless of which approach is taken, an element of compliance verification must be retained in the audit process to ensure these systems are fully implemented.

Notes

1. "Specification for Environmental Management Systems," British Standard BS 7750:1992, ISBN 0 580 20644 0, March 16, 1992.

2. Id., page 4.

3. Id., Annex, page 9.

Lawrence B. Cahill is a senior program director with ERM, Inc., and the principal author and editor of *Environmental Audits*, 6th Edition, Government Institutes, Inc., Washington, DC, 1989.

Case Study: Toward Effective Environmental Auditing at the TVA—Management Audits versus Compliance Audits

Myron L. Iwanski and John R. Thurman

Companies that incorporate Total Quality Management into their operations are plac-ing increased emphasis on identifying the root causes of deficiencies and problems. This is in keeping with the TQM principles identified by Deming in Out of the Crisis. *Deming states that quality comes not from inspection or from management by objectives or results, but from improvements made in the process and products in order to meet customer needs. Deming's approach demands a shift in focus from addressing symptoms to addressing causes. In this chapter, environmental management audits are presented as the best means to assure that adequate management controls are in place to protect the company, its managers and its employees from penalties associated with civil and criminal enforcement actions.*

Management audits are effective tools for defining the causes of compliance problems and fit well into the TQM approach. Management audits let the cus-tomer (auditee) know how to improve the process (compliance program) so that risks can be better managed. Such audits let management know of environmental risks associated with their operations and point out where additional controls are needed to manage these risks more effectively.

Environmental compliance audits, on the other hand, are less effective. Most companies, particularly those with new audit programs or with limited environ-mental auditing experience, rely on compliance audits. Such audits identify non-compliance with regulatory requirements and company procedures, and recom-mend actions needed to correct the specific nonconformances identified in the audit. But they seldom address the root causes of the noncompliance; consequently, their value to management is limited.

Several recent federal regulatory amendments and policy shifts underscore the need for companies to strengthen their total environmental programs. More effec-tive programs will better protect the company, its managers, and employees from criminal and civil prosecution, which can result in jail terms or fines. The enforce-ment policies of the U.S. Environmental Protection Agency (EPA) and U.S. Depart-ment of Justice (DOJ), together with the U.S. Sentencing Commission's sentencing guidelines, encourage corporations to establish effective programs as a means of reducing the frequency of violations. To be effective, companies will need audit programs that evaluate management control systems and audits that search for root causes of nonconformance. Compliance auditing alone is no longer sufficient to provide the information management needs to meet or exceed compliance requirements consistently.

Differences between Compliance Audits and Management Audits

Most internal environmental audit programs begin with compliance audits. In the electric utility industry, most companies now conduct compliance audits. Many are beginning to consider expanding their programs to include the examination of the adequacy of environmental management controls. This is in keeping with the trend in the internal auditing profession, which encourages evaluation of management controls and systems as an integral part of the audit. This kind of auditing tells management the extent of risk and potential liability—valuable information for any well-run business.

Typically, environmental compliance audits identify specific areas of nonconformance, e.g., improperly labeled PCB transformers, and report the problem to management with a simple recommendation for corrective action. The recommendation is then acted on to bring the facility into compliance, perhaps by marking PCB transformers with labels specified in the regulations. The root cause of the nonconformance is not examined. In a management audit, the auditor probes for the cause of the problem, which could be a lack of procedures, insufficient training of personnel, or something else.

Examples of questions that would be asked by the auditors in a management audit include the following:

- Has the importance of compliance with PCB regulations been communicated to employees by the facility manager?
- How was responsibility for labeling assigned?
- Did the person responsible for labeling have adequate training?
- Was there a self-assessment program at the facility to ensure that labeling responsibilities were carried out?
- Does the facility have a system for correcting deficiencies noted in self-assessments?

These kinds of questions get at the root causes and allow auditors to recommend actions that not only correct the existing condition but enhance the capability of the audited facility to avoid future problems. This approach lets management know that the facility has a program in place to manage for compliance over the long term. It helps management assess the quality of the compliance program and what actions are needed to strengthen it.

If the environmental audit team is to conduct successful audits of management controls, it will need more than basic audit experience and knowledge of regulatory requirements. It is imperative that the team have a high level of collective experience in understanding facility operations, how organizations and procedures work, and management control systems.

During a management audit, auditors typically interview high-level managers. This requires that they have substantial experience in obtaining and interpreting information on which accurate findings and appropriate recommendations can be based. They must also be able to maintain credibility with high-level managers and employees at all levels. It is one thing to report straightforward instances of nonconformance, such as the absence of a PCB label on a PCB transformer. It is quite another thing to explain clearly to a plant manager why there must be a draft self-assessment program or why the plant needs a formal records-retention system. Auditors must be able to talk about risks and liability. These words are part of today's business vocabulary; most managers know this language.

Management audits also require that much more time be invested in audit planning. Crafting good interview questions, audit plans, and checklists is time-consuming. Correspondingly, more time is spent interviewing management and staff at the facility.

Regulatory Authority Enforcement

Recent changes in environmental regulations and enforcement standards indicate a need for environmental auditors to move beyond traditional compliance audits into management audits. The U.S. Sentencing Commission's sentencing guidelines for corporations and federal agencies and employees convicted of federal crimes became effective on November 1, 1991. The guidelines mandate tougher penalties for individuals and organizations that violate environmental statutes. The guidelines also allow federal courts to show leniency when an organization has an "effective program to prevent and detect violations of the law." Accordingly, many companies are developing corporate compliance programs that go beyond basic compliance audits. The guidelines specifically identify the following actions as necessary for an effective program:

- Top management buy-in, support, and participation
- Establishment of a corporate environmental policy
- Communication of the policy to employees
- Delegation of responsibilities
- Written procedures
- Internal auditing

Corporate management is advised that simply having a compliance program, but not fully supporting and implementing it, is a serious mistake. Such an approach could actually increase the risk of serious penalties.

On July 1, 1991, the DOJ issued a policy detailing the factors it will consider in criminal prosecutions for environmental crimes. The policy states that DOJ will "consider the existence and scope of any regularized, intensive, and comprehensive environmental compliance program." The policy further states that audit programs should include "sufficient measures to identify and prevent future noncompliance" and that DOJ will consider whether internal "management audits" are done.

As environmental laws have been reauthorized, Congress has increased the penalties for environmental violations. Meanwhile, there has been a dramatic increase in the number of enforcement actions taken by EPA—particularly against senior managers. This accelerating pace of enforcement is expected to continue, further indicating the need for companies to aggressively and effectively manage environmental compliance. It seems clear that companies need an audit function capable of assessing the adequacy of the overall compliance program. Traditional compliance audits will not be enough.

Areas Examined in Management Audits

Management audits are known by a variety of names—management control audits, operational audits, and systems audits. Although the approach to gathering information varies, the factors to be considered include:

- **Risk Assessment**—The company should conduct an assessment to determine where its highest risks are and then develop a plan to address them.
- **Communication**—The facility manager should regularly communicate environmental policy to employees and emphasize the importance of compliance. The facility should also have a system for communicating environmental responsibilities and new regulatory requirements to employees. There should be a feedback mechanism for employees to communicate their environmental concerns and to advise management of potential violations.
- **Procedures**—The facility should have written environmental compliance procedures. These should be current, cover all pollution pathways, and be peer-reviewed for accuracy and completeness.
- **Responsibilities**—Responsibilities of staff involved in environmental compliance should be clearly written in procedures or job descriptions and understood by employees. Accountability for meeting these responsibilities and the consequences for not meeting them should be made clear.

- **Training**—The facility should have a documented training program that covers requirements and responsibilities for all employees involved in environmental compliance. Training should cover all pertinent compliance requirements and be at a level sufficient to meet the specific needs and responsibilities of the individuals involved.
- **Record Keeping**—The facility should have a formal record keeping system that allows easy retrieval of records.
- **Self-Assessment**—The facility should have a documented self-assessment program that lets facility management know if the facility is meeting environmental requirements and if nonconformances are promptly corrected once identified. This requires assigning environmental oversight responsibility to an individual at the facility who regularly conducts site inspections and reports results to facility management. Such self-assessments provide continuous feedback to management on the status of compliance and supplement the less frequent environmental audits of the facility.

Although the extent of formalization will vary depending on the size of the facility, its environmental risks, and company corporate culture, an effective environmental program should include each of the above components.

The Tennessee Valley Authority's Approach to Management Audits

The mission of the TVA's Environmental Auditing Department is to provide top corporate management and operations managers with thorough, timely, and accurate information on the effectiveness of management controls to minimize environmental risks and achieve compliance. The department conducts management audits of TVA facilities, programs, contractors and subcontractors, and lessees. Its objectives are

- To identify environmental risks
- To determine if adequate management controls are in place to control risks and maintain compliance
- To identify root causes of problems identified
- To recommend corrective actions

The TVA's Environmental Auditing Department uses two approaches in conducting management audits: (1) Programmatic audits look at management controls across the entire company in specific pollution media and regulatory areas, e.g., PCBs, used oil management, and asbestos management. (2) Facility management audits look at management controls at a single facility.

Over the past two years, department staff have completed companywide programmatic audits of the TVA's management of several regulated areas, including

- Used oil disposal
- Waste drum disposal
- Hazardous waste treatment and disposal contracting
- Battery recycling
- Asbestos management
- Hazardous waste transportation

These programmatic audits examine management controls, beginning at the corporate level and extending to facilities. Recommendations address a wide range of weaknesses. The weakness most often found has been the lack of an effective self-assessment process to assure management that regulatory and TVA procedural requirements are being met.

In the past several years, the scope of facility audits has expanded to include facility-level environmental management controls. As each audit team member reviews an individual regulatory area, he or she examines each element necessary for an effective environmental management system. Thus, while the facility audit continues to assess compliance with specific regulatory and procedural requirements, it now provides the needed input (evidence) for a management audit.

At the completion of each audit, the lead auditor consolidates the information obtained from interviews with managers and employees about management controls. This, along with information each auditor obtains on compliance in each regulatory area, is used to rank the overall compliance status of the operation. Operations are ranked into one of five categories:

- **Meets Regulatory and TVA Requirements**—The facility or activity is judged to be in compliance with applicable requirements included in the audit scope. It has a highly effective compliance program.
- **Substantially Meets Regulatory and TVA Requirements**—Audit results verify a high level of compliance. Only a few deficiencies were observed. These deficiencies represent isolated exceptions and the facility or activity is judged to have an effective compliance program.
- **Generally Meets Regulatory and TVA Requirements Except as Noted**— Several instances of nonconformance, some of which were judged significant, were observed. These reflect weaknesses in the compliance program.
- **Requires Improvement to Meet Regulatory and TVA Requirements**— Many instances of nonconformance, some of which were significant, were observed. These significant nonconformances reflect an ineffective compliance program.

- **Requires Substantial Improvement to Meet Regulatory and TVA Requirements**—Numerous significant nonconformances were identified, reflecting a highly ineffective or complete lack of a compliance program.

This ranking system considers both the current status of compliance (the information obtained in a traditional compliance audit) and the effectiveness of the environmental management controls.

Written audit reports are designed to be useful and therefore must be easily understood by management. The TVA's reports are designed to meet the customer's (auditee's) need. A typical report begins with an executive summary that focuses on significant matters and provides management with an overall compliance rating. It presents to management the extent of risk managers, employees, and the corporation are exposed to in the way of penalties. It also identifies actions needed to reduce the risks.

Conclusion

Recent changes in environmental regulatory requirements along with more aggressive enforcement policies and stricter federal sentencing guidelines indicate a need for companies to have effective total compliance programs. Environmental management audits are the best means to assure company managers at corporate and facility levels that adequate management controls are in place to protect the company, its managers, and its employees from penalties associated with civil and criminal enforcement actions. These audits can tell the customer (auditee) just how effective the compliance program really is.

The TVA has moved beyond basic compliance auditing to management auditing over the past few years. It has chosen an approach that uses the traditional compliance audit to collect the evidence on which the management audit is built. These audits are conducted at each facility. In addition, specific companywide programs that pose potential environmental risks are audited. As a result, the audits provide a more useful product than was provided previously by traditional compliance audits. Management audits not only assess the current compliance status, but more importantly, they provide management with the answer to four basic questions which, from a business perspective, are critical:

- Is the environmental compliance program functioning as intended by management?
- Are adequate controls in place where risks and potential liability exist?
- What are the implications or possible outcomes if controls are not added or improved?
- What can be done to improve the compliance program?

References

Buente, D.T., T.G. Echikson, J.L. Connaughton. "Developing and Implementing an Environmental Corporate Compliance Program." Paper presented at the Edison Electric Institute Conference on Corporate Compliance Programs Under the U.S. Sentencing Commission Guidelines, Edison Electric Institute, Washington, DC, 1992.

Deming, W.E. *Out of the Crisis.* Cambridge: Massachusetts Institute of Technology, 1992.

Edison Electric Institute. *Environmental Auditing Case Studies.* Washington, DC: Edison Electric Institute, 1991.

Edison Electric Institute. *Environmental Management Systems Handbook.* Washington, DC: Edison Electric Institute, 1989.

Greeno, J.L., G.S. Hedstrom, and M. DiBerto. *Environmental Auditing, Fundamentals and Techniques*, 2d ed. Cambridge: Arthur D. Little, Inc., 1987.

Iwanski, M.L., and J.R. Thurman. "Environmental Auditing—A Tool to Help Reduce Exposure to Liability." In *Proceedings Air & Waste Management 84th Annual Meeting.* Pittsburgh: Air and Waste Management Association, 1991.

Peters, B.J. "Revolution," *Internal Auditor*, Vol. 22, April 1992.

Sawyer, L.B. *The Practice of Modern Internal Auditing*, 2d ed. Alamonte Springs, Florida: Institute of Internal Auditors, 1981.

U.S. Department of Justice. *Factors in Decisions on Criminal Prosecutions for Environmental Violations in the Context of Significant Voluntary Compliance or Disclosure Efforts by the Violator.* Washington, DC: U.S. DOJ, 1991.

U.S. Sentencing Commission's Organizational Sentencing Guidelines, May 16, 1991 (56 Fed. Reg. 22,761).

Myron L. Iwanski is a lead environmental auditor with the Tennessee Valley Authority's Corporate Environmental Audits, and **John R. Thurman** is manager of environmental audits for the Tennessee Valley Authority.

Quality Management Initiatives Driving Change

GEMI's Environmental
Self-Assessment Program (ESAP)

5

Chris FitzGerald

The Environmental Self-Assessment Program was developed by the Global Environmental Management Initiative to provide practical measurement tools with which to implement the International Chamber of Commerce's Business Charter for Sustainable Development. This chapter describes the development of these measures and how they are applied.

In the past decade a number of cross-industry standards for corporate environmental quality have been promulgated, such as Responsible Care, BCNI, the Keidanren Principles, BAUM, CERES and the International Chamber of Commerce's Business Charter for Sustainable Development: Principles for Environmental Management (**Exhibit 1**). GEMI's *Environmental Self-Assessment Program* (Washington, DC, September 1992: The Global Environmental Management Initiative), or ESAP, is intended to bridge the gap between corporate "goals" for environmental performance and the day-to-day challenges and choices that in the aggregate constitute corporate environmental performance.

GEMI's ESAP was developed and tested over a twelve-month period by GEMI's Data Measurement Work Group comprised of representatives from thirteen member companies,[1] including GEMI and Deloitte & Touche. The purpose of the project was to provide practical measurement tools for assessing progress in implementing the ICC Business Charter. "Charters are fine, but how can they effect changes?" asks Ross Stevens of DuPont, who chaired the Data Measurement Work Group. "We set out to provide a semi-quantitative assessment on how a company is progressing toward charter principles, and how to prioritize its next efforts: where you'll get the most bang for your buck."

Approach

The Work Group began by reviewing member company assessment practices and other self-assessment programs, such as the CMA Self-Evaluation Form for assessing adherence to the Codes of Management Practices under the Responsible Care program. In principle, the ESAP could be applied by a single knowledgeable member of corporate staff, or by division managers. In developing measures specific to the

ICC Charter Principles, the Work Group's approach was characterized by:

- *Development of Program Elements:* The Work Group developed measurable activity-based elements for each of the sixteen ICC Principles. For example, Principle 12: Emergency Preparedness is stated in the Charter as "To develop and maintain, where significant hazards exist, emergency preparedness plans in conjunction with emergency services, relevant authorities and the local community, recognizing potential transboundary impacts." This broad principle is articulated at four activity levels reflecting typical U.S. corporate concerns and practices:

  12.1 Hazard and Incident Assessment

  12.2 Emergency Response Plans

  12.3 Product and Service Safety

  12.4 Employee Training

- *A Matrix Scoring System:* The ESAP reflects the fact that different companies will have different priorities for improvement in different activity levels. The scoring system includes weighting factors of 1-3 and formal performance level descriptors of 0-4. The performance level descriptors (see **Exhibit 2**) are a critical feature of the ESAP approach, as they provide an ordinal scale for measuring progress in program development on a consistent basis across all program elements. The descriptions are cumulative—i.e., a company cannot achieve level 3 unless it has already achieved and continues to maintain system performance as described in levels 1 and 2.

- *Management Systems Focus:* The ESAP is a measure of management *systems* performance rather than of pollution indicators such as TRIS values, incidents, or notices of violations. Thus, mere compliance on a case-by-case basis is the lowest rating—level 1. In levels 2 through 4 the evolution beyond compliance tracks a company's integration of environmental, health, and safety stewardship practices into mainstream business activities.

Exhibit 1: The Business Charter for Sustainable Development Principles for Environmental Management[2]

1. Corporate Priority
2. Integrated Management
3. Process of Improvement
4. Employee Education
5. Prior Assessment
6. Products and Services
7. Customer Advice
8. Facilities and Operation
9. Research
10. Precautionary Approach
11. Contractors and Suppliers
12. Emergency Preparedness
13. Transfer of Technology
14. Contributing to the Common Effort
15. Openness to Concerns
16. Compliance and Reporting

Exhibit 2: Performance Level Descriptions[3]

- **Not Applicable:** A "Not Applicable" rating indicates that a particular element is not relevant to a company's operations due to the nature of the company's industry.

- **Level 1—Compliance:** The company has a goal of regulatory compliance. At this initial level of development, the primary goal of environmental management is to achieve compliance with health, safety, and environmental requirements mandated by government laws and regulations, and to respond to problems promptly and responsibly. Efforts to manage environmental compliance and risk may occur on an as-needed basis or in an informal manner.

- **Level 2—Systems Development and Implementation:** This stage is characterized by the development and implementation of formal environmental management systems. These systems provide compliance management methods and also facilitate the company's efforts to reach environmental performance extending beyond regulatory compliance, to meet more comprehensive corporate policies. These systems also identify environmental investment opportunities that offer the greatest environmental and/or financial returns, considering costs and benefits.

- **Level 3—Integration into General Business Functions:** The company has formal systems to integrate environmental management concerns into its management functions and general business conduct on a regular basis. Environmental information and concerns are thus incorporated into all relevant business planning functions, such as corporate policies; capital budgets; product design, development, manufacture, and disposition; and marketing strategies, hiring decisions, implementation programs, and reporting. The environmental concerns include direct and indirect environmental impacts of products, operations, and services, extending beyond maintaining regulatory compliance.

- **Level 4—Total Quality Approach:** At this highest level, the integrated environmental management systems are applied to operations globally, and are continually evaluated for improvement opportunities. Improvements are implemented using leading technologies and management practices where feasible. A method exists to continuously improve company knowledge and prevent or reduce potentially adverse environmental impacts due to its operations. The full life cycle of products, operations, and services is evaluated in this effort, including direct and indirect or secondary effect on the environment.

- *Reliance on Supporting Documentation:* For each element the reviewer is required to note what documentation or other evidence has been used to verify the assigned scores. This *Basis for Assessment* assures that the assessment process can be replicated over time and verified independently.

Stevens also stresses that the ESAP results are intended to be maintained and updated internally, not published for comparison between companies. "We see the ESAP as an internal diagnostic tool, not to be seen by the outside world. The scoring is to help you track continuous improvement and focus on the best opportunities for improvement."

Applying the ESAP

The ESAP is intended to be conducted by a senior environmental professional (possibly but not necessarily with outside assistance) across all sixteen Charter principles. Within each program element the respondent determines the company's performance level and the relative importance of the element. For example, for program element 8.7, Pollution Control and Reduction (see **Exhibit 3**), the company score might be 2.0 if the respondent determines that the company not only *responds* to laws requiring pollution control (level 1), but also has *formal systems* to "identify potential spill risks and prioritize emissions sources and implement leading cost-effective solutions to reduce or prevent spills and emissions," and "Spill and emissions prevention, control, monitoring and warning systems exceed legal requirements." The respondent is free to use noninteger scores to reflect progress within a performance level—e.g., a score of 2.3 to indicate that levels 1 and 2 had been fully achieved and the company is making significant progress in integrating pollution prevention and reduction program systems with facility and process engineering and activity planning functions.

The respondent also assigns a relative importance weighting to the element on a scale of A (greatest importance), B (medium importance), and C (less importance). The weights are applied against the performance score at the principle level, where they are translated to integer values (3, 2, 1).

Calculating ESAP Scores

The ESAP scores are calculated at the principle level in a matrix combining performance and relative weights. Each element score is multiplied by its weight factor to produce a weighted score, and the score for the ICC principle is calculated as:

(Sum of Element Scores) ÷ (Sum of Weights) = Weighted Average Principle Score

Element	Score	Weight Factor	Weighted Score
x.1	2.3	2	4.6
x.2	2.5	3	7.5
x.3	2.0	2	6.0
Totals		7	18.1
Weighted Average Principle Score		18.1 /7 = 2.58	

Using the ESAP Score Results

What do these laboriously calculated numbers mean? Charles McGlashan, Deloitte & Touche's project manager for the ESAP development project, suggests that the ESAP offers value on two principal tracks: GAP analysis and benchmarking. "GAP analysis requires comparing a company's stated priorities to the results achieved," says McGlashan. "In testing the ESAP over the past year, we found it a very effective tool for GAP. By comparing the elements and principles which score highly on the importance factor to the high scores on performance, companies learned how effective their implementation systems were. Elements with low performance scores and high importance probably deserve a careful look in terms of opportunities for improvement." Over time the scores will gain meaning as barometers of the relative success of various continuous improvement efforts.

The ESAP can also serve as a benchmarking tool, allowing comparisons between operating units of a company. By conducting the ESAP process across the company, participants improved their understanding of how their various operating units approach environmental problems. Managers in the GEMI pilot program found that *the process* of assigning priorities and reconciling perceptions was in itself a hefty benefit of the ESAP review process.

The application of the ESAP to Work Group member companies helped highlight the gaps between which principles were considered most important and which principles were actually best implemented:

Performance Lags Perceived Importance

15. Openness to Concerns
16. Compliance and Reporting
 6. Products and Services
 9. Research
 5. Prior Assessment
10. Precautionary Approach

Perceived Importance Lags Performance

 1. Corporate Priority
 2. Integrated Management
 8. Facilities and Operation
 7. Customer Advice
14. Contributing to the Common Effort
 4. Employee Education
13. Transfer of Technology

Exhibit 3: Environmental Self-Assessment Program

Mark an "X" on the continuum which best estimates the overall performance level of your company. On the line next to the word "Score" write the number that corresponds to the "X" on the continuum. If an element is not applicable, put an "X" on the line next to "NA."

Performance Level

	Not Applicable	**1**	**2**
8.7 Pollution Control and Reduction		Corporation *responds* to laws requiring pollution control.	Formal systems exist to *identify potential* spill risks and prioritize emissions sources and *implement* leading cost-effective solutions to *reduce or prevent* spills and emissions. Spill and emission prevention, control, monitoring and warning systems *exceed legal* requirements.
	NA ———— 0	1	2
8.8 Employee Health and Safety		Corporation *responds* to employee health and safety laws.	System in place to *identify and prioritize* health and safety risks and implement cost effective risk reduction technologies and practices that *exceed legal* requirements.
	NA ———— 0	1	2

Elements

46

Principle 8: Facilities and Operations

"To develop, design, and operate facilities and conduct activities taking into consideration the efficient use of energy and materials, the sustainable use of renewable resources, the minimization of adverse environmental impact and waste generation, and the safe and responsible disposal of residual wastes."

3	**4**	**Element Importance** Please Assign an Importance Weighting to Each Element
		A = Greatest Importance B = Medium Importance C = Less Importance
Pollution prevention and reduction systems are **integrated** with facility and process engineering and activity planning functions. **Direct and indirect impacts** of facilities, operations and activities are addressed. A system exists to **measure progress** toward spill and emission reduction goals.	Pollution prevention and reduction systems are continuously **evaluated** through total quality management techniques to identify and implement improvement opportunities. Systems exist to **solicit, accept, and respond** to input and feedback from employees and appropriate external sources (e.g., regulators, community leaders, technical experts, and industry leaders.)	A B C
2	3	4 Score: _____
Employee health and safety considerations are **integrated** with the planning and management systems of business functions. **Direct and indirect impacts** of facilities, operations and activities on employee health and safety are addressed. Systems exist to **measure progress** toward corporate health and safety goals.	**Systems are continuously evaluated** through total quality management techniques to identify and implement opportunities for improvement. Systems exist to solicit, accept and **respond to input** and feedback from employees and appropriate external experts (e.g., medical community, industry leaders, health and safety professionals.)	
2	3	4 Score: _____

Exhibit 3: (continued)

OVERALL RATING

Principle 8

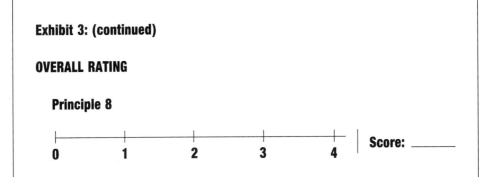

Score: _____

BASIS FOR ASSESSMENT

Please note for your company's records the documentation or other evidence you would use to verify the score assigned for each element:

Element 8.1 Internal Operating Standards/Practices

Element 8.2 Solid and Hazardous Waste Reduction and Treatment

Element 8.3 Waste Residue Management and Disposal

Element 8.4 Energy Minimization Program

Getting the ESAP

GEMI is sharing the ESAP widely in order to facilitate implementation of the Business Charter. Copies can be obtained for $25.00 by writing:

The Global Environmental Management Initiative
2000 L Street, N.W., Suite 710
Washington, DC 20036

The ESAP has received substantial interest from the EPA, UNEP, and industry associations, who are making their members and partners aware of it as well.

Notes

1. In addition to DuPont, the participating companies included Allied-Signal, Eastman Kodak, Procter & Gamble, Dow Chemical, BFI, Digital Equipment Company, Apple, Occidental Petroleum, Weyerhaeuser Company, and the Southern Company.

2. Paris: The International Chamber of Commerce. May 1992, Publication 210/356A. Adopted on November 27, 1990 and first published in April 1991.

3. The Global Environmental Management Initiative, *Environmental Self-Assessment Program* (Washington, DC, September 1992), p. 16.

Chris FitzGerald, the editor-in-chief of *Total Quality* Environmental *Management*, is a consultant in environmental information management and teaches courses on environmental software selection and implementation.

Case Study: Using GEMI's Environmental Self-Assessment Procedure (ESAP) to Evaluate Environmental Performance

6

Robert R. Morton

With increasing expenditures on improving environmental management, there comes a need to determine a return on this investment by measuring performance. One such means of measurement, GEMI's environmental self-assessment procedure (ESAP), is based on a goal of meeting leadership standards and is the focus of this case study. Designed to be a self-assessment tool, the ESAP reflects a company's perceived rating of environmental performance. This perception can be different from actual performance, depending on the objectivity exercised and the level of compliance assurance information available.

Business stakeholders are being pressured more and more these days to become environmentally responsible. For example, regulatory agencies are continuing to increase the effectiveness of their enforcement efforts by using improved techniques for detecting violators and by employing creative compliance incentives. In response, many companies are focusing their attention on environmental management, resulting in increased spending.

Other stakeholders—company employees, investors, and consumers—are all expecting more than just compliance with the law. They want to be associated with *proactive* companies that demonstrate leadership in defining environmental quality. Because of this, many companies have intensified their commitments to environmental quality, resulting in dramatic impacts on company operations such as auditing. With so much attention being paid to environmental management, a keen interest has developed in determining how to measure aspects of these efforts.

To begin measuring, it is necessary to have a standard to measure against. One of the most widely endorsed standards for environmental management is the International Chamber of Commerce's Business Charter for Sustainable Development (ICC principles). There are sixteen ICC principles (**Exhibit 1**) which together provide a framework for the various aspects of environmental management. More than 1,200 companies have endorsed the ICC principles, including a group of leading companies dedicated to promoting high-level environmental performance by putting into practice Total Quality Management principles. This group, the Global Environmental Management Initiative (GEMI), has developed a standardized method, the environmental self-assessment procedure (ESAP), for companies to assess their environmental performance against the ICC principles.

The ESAP format is designed to rate the effectiveness and implementation of elements that comprise each characteristic of environmental management systems. ESAP scoring is based on a scale of 0 to 4 with a score of 1 characterized by a general goal to achieve substantial regulatory compliance. A score of 2 represents development and implementation of environmental management systems. A score of 3

9. Research

To conduct or support research on the environmental impacts of raw materials, products, processes, emissions and wastes associated with the enterprise and on the means of minimizing such adverse impacts.

10. Precautionary approach

To modify the manufacture, marketing or use of products or services or the conduct of activities, consistent with scientific and technical understanding, to prevent serious or reversible environmental degradation.

11. Contractors and suppliers

To promote the adoption of these principles by contractors acting on behalf of the enterprise, encouraging and, where appropriate, requiring improvements in their practices to make them consistent with those of the enterprise and to encourage the wider adoption of these principles by suppliers.

12. Emergency preparedness

To develop and maintain, where significant hazards exist, emergency preparedness plans in conjunction with the emergency services, relevant authorities and the local community, recognizing potential transboundary impacts.

13. Transfer of technology

To contribute to the transfer of environmentally sound technology and management methods throughout the industrial and public sectors.

14. Contributing to the common effort

To contribute to the development of public policy and to business, governmental and intergovernmental programs and educational initiatives that will enhance environmental awareness and protection.

15. Openness to concerns

To foster openness and dialogue with employees and the public, anticipating and responding to their concerns about the potential hazards and impacts of operations, products, wastes or services, including those of transboundary or global significance.

16. Compliance and reporting

To measure environmental performance, to conduct regular environmental audits and assessments of compliance with company requirements, legal requirements and those principles and periodically provide appropriate information to the Board of Directors, shareholders, employees, the authorities and the public.

represents the presence of mature systems now being integrated into general business functions. A score of 4 represents the best score and is characterized by application of proactive leadership techniques and practices, including TQM principles.

Typically, not all the criteria for a particular score are met. For example, some criteria needed for a score of 2 may not be met while at the same time some criteria for a score of 3 for the same element are met. This may result in a rating performance between 2 and 3.

The relative importance of each element is also evaluated (importance factor) based on a ranking of A to C (or 1 to 3), with A representing greatest importance and C representing the least importance. Each score element is multiplied by the importance factor to determine an importance element score. An importance average score for each ICC principle (average principle score) is determined by adding together all important element scores and dividing the result by the sum of all the importance factors.

Case Study

Recently, a multinational, speciality chemical manufacturer hired an environmental management consultant to develop an approach for evaluating and benchmarking its environmental performance. The company has been a longtime leader in its specialty, expanding from a U.S. base of operations to more than a dozen countries on five continents. The company is centralized, with a large corporate environmental staff, including an environmental auditing group.

The environmental management audit designed consisted of a complex review of technical, regulatory, and organizational components of the company's systems and programs. The corporate office and various manufacturing facilities were audited, with the following objectives:

1. To ensure that a high-quality, comprehensive environmental management system exists at all levels of the organization.
2. To develop a more complete understanding of facility processes, internal controls (management and engineering), organization, and responsibilities with respect to applicable environmental regulations.
3. To identify current and past environmental management practices that may affect the company's understanding of current environmental managements systems, and correct those practices that adversely affect the company's ability to achieve and maintain compliance.
4. To ensure that systems are established to identify and respond to changes in corporate, statutory, and regulatory requirements and that those systems effectively address the interrelationships among various parts of the organization.
5. To enhance existing systems or establish new ones by evaluating the overall effectiveness of current management systems.

As an aspect of this approach, various uses of the ESAP were incorporated. The first use of this tool was for self-assessment as originally designed. Key individuals from the corporate office and various manufacturing locations completed the ESAP. This represented the company's perception of how its environmental performance rated.

Next the ESAP was used by audit teams to evaluate each of the facilities audited. In this instance, no importance factors were applied. Average principle scores (APSs) were calculated by adding the individual element scores and dividing by the number of elements. This use of the ESAP served as the fact-based or "reality" evaluation of the company's performance. The results of scores and various means used for comparison for one of the audited facilities are discussed below.

Company ESAP Results

There were four company employees who completed the ESAP for Facility X. **Exhibit 2** indicates the average principle scores without importance factors for each of the sixteen ICC principles. Average scores for all principles ranged between 1.75 and 2.5. This indicates that the respondents believe there is an environmental management program in place and that it is in either the developing or implementing stage and facilitates the objectives of corporate policy and regulatory compliance. It also indicates that the respondents believe that there is room for considerable improvement to fully integrate these systems into general business functions.

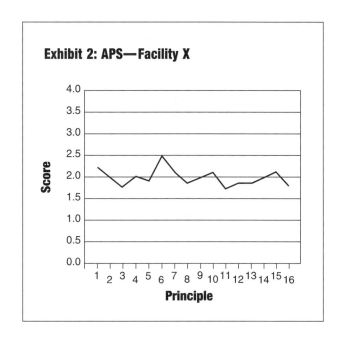

Exhibit 2: APS—Facility X

The narrow range of average scores reflects a belief that performance relative to all ICC principles is consistent. The principle receiving the highest average score was Principle 6, "Products and Services." The principle receiving the lowest average score was Principle 11, "Contractors and Suppliers." However, the narrow range by which the principles receiving the highest and lowest average score differ (less than 0.75) is an indication that the respondents did not perceive much difference in the performance for even these two principles.

Auditors and Company Comparison

Exhibit 3 represents a comparison of the average principle scores between company employees and the auditors for Facility X. The auditor scores varied more than the company scores, ranging from 1.20 for Principle 16, "Compliance and

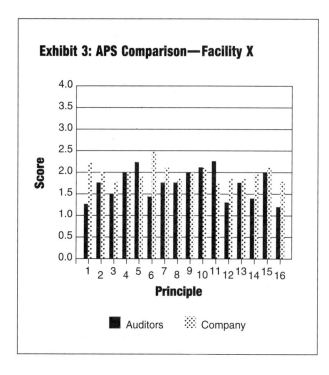

Exhibit 3: APS Comparison—Facility X

Reporting" to 2.25 for Principle 11, "Contractors and Suppliers." Both company (1.8) and auditors (1.20) scored Principle 16 low, primarily due to the Corporate Auditing Group having just recently been formed. However, the company scored Principle 11 lowest (1.75) while the auditors scored it highest (2.25).

The Auditors also scored Principle 5, "Prior Assessment," higher than the company (2.20 to 1.90). The disparity between scores for Principle 1, "Corporate Priority" (company 2.83, second highest and auditors 1.25, second lowest) was larger than even Principle 11. The auditors consistently found throughout the company a perception that environmental management was a higher priority than what was indicated by the information the auditors reviewed.

Comparison to Other Companies

As depicted in **Exhibit 4**, the ESAP completed by the company for Facility X was compared to those completed by six other manufacturers. Generally, the six other companies scored most of the principles between 1.5. and 2.5. Lowest scores were 1.0 and highest scores were 3.0. One score for Principle 1 was 3.5. This indicates that these companies believe that they are generally at a stage of progress where they are about to or have developed/implemented systems to maintain consistent compliance with regulations.

This trend varies for the different principles. Some principles that are not as far along are at the stage of responding/reacting to governmental laws and regulations and company policies, or in between this stage and development of systems. Other principles are beyond systems development and are now about to be or are already integrated across all functions and levels in the business.

The three highest average scoring principles by decreasing order were Principle 1, "Corporate Priority," Principle 14, "Contributing to the Common Effort," and Principle 16, "Compliance and Reporting." The three lowest average scoring prin-

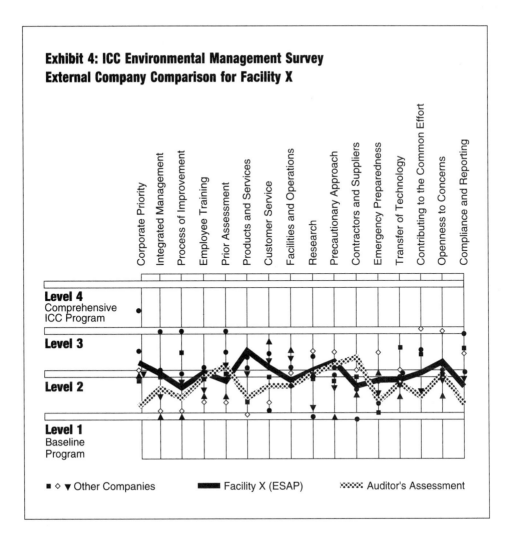

Exhibit 4: ICC Environmental Management Survey
External Company Comparison for Facility X

Level 4
Comprehensive
ICC Program

Level 3

Level 2

Level 1
Baseline
Program

■ ◇ ▼ Other Companies   ▬▬ Facility X (ESAP)   ⋯⋯ Auditor's Assessment

ciples by increasing order were Principle 11, "Contractors and Suppliers," Principle 2, "Integrated Management," and Principle 4, "Employee Training." Facility X compares favorably to these other manufacturers, falling within the range of scores for most of the principles.

Improvement Opportunities

Exhibit 5 depicts the average principle score plotted against the importance factors for the ESAP completed by each of the company employees. Exhibit 5 is divided into octants with the upper left representing a combination of highest importance and lowest score. Principles scored in this octant (Octant 1) represent the best opportunities for improvement. While for Facility X many principles are deemed to be highly important, none of them requires critical attention to assure

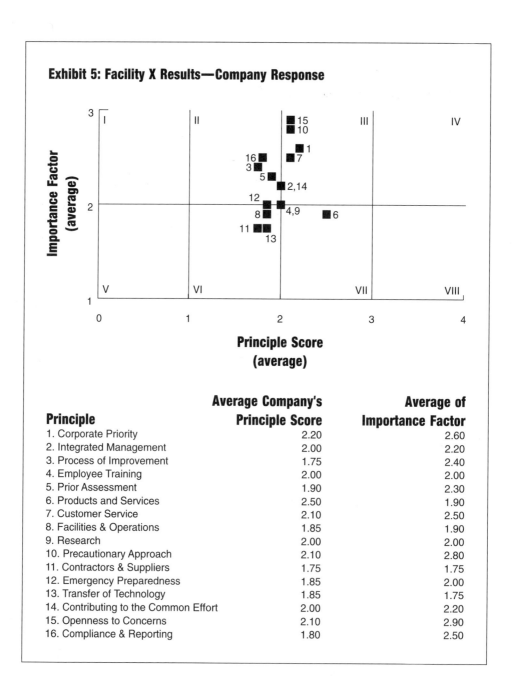

Exhibit 5: Facility X Results—Company Response

Principle	Average Company's Principle Score	Average of Importance Factor
1. Corporate Priority	2.20	2.60
2. Integrated Management	2.00	2.20
3. Process of Improvement	1.75	2.40
4. Employee Training	2.00	2.00
5. Prior Assessment	1.90	2.30
6. Products and Services	2.50	1.90
7. Customer Service	2.10	2.50
8. Facilities & Operations	1.85	1.90
9. Research	2.00	2.00
10. Precautionary Approach	2.10	2.80
11. Contractors & Suppliers	1.75	1.75
12. Emergency Preparedness	1.85	2.00
13. Transfer of Technology	1.85	1.75
14. Contributing to the Common Effort	2.00	2.20
15. Openness to Concerns	2.10	2.90
16. Compliance & Reporting	1.80	2.50

regulatory compliance. However, a concerted effort must be made to continue to move toward full integration of environmental management systems. Highly important principles located in Octant 2 and requiring the most improvement are Principles 3, 5, and 16.

Exhibit 6 depicts the average principle score completed by the audit team

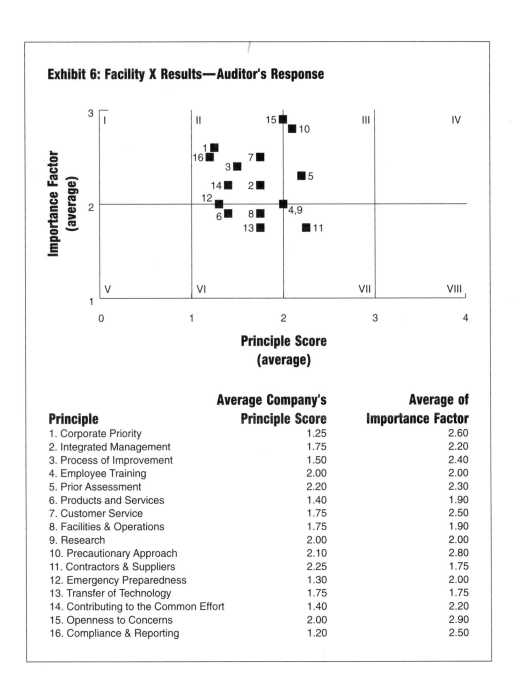

Exhibit 6: Facility X Results—Auditor's Response

Principle	Average Company's Principle Score	Average of Importance Factor
1. Corporate Priority	1.25	2.60
2. Integrated Management	1.75	2.20
3. Process of Improvement	1.50	2.40
4. Employee Training	2.00	2.00
5. Prior Assessment	2.20	2.30
6. Products and Services	1.40	1.90
7. Customer Service	1.75	2.50
8. Facilities & Operations	1.75	1.90
9. Research	2.00	2.00
10. Precautionary Approach	2.10	2.80
11. Contractors & Suppliers	2.25	1.75
12. Emergency Preparedness	1.30	2.00
13. Transfer of Technology	1.75	1.75
14. Contributing to the Common Effort	1.40	2.20
15. Openness to Concerns	2.00	2.90
16. Compliance & Reporting	1.20	2.50

plotted against the company-determined importance factors for the ESAP. Once again, there are no scores that fall into Octant 1. However, there are many more scores than in Exhibit 5 which fall into Octant 2. In particular, Principle 1, "Corporate Priority," is rated by the auditors to be the best improvement opportunity. Exhibit 5 indicates that "Corporate Priority" was not an area of concern.

Conclusion

GEMI's ESAP is proving to be an excellent tool for measuring environmental management. Originally designed to be a self-assessment tool, the ESAP reflects a company's perceived rating of environmental performance.

Where compliance assurance information is not substantial or derived objectively, it may be helpful to conduct an independent environmental performance audit. This exercise may not only result in a fact-based assessment but may point out differences with company management's perception of performance. This type of analysis can facilitate development of a strategic plan for environmental management by identifying areas considered important and requiring improvement. The ESAP could also be used as a benchmarking tool to regularly measure progress and monitor performance in accordance with strategic goals and objectives.

Robert R. Morton, REM, is the corporate director of environmental management services for ATEC Associates, Inc., a national environmental consultant headquartered in Indianapolis. He is a member of a subcommittee on environmental performance evaluation for the U.S. Technical Advisory Group (TAG) to the International Organization for Standardization (ISO) technical committee on environmental management (ISO/TC207). The author thanks Bob Gurdikian and Dan Lewis for graphic support and Bruno Maestri and Dave Wilson for their suggestions.

Certification of Environmental Management Systems— for ISO 9000 and Competitive Advantage

7

Suzan L. Jackson

ISO 9000 has become the buzzword of many industries worldwide as they strive to gain competitive advantage by registering their quality systems. At the same time, environmental performance and improvement is becoming increasingly important in the global marketplace. Work has begun to integrate these two important concepts into a new one: certification of environmental management systems. This chapter explains the new standard and why companies need to recognize and react to their international environmental impact.

ISO 9000 is an international standard that describes elements of an effective quality system. It was written by Technical Committee (TC) 176 of the International Organization for Standardization (ISO). ISO 9000 can apply to any business, anywhere in the world, so its requirements are very generic. It specifies the elements of a system that need to be in place in order to manage quality effectively, but it does not specify how those elements should be implemented. The "how" is left up to the user—ISO 9000 does not tell you how to run your business. In this way, it is flexible enough to be useful to any type of business.

What Is ISO 9000?

ISO 9000 is actually a series of five standards—ISO 9000 through ISO 9004. The first and the last of these standards (9000 and 9004) are advisory standards. Their purpose is to provide guidance to the user. The remaining three standards, ISO 9001, 9002, and 9003, are contractual standards to which a business may choose to register itself. Each describes a quality system model. A business chooses one of these three, depending on the type of business involved. (See **Exhibit 1.**)

ISO 9003 is the most limited of the contractual standards and is meant for businesses that only do final inspection and testing—no manufacturing, no design, no servicing. Due to its limited scope, ISO 9003 is used by only about 5 percent of the businesses that register their quality systems worldwide.

ISO 9002 contains all twelve of the elements of 9003 but adds to these, for a total of eighteen quality system elements. ISO 9002 is applicable for any business that either manufactures a product or supplies a service. About 75 percent of the worldwide registrations are to ISO 9002.

The most comprehensive of the three standards is ISO 9001. It adds two additional elements to ISO 9002—one on design and one on after-sales servicing. So if design/development or after-sales servicing is an integral part of your business, then ISO 9001 is the appropriate standard.

Quality System Registration

The ISO 9000 standards are being used worldwide to register quality systems. Registration occurs when an independent, accredited third party audits a company to certify that its quality system meets the basic requirements of the appropriate ISO 9000 standard. The use of an accredited auditing organization (a registrar) and an international standard means that this registration could be recognized by customers worldwide as proof that the company has a system in place to assure quality.

Quality system registration is quickly becoming a competitive advantage worldwide and even a market requirement in some industries. Companies all over the world are working to implement a comprehensive quality system and get it registered. Fifty-three nations have adopted ISO 9000 as their national quality standard. In the United Kingdom, where quality system registration has been in place for eight years, there are over 16,000 registrations to ISO 9000. Most other European countries have between 200 and 1,000 registrations to date, and the United States had 400 as of August 1992. (See **Exhibit 2.**) In the U.S., the machinery, electronic, and chemical industries are all adopting ISO 9000 quite aggressively. (See

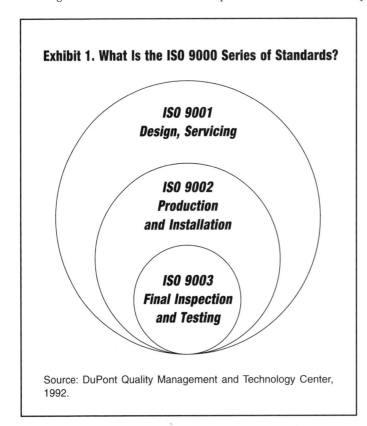

Exhibit 1. What Is the ISO 9000 Series of Standards?

ISO 9001
Design, Servicing

ISO 9002
Production
and Installation

ISO 9003
Final Inspection
and Testing

Source: DuPont Quality Management and Technology Center, 1992.

Exhibit 3.) DuPont, leading the United States in ISO 9000 registrations, has 70 registrations in the United States and 160 worldwide.

Although many of these ISO 9000 efforts are market-driven, the companies using ISO 9000 are finding out that there are many internal benefits that greatly outweigh the effort required to implement such a system. At DuPont, businesses have reported major cost reductions and improvements in product quality, productivity, and customer satisfaction due to implementation of ISO 9000 quality systems. One plant site increased its first-pass yield from 72 percent to 92 percent. A DuPont Electronics business reduced its site costs by $3 million, while improving on-time delivery from 70 percent to 90 percent and decreasing product defects from 500 ppm to 150 ppm. A chemicals plant reduced its product cycle time from 15 days to 1.5 days. Benefits like these have been achieved by businesses all over the world.

Exhibit 2: ISO 9000 Registrations Worldwide Estimates–October 1992

United Kingdom	25,000 -	30,000
Germany	1,000 -	1,500
Australia	500 -	600
United States	400 -	450
Netherlands	200 -	400
Canada	200 -	250
Switzerland	200 -	250
France	100 -	200
Singapore	100 -	150
Spain	50 -	100
Japan	50 -	100
New Zealand	25 -	50

Source: DuPont Quality Management and Technology Center, October 1992.

Exhibit 3: United States ISO 9000 Registrations by Industry–August 1992

Industrial & Commercial Machinery and Computer Equipment	86
Chemicals and Allied Products	80
Measuring, Analyzing, and Controlling Instruments	66
Electronic and Other Electrical Equipment and Components	53
Fabricated Metal Products, Except Machinery & Transportation	32
Stone, Clay, Glass, and Concrete Products	15
Paper and Allied Products	11
Business Services	8
Textile Mill Products	8
Primary Metal Industries	8
Other	33
TOTAL	**400**

Source: *Quality Systems Update*, August 1992.

International Environmental Scene

Given the success of ISO 9000 worldwide, many businesses have begun to expand the scope of their quality management system to include other aspects of their business; environmental management has been one area of focus. Meanwhile, the European Community (EC) has realized that in order to facilitate free trade, environmental aspects must be managed. These two paths have converged in the formation of the Strategic Advisory Group for the Environment (SAGE).

Strategic Advisory Group for the Environment

SAGE was established by the ISO and the International Electrotechnical Committee (IEC) in 1991 to make recommendations regarding international standards for the environment. SAGE concluded that an environmental management system (EMS) was a critical element in achieving environmental excellence and in meeting future environmental needs worldwide. An EMS provides a way to achieve a company's environmental performance goals, using the company's environmental policies and principles as a base. For the chemical industry, an effective EMS is one element of Responsible Care. For any business, it is a part of sustainable development, defined by SAGE as "...operating activities [that] meet the needs of present stakeholders (shareholders, employees, customers, and communities) without impairing the ability of future generations to meet their needs."

SAGE's recommendations stated that a technical committee should be established in the ISO to develop an international environmental management system standard. Like all international system standards, it should be generic so that it could be used by any industry in the world. In addition, SAGE recommended that the new environmental standard should

- Fit with existing management system standards (i.e., ISO 9000)
- Describe best practices in environmental management
- Provide consistency worldwide
- Provide a model for elements of an effective environmental management system
- Not include performance criteria (these should be left to regulatory bodies)
- Include requirements for leadership commitment
- Be voluntary
- Add value to an organization when applied
- Be challenging, yet available to and within the capability of any business worldwide
- Include requirements for communication to stakeholders
- Link to ISO 9000 and other management systems standards through the use of common language to enable a single cohesive management system (see **Exhibit 4**)
- Be flexible

These characteristics encompass many of the characteristics of ISO 9000. Besides authoring the ISO 9000 series, TC 176 has also authored "Vision 2000: A

Exhibit 4: Strategic Vision for Integrated Quality Management System Standards

Standard Hierarchy

Generic Management Systems

Generic Management System

Management System Models for Specific Areas of Concern

Product Quality	Service Quality	Environmental Quality	Health and Safety Quality

Supporting Procedures Guidelines Criteria

Auditing
Customer Service
Life Cycle Analysis
Impact Assessment
Codes of Practice
Management Review
Performance Evaluation

Source: ISO/IEC/SAGE SG1 Document 46: Position Paper, September 1992.

Strategy for International Standards' Implementation in the Quality Arena During the 1990s," which describes the TC's vision of the future of quality system standards. One aspect of Vision 2000 is that a single international standard exists for consistent application worldwide. This single standard may then be supplemented by guidance documents to assist various industries in translating the standard's requirements for their own businesses. Vision 2000 advocates that these guidance documents be written by the same international committee that authored the standard to avoid proliferation of many different interpretative guides. TC 176 has in fact authored guidance documents for the process, software, and service industry segments.

SAGE's recommendations are in line with TC 176's Vision 2000 document. In addition to the above list, SAGE recommends that application guides be written when needed for specific industries to complement the generic international standard.

A SAGE subgroup has been formed on environmental auditing. SAGE notes that there needs to be close cooperation between this subgroup, other SAGE subgroups, and other groups working on international auditing standards. Specifically, the need for a strong link with ISO 10011, the set of international standards on quality auditing, is mentioned. This further integration of quality and environmental system standards would allow integration of management systems as well as integration of system audits, whether external or internal.

The EC and the Environment: Community Eco-Management and Audit Scheme

The EC has proposed a regulation to encourage businesses to continuously review and improve their environmental performance. This Community Eco-Management and Audit Scheme (previously named Eco-Audit) would be voluntary and would include two parts: an EMS and a verified public statement of performance.

As currently proposed, the environmental management system requirement could be met by internal auditors (if the company operates within an ISO 9000 system) or by external assessment. In either case, the auditors would have to meet the requirements of ISO 10011. The EMS would include, among other elements, written environmental policies and internal environmental auditing.

The public statement would report data to describe and quantify the company's environmental performance and would need some sort of validation. This validation, which would likely come from an accredited verifier, would verify that the data arise from a certified EMS and that it is compatible with the previous year's statement. Ideally, the same accredited organizations could verify the public statement, audit the EMS, and possibly also register the quality system against ISO 9000. In any case, the EC would like to avoid the need for a separate certification scheme, which could create greater costs and bureaucracy for companies.

The EC voted on the adoption of the Community Eco-Management and Audit Scheme in December 1992. Eleven of the twelve member nations voted for the proposed regulation; Germany voted against it. The proposal will be considered again in March 1993. Given this delay, registration within this scheme will be available in the fourth quarter of 1994, if it passes its March vote.

EMS Standards: Two Approaches

Currently, there are two different schools of thought on the integration of quality systems and the environment. One is to apply the ISO 9000 standards to environmental systems. The other is to create a separate standard for environmental management systems. Work is progressing on both sides of this issue and it is likely that the two approaches will coexist in some industries.

Applying ISO 9000 to the Environment

This approach is being developed primarily within the chemical industry. The United Kingdom's Chemical Industries Association (CIA) has published

"Responsible Care Management Systems: Guidelines for Certification to ISO 9001—Health, Safety, and Environmental Management Systems in the Chemical Industry." The booklet is patterned after ISO 9001 and is meant to guide organizations in applying their existing ISO 9000 registered quality system to the areas of safety, health, and the environment. This approach is consistent with Vision 2000 and allows for the same basic management system to be used for all areas of a business.

The guide was written with the chemical industry's Responsible Care program in mind. Although an EMS is only one part of Responsible Care, this interpretative guide could be helpful in integrating Responsible Care with existing and future quality and environmental initiatives.

The CIA's guide has a larger scope than just environmental management in that it also includes safety and occupational health. This was done deliberately in anticipation of safety and health management system requirements similar to the proposed environmental requirements (Community Eco-Management and Audit Scheme). The CIA's interpretative guidelines are currently being piloted by ten chemical industry companies in the United Kingdom. If these pilots go as planned, accredited certification of an EMS to these guidelines would be available by July 1994.

Environmental Management System Standard: BS 7750

The British Standards Institute (BSI) has developed and published an environmental management systems standard called BS 7750 (the British equivalent of ISO 9000 is BS 5750). This is a new and separate standard for EMS only, and includes requirements for environmental policies, review and assessment of environmental performance, continuous improvement, communication of performance to the public, and internal auditing.

BS 7750 parallels ISO 9000 in many ways, describing a similar generic model for a management system. The environmental standard has a larger scope than ISO 9000, but with ISO 9000 already in place, BS 7750 would be easier to implement. ISO 9000 provides a foundational quality system on which to build higher-level quality initiatives or broader management systems. Both ISO 9000 and BS 7750 have similar requirements in the areas of management commitment and involvement, internal auditing, the foundation of company policies, and the continual review of audit results versus those policies to encourage continuous improvement.

BS 7750 has been piloted in the United Kingdom by ten companies in the chemical industry. Accredited certification to BS 7750 should be available by July 1994. BSI is also working on a management system standard for safety and health, which would be called BS 8750.

The Issues and the Future

Although these two different approaches seem at odds with each other, both are currently being piloted. With the SAGE recommendations for an international standard for EMS, it seems less a question of what will happen and more a question of when it will happen.

Either of the current approaches can work. Although both encompass the same basic principles, each has its advantages: A separate environmental standard means less interpretation is needed, whereas the application of ISO 9000 to EMS means greater potential for integration. Rather than become entangled in the argument of which approach is best, it would be more beneficial to simply acknowledge that EMS certification is coming and strive within each of our own organizations to apply these basic principles now.

Many of DuPont's European customers are already asking for or requiring an EMS. Besides this kind of market pressure, it is very likely that implementing an EMS will garner the same kind of internal benefits that ISO 9000 quality system implementation has. Ron Zelonka, DuPont of Canada's general manager-fluorochemicals and the chairman of DuPont of Canada's Business Environmental Stewardship Committee, has proposed that all of DuPont of Canada's fluorochemicals businesses certify their EMS; many of the businesses will start down that road in 1993. Regardless of the details of each business' EMS, Zelonka states, "the need for an environmental management system and the need to conform to the environmental management system (whatever the specific system is) will be common to all businesses."

With the increasing focus on quality system registration, the environment, and unrestricted trade worldwide, it is obvious that some sort of EMS certification will become necessary. Like ISO 9000, it is likely to be voluntary but highly market-driven. Given the implications of environmental matters on communities world-wide, it is also likely to be strongly driven by the consumer and the public. Environmental management system certification is on its way, in one form or another.

Suzan L. Jackson is a consultant and instructor in DuPont's Quality Management and Technology Center in Newark, Delaware, specializing in the ISO 9000 Standards and Continuous Improvement. Her DuPont experience includes roles as a process engineer and manufacturing site quality coordinator. Her experience with ISO 9000 includes authoring site documentation, training all levels of personnel, conducting quality audits against ISO 9000, and consulting both within DuPont and externally on implementation of an ISO 9000 quality system.

The European Eco-label and Audit Scheme: New Environmental Standards for Competing Abroad

8

John J. Kirchenstein and Rodger A. Jump

Businesses outside the European Community (EC) will soon discover that pressure is mounting for their products to meet minimum environmental standards now being drafted by the EC. Companies will be pressed to demonstrate that their products and their production facilities and operations (1) help preserve, protect, and improve the environment, (2) contribute toward protecting human health, and (3) ensure a prudent and rational use of natural resources. The EC is offering two avenues to companies: the Eco-label to provide evidence that a product complies with the EC environmental standards and the Audit Scheme to assure potential consumers that a company's operations and facilities do likewise. This chapter presents an overview of the EC Eco-label and Audit Scheme processes and requirements in order to help auditors and environmental managers prepare foreign businesses for commerce with the EC.

The 1957 Treaty of Rome (Article 130r) specifies that an objective of the EC is to "preserve, protect, and improve the quality of the environment, and to contribute toward protecting human health and to ensure a prudent and rational utilization of natural resources."

The EC has been very proactive in addressing environmental issues. Since 1972, the EC has produced over 200 legislative measures concerning the environment. This steady environmental thrust has produced a large volume of regulations that have provided constant challenges to businesses. The issues include plant site acquisition and potential liabilities associated with prior use of the land; cradle-to-grave environmental monitoring of the manufacturing process; product labeling, marketing, and distribution; ultimate disposal of residuals and packaging; environmental management systems and their audits; as well as more specific requirements concerning employee working conditions.

Two environmental initiatives have recently come to the forefront: environmental labeling (*Eco-labeling*) and environmental auditing (*Audit Scheme*). Both of these are being vigorously pursued by the EC member nations because the EC will require their adoption in the very near future. Businesses outside the EC must become aware of these initiatives because they will affect their products, production facilities, and operations.

Background

The Eco-label effort by the EC is expected to bring harmony in an arena where a variety of labels has sometimes presented confusion to EC consumers and businesses. For instance, a green label that concerns 4,000 products and affects 80 percent of consumers has existed in Germany for seven years. The major French chains Monoprix, Prisunic, Carrefour, and Intermarché have together instituted their own green logo. In 1992, the Association Française de Normalisation (AFNOR), the French standards making body, was preparing to issue its own label, *NF Environnement*, which is also voluntary.

The International Standards Organization (ISO) established the Strategic Advisory Group on the Environment (SAGE) to study the need for environmental standardization. SAGE, in turn, recommended that the ISO press for environmental standards. ISO, accordingly, set up an EC working group to develop standards. The working group selected product groups and designated a lead country to identify Eco-label award criteria for each assigned product. The product groups that were selected and the assigned lead assessor countries are shown in **Exhibit 1**.

France was designated the lead nation for paints, varnishes, and related products.

Exhibit 1:
Eco-labeling Product Groups and Lead Country

Kitchen towels	Denmark
Toilet tissue	Denmark
Photocopier paper	Denmark
Writing papers	Denmark
Building insulation materials	Denmark
Textiles	Denmark
Laundry detergents	Germany
Dishwasher detergents	Germany
Household cleaning products	Germany
Shampoo for automobiles	Germany
Batteries	France
Paints and varnishes	France
Paper and plastic waste bags	France
Shampoos	France
Washing machines	UK
Dishwashing machines	UK
Light bulbs	UK
Soil improvers	UK
Hair styling agents	UK
Antiperspirants	UK
Deodorants	UK
Shoes	Netherlands
Cat litter	Netherlands
Domestic heating systems	Germany (awaiting further details)
Refrigerators and freezers	Italy
Packaging materials	Italy (underpinning study)
Building materials	Italy (awaiting further details)
Ceramic tiles	Italy

Source: UK Department of Trade and Industry, May 1992 (referencing the EC Working Group for the Development of Environmental Criteria) and updated by EC Official Journal entries, September 1993.

France enlisted the aid of AFNOR to draft the criteria and technical requirements. The criteria were derived from cradle-to-grave life cycle analyses of the environmental performance of the products. AFNOR finalized the norm, *NF Environnement Label, Technical Rules Applicable to Paints, Varnishes, and Related Products,* in March 1992. It was the intention of AFNOR to issue a French standard until the EC Eco-labeling process was in operation. However, it appears that the AFNOR-designed *NF Environnement* process parallels the EC Eco-label process so that it will be relatively simple for France to make the transition to the EC requirements. AFNOR also generated a list of approved laboratories to conduct specific tests for vendors to demonstrate that their products meet the evaluation criteria.

The Eco-label Procedure

The Eco-label regulation was adopted by the EC Council of Environmental Ministers on March 23, 1992. The regulation provides a voluntary, self-financed procedure to encourage manufacturers to reduce the environmental impact of their products, inform consumers about the environmental performance of their products, and facilitate trade of environmentally benign products. Products that conform to the EC's health, safety, and environmental standards will be awarded an Eco-label after the product goes through the review and approval procedure as outlined in **Exhibit 2**. The Eco-label is shown in **Exhibit 3**.

The EC regulation further requires that each member state must designate a "Competent Body" to carry out the functions of Eco-labeling, such as assessing applications for labels and making contractual arrangements with Eco-label applicants and recipients of awards. The Competent Body can recommend award of the Eco-label if the product meets the EC environmental criteria. Final award follows only after the other eleven member states and the Commission concur. The product may receive the Eco-label within thirty days if no objections arise. There is a formal appeal procedure to be followed

---

Exhibit 2: Procedure for Awarding Eco-labels

1. The manufacturer (or importer) submits an application to the Competent Body.

2. The Competent Body in an EC state recommends the award and informs the European Commission (the governing body of the EC) and the other member states.

3. Should there be no objection after 30 days:
   a. A contract is signed between the Competent Body and the manufacturer (or importer).
   b. A list of products covered by the contract is published.

4. Should there be an objection:
   a. Resolution of the objection is attempted for 15 days.
   b. If the objection still stands after 45 days, the matter is referred to the Regulatory Committee (all EC members and the Commission).

in case of objections. For imported products, the importer will need to apply for the Eco-label award. The same criteria apply for imports as for products manufactured within the EC.

The member nations, as well as the EC working group, debated long over the content of the Eco-label contract specifications before agreeing on fees. The application fee alone is ECU 400 (1 European Currency Unit = $1.12 in January 1994). The fee is payable to the EC member state Competent Body where the product is entered into the EC or the member state where it is manufactured or first marketed.

Successful applicants are required to sign a licensing agreement with the member state Competent Body that awarded the Eco-label specifying the conditions of display and the effective period of the label. The annual license fee has been set by the EC Commission as .15 percent of the annual product sales within the EC at factory prices plus value-added tax (VAT). The minimum fee is ECU 500.

It is interesting to compare the costs of acquiring the Eco-label with the cost of acquiring the AFNOR *NF Environnement* label. The fees for the AFNOR label are about $2,500 for drawing up the technical rules for each applicant, $1,300 for processing costs, $1,200 per day for plant inspections, plus unspecified costs for testing a product, and $1,500 minimum for an annual royalty for use of the *NF Environnement* label. All these costs are subject to the value-added tax.

AFNOR recently has been designated the Competent Body by the EC for administering the Eco-label for paints and varnishes. This action would appear to do away with the need for an *NF Environnement* label for paints and varnishes. As of September 1993, twenty firms had applied for the Eco-label for some 100 water-based paints. No applications had been filed for paints based on solvents other than water. AFNOR declined as of September 1993 to provide any of the names of the firms that have applied because the applications were still in process.

The United Kingdom (UK) responded positively by designating a Competent Body to administer the Eco-labeling process. To assure that the body is independent but official, and to demonstrate that it has authority and is impartial, a non-departmental public body was created. On March 5, 1992, Dr. Elizabeth Nelson (chairwoman of a private consulting group) was named as the first head of the UK's official Eco-labeling body. Dr. Nelson is assisted by a board to accomplish the requirements set forth in the EC Eco-labeling regulation.

In May 1992 the UK-led dishwasher Eco-labeling group produced a pilot Eco-labeling criteria document. The criteria were derived from a life cycle analysis of the product. The key criteria, or mandatory threshold levels, are those values that may not be exceeded without making the product unacceptable for award of an Eco-label.

The following key criteria pertain to dishwashers:

- Energy consumption
- Water consumption
- Detergent consumption

Additional best-practice criteria were also set, but at less challenging levels than the key criteria:

- User instructions
- Encouragement to recycle certain components
- Performance criteria

The dishwasher document is typical of the other product Eco-labeling documents. Some documents, such as those for paper and paper products and the one on paints, varnishes, and related products, contain specifications that more precisely define threshold levels. For example, the acceptable level of glycol and derivatives is set at less than 5 percent by weight of the paint product and any substances classified as carcinogenic, mutagenic, or teratogenic (causing fetal malformations) as per EC directives numbers 79831 and 83467 are prohibited altogether.

Businesses should take note that the EC Eco-label regulations for products spill over into *how* the products are manufactured. The statement "The Eco-label shall in no case be awarded to products manufactured by processes which are likely to harm significantly man and/or the environment" clearly goes beyond the can of paint sitting on the store shelf.

Recycling

Recycling will receive increased emphasis in all categories. Recycling has become a worry to U.S. exporters because it is the most difficult part of a product's life cycle for a foreign firm to address. Recycling of the firm's product at the end of its operational life presents a number of problems for a foreign firm that a domestic firm can handle with comparative ease. For example, how would a U.S. manufacturer or exporter of dishwashers manage recycling in an EC country?

Germany has already implemented its own strict recycling laws that have forced packaging redesign for even the smallest products.

Audit Scheme

The EC recognized that both social and industrial pressures signaled a need for improved environmental business policies and effective management systems to supervise environmental practices. As a result, in 1992 the EC proposed a regulation encouraging voluntary participation by industries in a Community environmental auditing process called Eco-audit. The process has since been renamed Audit Scheme. The EC Council Regulation was adopted in 1993.

EC members are reviewing a draft ISO Audit Scheme document prepared by a Canadian group. Antoine Cayla, AFNOR delegate to SAGE, expressed the view in September 1992 that the Canadian draft would require very little revision to be acceptable to the EC.

The EC Audit Scheme plan relates principally to sites where industrial activities are conducted. Its purpose is to evaluate and improve the environmental performance of industrial activities and provide relevant information to the public. The participants will be urged to

- Establish internal environmental protection systems
- Keep the public informed about their environmental performance
- Have their public statements verified by an accredited environmental auditor

The environmental protection systems will have to take into account the EN 29000 series of standards (the ISO 9000 quality assurance series of standards as adopted by the EC) and any future standard specifically set forth for environmental management systems.

Those companies (sites) in the EC participating in the Audit Scheme will be listed in the Official Journal of the European Communities. The list will be updated annually based on notice from the Competent Bodies that the participating companies have submitted timely, verified environmental statements. The statements must cover all significant environmental issues relevant to the site. Sites will not be judged on quality of environmental performance but rather on the accuracy of the content of the statements. The process requires independent verification of the statements by accredited environmental auditors. Details of the verification procedures have not yet been finalized.

Companies or sites appearing on the official list of Audit Scheme participants will be authorized to display an Audit Scheme logo for public relations purposes. The Audit Scheme logo is shown in **Exhibit 4**, together with three statements, at least one of which must be used in conjunction with the logo.

Unlike the Eco-label, the Audit Scheme logo may not be displayed on a product. Audit Scheme logos, when used with the appropriate phrase in advertisements or on company stationery, will have to include a statement to indicate that the logo is related to a site verified by an audit. Each site that is registered will need to establish an "internal environmental protection system." Depending on the potential overall environmental impact of the site activity, the auditing frequency could vary from one to three years. An annual audit would be conducted for sites with a high environmental impact, every two years for moderate-impact sites, and every three years for low-impact sites.

AFNOR developed their Norm 30200 as part of the Audit Scheme. The norm was completed May 1993 and implements the environmental portions of ISO 9000.

Exhibit 4: The Audit Scheme Logo

This logo must be used in conjunction with one of the following phrases, as appropriate:

- All our production sites in the EC participate in the Audit Scheme process.
- All our production sites in (name of Community Member State) participate in the Audit Scheme process.
- The following production sites of our company participate in the Audit Scheme process.

Source: Annex III, Audit Scheme, Official Journal of the European Committees C76/02, March 27, 1992.

United Nations Cleaner Production Program

The Cleaner Production Program was inaugurated by the United Nations as a result of the Earth Summit held in Rio in June 1992. The Cleaner Production Program, headquartered in Paris, was chartered to assist all nations, and especially nations with emerging economies, to plan for cleaner production as an intrinsic part of their economic development. It would appear that the United Nations could borrow from the EC Audit Scheme or the efforts of the ISO in order to help promote worldwide standards; however, the small, overworked Cleaner Production Program staff has few resources to devote to such coordination.

Environmental Management Standards

During the life of the Eco-label license or the registration period of the Audit Scheme, participating manufacturers must maintain their products and their industrial activities in conformance with the criteria for their products and operations. The company's quality manuals will need to emphasize documentation of procedures, adherence to specifications, legal requirements, and other requirements of society. Indications are that establishment of a responsive quality management system (QMS) that is heavily oriented toward Total Quality Management would be a precondition to attempting Eco-labeling or applying for Audit Scheme registration.

The British Standards Institution (BSI) began in 1990 to prepare a standard that would provide an independent professional assessment for all aspects of a company's environmental performance against national standards and codes of practice. The resulting document was BS 7750, "Specification for Environmental Management Systems," published in March 1992. The final selection of the standards number (7750) was a deliberate action to link the new environmental management standard to the BSI and the international quality systems standards (BS 5750/EN 29000/ISO 9000).

As occurred in the writing of ISO 9000, when BS 5750 was used by the ISO as the leading source, Bernardo Delogu (Director General of the EC Directorate on Environment, Nuclear Safety and Civil Protection) commented on BS 7750 as being the model for the comparable European standard. He said, "It is clear that it [BS 7750] could later be transferred easily into a European Standard....[I]t could even be more important than before." At the ISO level, the ISO/International Electrotechnical Commission (IEC) working group on environmental management is gathering source material to write an international standard. However, it is likely that the ISO will rely heavily on the EC Audit Scheme regulation and incorporate the BS 7750 experience in the proposed international standard on environmental management systems.

BS 7750 is a management tool and as such its use is entirely voluntary in relation to the EC Audit Scheme plan. BS 7750 is not a substitute or implementing instrument for the EC Audit Scheme plan although it complements and is consistent with the plan. The standard provides a suggested environmental management system that would satisfy the EC Audit Scheme management system requirements.

BSI will be monitoring the application of the standard across a wide range of sectors. The experiences gained during the pilot application are being reviewed beginning in September 1993, together with reactions and progress of the EC Audit Scheme, and a revision may follow.

Employment of BS 7750 would be useful to any firm seeking to strengthen its TQM by the inclusion of environmental management policy and procedures. The standard defines environmental management system requirements to include guidance on the preparation of policy, organization, documentation, operational control, records, audits, and periodic management reviews.

Since BS 7750 shares common quality management system principles with BS 5750, British organizations are opting to follow BS 5750/ISO 9000 guidelines when forming their environmental management systems. Other Europeans, anticipating a comparable European standard, are doing likewise. Established procedures for the assessment of compliance with BS 5750 are also applicable to assessment of compliance with BS 7750. A good number of international and American organizations have already achieved registrations to ISO 9000; therefore, incorporation of the BS 7750 specifics would pose no problem.

According to Ann C. Perry, Union Carbide's institute plan quality manager, "ISO 9000 has a positive cascading effect throughout the organization. It helps to improve safety, management, R&D, and other functions as well." Similar thoughts have been expressed by many of the quality experts from ISO 9000-registered firms throughout the world, including Digital Equipment Corporation, DuPont, 3M Company, and Sun Microsystems.

Momentum is gathering in other nations, such as France, for adoption of environmental management system standards. The *Technical Rules Applicable to Paints, Varnishes, and Related Products* published by AFNOR provides for audits "to ensure that the products benefitting from the *NF-Environnement* label are permanently manufactured in accordance with the certified characteristics, where necessary *setting up a quality assurance system* complying with the prevailing standard" (emphasis ours).

The Current Status in the United States

An informal survey of ten U.S. firms conducted by the authors revealed that most of the businesses surveyed were not aware of the Eco-label or Audit Scheme. Some of the firms selected for the survey were cited in a recent *World Trade* magazine article concerning ISO 9000, and some were cited in a *Business Week* article in 1992 as being some of the most aggressive small U.S. exporters. Several of the staff surveyed expressed the mistaken view that complying with ISO 9000 was probably tantamount to meeting Eco-label and Audit Scheme requirements.

The Green Cross and the Green Seal are two standards bodies that were established in the United States over the past few years by environmental activist groups. Their effectiveness has been limited partly because it has not been demonstrated to the U.S. business community that securing the Green Cross or the Green Seal would benefit business. AFNOR staff in Paris obtained copies of a Green Seal standard concerning recycled motor oil and another on printing and writing paper. The AFNOR staff seemed to have the impression that the Green Seal standards had the stature of an ASTM or ASQC standard.

Without the support of American business, it is doubtful whether the Green Cross or Green Seal standards will assume the force of ASTM, ASME, or ASQC standards. The Green Cross and Green Seal organizations seem more oriented toward political activism as evidenced by Mikhail Gorbachev recently aligning himself with Green Seal efforts to "reform the toxic economies" of the world.

Conclusion

Businesses outside the EC must become aware of the mounting pressures that will impact their products, production facilities, and operations resulting from environmental standards being implemented by the EC. In most of the EC countries the standards are still voluntary. However, it appears to be only a matter of time before the standards become mandatory and exports to the EC will need to conform. Also, we expect that within ten years many of the Eastern and Central European countries will have caught up with the EC in their environmental program requirements. In fact, some Eastern and Central European countries already have more stringent emission standards than their Western neighbors. Businesses outside the EC should become familiar with Eco-label, Audit Scheme, and the existing European standards for environmental management systems.

As for the impact of upcoming EC environmental standards on U. S. industry, Joseph Cascio, program director of product safety and chemical management for IBM, predicts, "Four years from now American plants will have to be certified to environmental standards in order to sell their products in Europe." American business must not hesitate to develop environmental strategies for near-term implementation.

However, it is evident from this survey of the field of environmental standards that there is much flux and uncertainty for business decision makers to contend with, as is demonstrated by the number and diversity of bodies bidding to establish environmental standards. The EC, the United Nations, Green Seal, the International Standards Organization, the ASTM, and so on are well intended. However, their combined effect presents a world of confusion to U.S businesses that export or plan to export. The best advice is for each business to actively support establishment of cost-effective standards through long-recognized standards bodies and to stay informed.

John J. Kirchenstein is senior international consultant to Tennessee Associates International (TAI) of Maryville, Tennessee. With offices in fifteen countries, TAI specializes in melding a firm's functional and organizational capabilities to create a quality management system for continuous improvement of products, services, and processes.

Rodger A. Jump, PE, is president of International Business Consultants (IBC), Rockville, Maryland, and worked on the startup of the Environmental Restoration Program for the U.S. Department of Energy at Oak Ridge, Tennessee, and at DOE headquarters in Washington, D.C. Mr. Jump recently joined Smith, Barney, Shearson in Washington, DC.

Environmental Auditing and the New ASTM Standards: A Useful Management Tool or an Enforcement Time Bomb?

9

William P. Gulledge

ASTM is now developing standard guides to precisely identify and define new auditing practices. These include a guide for assessing the effectiveness of an organization's environmental management program. They are reproduced here to encourage further discussion and participation in the auditing community.

During the past fifteen years, environmental auditing has served business, industry, government, and the general public in a variety of ways. What started as a use for environmental auditing to assess compliance has grown into other specialty audits such as measuring the effectiveness of an environmental management system or evaluating the success of a pollution prevention program. Today, environmental auditing has widespread use from ensuring compliance to assisting in total quality management.

An environmental audit must be distinguished from an environmental assessment. An environmental assessment, such as the procedure described in ASTM Standard E 1527-93 for conducting a Phase I environmental site assessment for commercial real estate, is a definitive study and conclusion to determine if certain environmental conditions exist. The goal is to identify recognized environmental conditions that adversely impact or may impact human health or the environment.

Normally, an environmental assessment is less rigorous and more subjective than an environmental audit. As commonly known, an environmental audit is a systematic, documented, objective, investigative process of a site, business or government entity or environmental program, to determine compliance with environmental laws and regulations or other corporate or government policies.

Most environmental audits are used to determine site compliance with applicable environment, health or safety requirements. Environmental compliance audits formally originated in the 1970s, and the chemical and petroleum industries are considered to be the founders of compliance audits. Enforcement actions in the late 1970s by the Security and Exchange Commission against certain manufacturers required these companies to develop environmental auditing programs.

The essentials of internal environmental auditing programs are the same as they were twenty years ago. These essentials include:

- Audit program development and support by top management;
- Selection and training of auditors;
- Prioritization of sites for conducting audits;
- Reporting of audit results and preparing schedule to correct deficiencies identified in the audit; and
- Follow up to correct deficiencies and prepare reaudit schedule.

During the late-1970s until the mid-1980s, the U.S. Environmental Protection Agency (EPA) had an active interest in environmental auditing. Emerging from an initial position of requiring third-party audits and later evaluating incentives to conduct audits, EPA finally issued, in 1986, an environmental auditing policy that encouraged voluntary compliance audits. EPA wanted to encourage private auditing programs and study successful programs so that other companies, particularly smaller businesses, could get a head start on developing environmental auditing programs on their own. (For further discussion of the history of environmental auditing, see *Air Emissions, Baselines and Environmental Auditing*, edited by Jacqueline Shields, Van Nostrand Reinhold, 1993.)

Important Environmental Auditing Issues

EPA's interest in environmental auditing declined in the late 1980s. However, several important issues related to the conduct and use of environmental audit information have emerged from users of environmental audits. The primary issue is the possible use by regulators of information obtained in an audit against a regulated entity. Are there privileges and immunities that can be offered? Several government guidelines have attempted to clarify the government's position.

EPA has the authority and has successfully obtained environmental auditing results for selected enforcement actions. More frequently, the Agency has interpreted one of the benefits of environmental auditing, establishing and implementing comprehensive environmental auditing programs, as a provision in enforcement consent decrees. On July 1, 1991, the Department of Justice (DOJ) attempted to clarify factors for bringing criminal prosecutions for environmental violations, and at the same time, continue to encourage self-audit programs.

DOJ's policy can be summarized as companies with established, well-staffed, and well-funded environmental auditing programs that act on findings and recommendations discovered in an audit may receive mitigation consideration for environmental compliance violations. Discretion is given to the individual prosecutor.

ASTM Standards for Environmental Auditing

Despite the government's attempts at clarifying liability, most companies and many government agencies believe that the advantages of environmental auditing far outweigh any perceived liability. Members of ASTM Subcommittee E-50.04 on Environmental Performance Standards, who are active environmental auditors, identified the need to provide further guidance on environmental compliance auditing. The guidance was needed to address several legal issues including privileges and immunities from prosecution, reporting of environmental violations, liability of the auditor, and attorney/client privilege. At the same time, a good technical guide was needed to outline major elements of a compliance audit.

An environmental auditing section was created under Subcommittee E-50.04 in 1993. Two standards are in draft form and are undergoing subcommittee review and ballot. The first one is a standard guide for environmental compliance audits. This standard addresses the legal and technical objectives mentioned above. The standard is very specific to U.S. environmental laws and regulations, for use by U.S. interests, but is designed to be compatible with any international auditing standards that may be approved by ISO.

The environmental compliance auditing draft standard includes the following topics:

- Audit Team Staffing and Qualifications;
- Elements of the Environmental Regulatory Compliance Audit;
- Pre-Visit, Site Visit, and Post-Visit Activities;
- Evaluation and Report Preparation.

E-50.04's second environmental auditing draft standard is not compliance based, but is instead a guide for assessing the effectiveness of an organization's environmental management program. It's essentially an environmental management systems audit. The guide includes an overview of subjects that should be evaluated for the audit and outlines major attributes of a successful auditing program. Topics discussed in this draft include:

- Auditor Independence;
- Professional Proficiency;
- Audit Scope of Work and Performance of Audit Work;
- Reporting, Quality Assurance, and Followup.

Both draft standards are being revised.

Standard Guide for the Study and Evaluation
of Corporate Environmental Management Systems

Approved March, 1992, as an Environmental Auditing Standard
by the Institute for Environmental Auditing, Alexandria, VA

ASTM Subcommittee E-50.04 on Environmental Regulation Performance Standards

Ballot Draft #1- September 13, 1993

1. Scope

1.1 Purpose: This standard defines minimum acceptable practices for the study and evaluation of environmental management systems. It is intended to be sufficiently flexible to be adapted to the particular circumstances of individual audits of such systems.

This standard is intended to govern the conduct of environmental audits of environmental management systems. Those who evaluate environmental management systems owe a responsibility to both management and a board of directors, providing both with information about the adequacy and effectiveness of the organization's system of environmental management.

1.2 Types of Environmental Audits: Environmental audits of environmental management systems are only one of several types of environmental audits routinely performed. While standards are needed to govern all of the types of environmental audits that are performed, these standards relate solely to audits of environmental management systems. Accordingly, whenever the terms "environmental audit," "environmental auditing," or "environmental auditor" are used in this standard, they are intended to apply solely to audits and auditors of environmental management systems.

1.3 Independence: Those who study and evaluate environmental management systems must be independent of the activities they audit. Independence permits those who provide the evaluation to perform their work freely and objectively.

1.4 Other Considerations: In setting these standards, the following developments were considered:

• All levels of management, as well as boards of directors, can be held accountable for the adequacy and effectiveness of their organization's systems of environmental management.

• No generally accepted standardized approach for studying and evaluating environmental management systems currently exists. Several standards have been proposed by international standards setting organizations (see Appendix A).

• Internal environmental management systems vary widely, and no generally accepted practices for providing such management have yet been established. However, in an appendix to a Federal Register environmental auditing policy statement (Vol. 51, No. 131, pages 25008 to 25010, July 9, 1986), the Environmental Protection Agency (EPA) has provided some general guidance that may be useful.

The responsibilities and functions of the environmental auditor should be related to the scope and complexity of environmental management systems in place in the organization. The auditor should not be expected to assess compliance with laws and regulations, but rather the organization's system of determining non-compliance and its response thereto. In all cases, however, the environmental auditor is responsible for providing management and the board of directors with an objective, systematic, and documented evaluation of the environmental management systems under review.

2. Referenced Document

2.1 ASTM Standards: (Hold for reference to ASTM compliance environmental auditing and pollution prevention standards)

3. Terminology

3.1 Scope: This section provides definitions and descriptions for many of the words used in this guide.

3.2.1 Definitions: "Environmental management systems" are those policies, procedures and activities effected by the entity's board of directors, management and other personnel, which are designed to provide reasonable assurance that environmental objectives are being achieved.

3.2.2 "Environmental auditing" is a systematic, documented, periodic and objective review of conditions, operations, and practices related to meeting environmental requirements.

3.2.3 "Environmental policy" is a statement of principles regarding an organization's intent to meet environmental objectives.

4. Significance and Use

4.1 Uses: This standard is to be used by organizations and individuals for assessing the environmental management program of an entity (company, site, municipality, government). Results of the assessment may be used by the organization or individual at their discretion. Generally, the results of an environmental management program assessment are for internal use and not for public distribution.

4.2 Clarification on Compliance Use: This standard is not a compliance environmental audit. In order to completely determine a facility's compliance status, a more detailed review of compliance issues is warranted.

5. Independence

Environmental auditors should be independent of the activities they audit. When environmental auditors are independent, they are best able to provide impartial and unbiased judgments that are critical to a successful audit. Independence is achieved through organizational status and objectivity.

5.1 Organizational Status: The organizational status of environmental auditors should make clear the importance of the function while ensuring an unbiased view.

5.1.1 For internal environmental auditors, clear support from senior corporate management, preferably the board of directors, should be expressed so that the auditors are assured of freedom from interference to complete their work. This should include the following:

- The individual within the entity who is responsible for environmental auditing should report to someone, such as a member of the board of directors, with the authority to ensure broad audit coverage, adequate consideration of audit reports, and appropriate action taken on audit recommendations.

- The individual within the entity who is responsible for environmental auditing should communicate directly with a member of executive management or the board of directors on a regular as well as special issue basis. Significant audit findings, program status, work schedules and budgets should be reported in writing at least annually to a member of executive management or the board of directors.

- Executive management of the entity should concur in the selection of the individual responsible for environmental auditing.

- The entity should have a written charter, approved at the appropriate level within the entity, that defines the purpose, authority, and responsibility of the internal environmental auditing function.

5.1.2 For external environmental auditors, their purpose and scope should be consistent with and coordinated with the internal environmental audit function (if one exists). Additionally, they should:

- Certify that both the audit firm and the individual auditor(s) have no relationship, for example through work, ownership, or personal mechanisms, that could bias their independence. The firm should establish procedures to enable it to provide the certification.

- Disclose any relationship, considered in making the above certification.

- Attest to the strict confidentiality they will employ in completing an audit, so long as the auditor has no independent obligation to disclose certain findings of the audit.

- Demonstrate a commitment to professional and ethical standards generally accepted in the environmental auditing profession such as maintaining membership in professional organizations and adhering to established codes of ethics.

5.2 Objectivity: Environmental auditors should be objective in performing audits. Objectivity is a mental attitude that enhances an unbiased view of facts and facilitates fair judgment on audit matters. Objectivity requires that environmental auditors have an honest belief in their work product and that no significant quality compromises are made.

5.2.1 Internal environmental auditors should not be assigned to projects where their ability to exercise objective professional judgment is compromised, such as:

- Where personal or professional conflict of interest exists.

- When auditors become accustomed to a certain facility or operation such that they lose their objectivity due to familiarity.

- Where auditors assume operating responsibility for departments they may audit.

- Where auditors are presently assigned to departments that they may audit.

- Where auditors were involved in the design and installation of the environmental or pollution control systems being audited.

Environmental auditors should not audit environmental or pollution control systems where they are directly involved in the actual operations of such systems.

5.2.2 External environmental auditors, both the auditing firm and the individual auditor(s), in addition to the preceding standards for internal environmental auditors, should also have no ownership or operating interest in the entity, facility or process being audited. Environmental auditors should have the absolute freedom to refuse or withdraw from projects where they have a real or apparent conflict of interest.

6. Professional Proficiency

Environmental audits should be performed with proficiency and due professional care. Professional proficiency is determined when the audit team collectively has the knowledge and skills needed to carry out its audit responsibility. Individual auditors should maintain the standards for the specific discipline they represent or professional organization with which they are affiliated, including any established code of ethics.

6.1 Knowledge: Environmental audit teams should have collective knowledge in all areas essential to the performance of environmental audits. This knowledge could include, but is not restricted to, management information systems, engineering, control systems, management systems, accounting, finance, statistics and law. Further, each auditor should have an appreciation for management principles, environmental issues, quantitative methods, and computerized information systems.

6.2 Skills: Environmental auditors should have demonstrated competence in key audit skill areas, including, but not restricted to:

1. Interpersonal: skills in dealing with people, understanding human relations and maintaining a positive attitude.

2. Communication: competence in verbal and written communication so that audit findings and recommendations can be effectively conveyed.

3. Organization: ability to organize, in a logical manner, work objectives and the process being audited.

4. Analytical Skills: ability to apply rational thought and a systematic approach to the performance of the audit.

6.3 Continuing Education: Environmental auditors should seek to maintain and enhance their competence in relevant knowledge and skills. They should maintain their standing in the professional discipline they represent and maintain a current understanding of auditing tools and techniques. Relevant continuing education may be obtained through membership and participation in professional societies; attendance at conferences and seminars, college courses, in-house training, and participation in research projects. The majority of continuing education activities should be related to environmental and auditing issues.

6.4 Due Professional Care: Environmental auditors should exercise due professional care. This calls for being alert to the possibility of wrongdoing, errors and omissions, inefficiency, waste, ineffectiveness, and conflict of interest. When the auditor suspects wrongdoing, he should report his findings to management. If management does not take corrective action, the auditor should notify the board of directors (or appropriate committee). If the board does not take corrective action, the auditor should consider resigning from the engagement.

Due professional care also means using reasonable skill and judgment in performing the audit and evaluating operating standards to determine if they are acceptable. Auditors should exercise due professional care and caution in pursuing indications of acts of noncompliance and should follow applicable legal requirements in notifying the proper authorities of acts of noncompliance. In cases where applicable legal requirements are vague, authoritative interpretation should be sought either from legal counsel or from regulatory agencies.

7. Audit Scope of Work

The scope of the audit or an organization's environmental management system should encompass all the policies, procedures and practices in place in the organization designed to identify and assess environmental matters. The scope of the audit should be clearly defined before the audit begins. The scope may be revised to address specific objectives of a particular audit.

7.1 Scope of Audit: The scope of the environmental management system audit should encompass the adequacy and effectiveness of the organization's system of environmental management control:

- *Adequacy:* The system provides reasonable assurance that the organizations environmental objectives will be met.

- *Effectiveness:* The system is functioning as intended.

7.2 Environmental Objectives: The entity adopts objectives and designs policies, practices, and procedures in light of those objectives. Management is responsible for establishing the environmental management systems. The objectives of environmental management control are to ensure: (1) compliance with management's environmental practices, procedures, and with applicable laws and regulations; and (2) the reliability and integrity of information relating to environmental matters.

- The audit should include a review of the systems established to ensure compliance with those policies, practices and procedures which could have a significant impact on environmental operations and reports, and should determine whether the organization is adhering to the established policies. Auditors should determine whether the systems are adequate and effective.

- The audit should also include a review of environmental operations or programs to ascertain whether results are consistent with established objectives and goals and whether programs are being carried out as planned.

- Environmental auditors should review the reliability and integrity of information generated by the environmental management system and the means used to identify, measure, classify, and report such information.

7.3 Elements of Audit: At a minimum, the audit should include, but not be limited to, the following elements of an environmental management system:

- Written environmental management/control policy statement.

- Delineation and documentation of lines of authority and responsibility for environmental management programs.

- Implementing procedures for all environmental management programs.

- Written communication of environmental goals and commitments to employees, customers, stockholders, suppliers, and the public.

- Existence, organizational placement and adequacy of the internal environmental audit function, if one exists (applicable to external audits).

- Adequacy of resources devoted to environmental management.

- Management commitment to corrective action and remediation based on audit results.

- Management commitment to appropriate and relevant education and training.

- Existence and adequacy of environmental risk assessment methodologies.

- Internal and external reporting procedures relating to environmental activities, expenditures, liabilities and risks. This includes activities which affect, or have the potential to affect, the environment, and are relevant to the organization's environmental policy and objectives.

- Systems to encourage and institutionalize quality in environmental management.

8. Performance of Audit Work

8.1 Planning the Audit: Environmental auditors should plan each audit. Audit plans should be in written form and include:

— The audit objectives and scope of work.

8.1.1 Specific audit objectives should clearly explain what the audit is to accomplish. The scope of audit work should be clearly defined, and should include the time period audited.

The audit objectives will generally involve the review of the company's policies and procedures that have been designed to attain management's environmental objectives. One of the auditor's responsibilities is to provide reasonable assurance that design of the Company's policies and procedures is proper to achieve such environmental objectives.

— The criteria necessary to evaluate the systems subject to audit.

8.1.2 The organization's environmental management system should be evaluated against reasonable criteria which have either been established by a recognized body or are stated in a sufficiently clear and comprehensive manner for a knowledgeable reader to be able to understand.

Guidance included in the EPA's Environmental Auditing Policy Statement (51 Fed. Reg. 25004, July 9, 1986) may embody reasonable criteria for this purpose. Criteria promulgated by other regulatory agencies and other bodies composed of experts that follow due-process procedures, including procedures for broad distribution of proposed criteria for public comment, would also be considered reasonable criteria for this purpose. The criteria may also encompass existing practices, programs and policies of other applicable industry organizations or the consideration of available and pertinent literature.

— Information about the activities to be audited.

8.1.3 The information needed by the auditor to plan an environmental audit varies with the audit objectives and the entity to be audited. Information to be obtained and recorded includes:

- Background information about the environmental laws and regulations that apply to the entity, the entity's history and current environmental objectives, its principal locations, and similar information needed by the auditor to understand and carry out the audit protocol.

- The key systems and procedures used for managing environmental activities and for evaluating and reporting on environmental activities.

- Size and scope of the entity's environmental activities.

- Areas in which there may be control weaknesses or lack of compliance with laws and regulations. Tests to determine the significance of such matters are generally conducted in the detailed audit work as specified in the audit protocol.

- Development of facility specific checklists to ensure comprehensive coverage of audit elements.

— The resources necessary to perform the audit.

8.1.4 Sufficient time and budget resources should be available to complete the audit.

Proper staffing of the audit team is also important. Staff planning should include:

- Assigning staff with the appropriate skills and knowledge for the job.

- Assigning an adequate number of experienced staff and supervisors to the audit. Consultants should be used when necessary.

8.1.5 During the audit, an auditor may encounter matters potentially material to the audit objectives that require special knowledge. The auditor may consider using the work of a technical consultant (see guidance in section 8.4). When planning the audit, the auditor should be alert to such a need in order to plan accordingly.

— The audit protocol.

8.1.6 A written audit protocol is essential to conduct the audit efficiently and effectively, and should be prepared for each audit. The audit protocol should provide:

- In reasonable detail, a description of the audit steps and procedures that the auditor believes are necessary to accomplish the objectives of the audit.

- The method of documenting work performed.

- The method of reporting to management.

- The types of personnel to be interviewed during the audit, and specific lines of inquiry to be addressed.

— Environmental laws and regulations.

8.1.7 Management is responsible for establishing an effective system of control to provide reasonable assurance of compliance with applicable environmental laws and regulations. Auditors should consider the entity's controls that relate to environmental laws and regulations. This requires that those planning the audit be knowledgeable of the compliance requirements that apply to the subject under audit, and of any applicable reporting requirements that may apply to instances of noncompliance. When audit steps and procedures indicate that acts of noncompliance have or may have occurred, the auditor needs to determine the extent to which these acts significantly affect the audit results. Auditors should exercise due professional care and caution in pursuing indications of acts of noncompliance and should follow applicable legal requirements in notifying the proper authorities of acts of noncompliance.

8.2 Preparing for the Audit- Adequate pre-audit preparation is critical to the successful completion of any audit function, and should include:

1. Thorough review of environmental management system documentation and facility operational information.

2. Establishing lines of communication with designated facility points of contact and coordinating with points of contact to resolve logistical issues such as facility access, scheduling interviews and meetings, and arranging for facility tour if deemed necessary.

8.3 Examining and Evaluating Information- Environmental auditors should collect, analyze, interpret, and document information to support audit results.

8.3.1 Evidence should be obtained to afford a reasonable basis for the environmental auditors' judgments and conclusions regarding the organization, program, activity, or function under audit. A record of the auditors' work should be retained in the form of working papers.

Evidence can be categorized as physical, documentary, testimonial and/or analytical:

• Physical evidence is obtained by direct inspection or observations. It may be documented in the form of memoranda summarizing the matters inspected or observed, photographs, charts, maps or actual samples.

• Documentary evidence consists of created information such as letters, contracts, accounting records, management reports, and management information on performance.

• Testimonial evidence is obtained from others through statements received in response to inquiries or through interviews.

• Analytical evidence includes computations, comparisons, reasoning, and separation of information into components.

8.3.2 Information should be sufficient, relevant and competent in order to provide a sound basis for audit findings based on the criteria upon which the audit was based. Statements important to the audit should be corroborated when possible with additional evidence. Testimonial evidence also needs to be evaluated from the standpoint of whether the individual may be biased or only have partial knowledge about the area. Recommendations developed from the findings may be included, but are not required by this standard.

8.3.3 Sufficient information is factual, adequate, and convincing so that a prudent, informed person would reach the same conclusions as the auditor. Sufficiency includes the presence of enough evidence to support the auditors' findings, conclusions, and any recommendations.

8.3.4 Relevant information supports audit findings and recommendations and is consistent with audit criteria and objectives. Relevance refers to the relationship of evidence to its use. The information used to prove or disprove an audit finding is relevant if it has a logical, sensible relationship to that issue.

8.3.5 Competent information is valid and reliable. Auditors should carefully consider whether reasons exist to doubt the validity or reliability of the evidence.

The following presumptions are useful in judging the competence of evidence. However, these presumptions are not to be considered sufficient in themselves to determine competence:

- Evidence obtained from an independent source is more reliable than that secured from the audited organization.

- Evidence developed under a good system of control is more reliable than that obtained where such control is weak, unsatisfactory, or nonexistent.

- Evidence obtained through physical examination, observation, computation and inspection is more reliable than evidence obtained indirectly.

8.3.6 The evidence to support the findings, judgments, and conclusions in the report must be in written form. Organizations performing audits need to establish policies and procedures for the preparation and maintenance of audit documentation, including safe custody and retention for a time sufficient to satisfy legal or other applicable requirements. Documentation should:

- Contain the written audit protocol.

- Contain adequate summaries of the findings of the audit.

- Be dated and signed by the auditor.

- Be reviewed by a supervisor, if appropriate (the review should be evidenced in the working papers).

- Be complete, accurate, and succinct to provide proper support for findings, judgments, and conclusions, and to enable demonstration of the nature and scope of the audit.

- Be understandable without oral explanations.

8.3.7 The process of collecting, analyzing, interpreting, and documenting information should be supervised to provide reasonable assurance that the auditor's objectivity is maintained and that audit objectives are met.

8.4 Technical Consultation: In performing an audit of the entity's environmental controls, an auditor may use the work of a specialist when expertise outside of the audit team is required. The auditor should be satisfied with the professional qualifications and reputation of the specialist by inquiry or other procedures and should consider the following:

- The professional certification, license, or other recognition of the competence of the specialist in his/her field, as appropriate.

- The reputation and standing of the specialist in the views of his/her peers and others familiar with his/her capability or performance.

- The relationship, if any, of the specialist to the client.

An understanding should exist among the auditor, the entity being audited, and the specialist as to the nature of the work to be performed by the specialist. This understanding should be in written form.

The auditor should obtain an understanding of the methods or assumptions used by the specialist to determine whether the work is suitable for corroborating the audit findings.

9. Reporting

Environmental auditors need to report the results of their audit work. Written audit reports are required to communicate the results of the environmental audit.

9.1 The environmental auditor's report should contain—

1. A description of the scope of the audit, including the audit objectives. This may include identification of the assertion that is being reported on (see 9.2 below).

2. The date of the environmental audit.

3. A statement that the audit was conducted in accordance with generally accepted environmental auditing standards.

4. A statement that the establishment and maintenance of environmental management controls is the responsibility of management.

5. A statement that the environmental audit was not specifically designed to evaluate compliance with specific laws and regulations.

6. If appropriate, a conclusion about whether the auditee's assertions regarding environmental management practices are in conformity with the established or stated criteria against which it was measured. (See discussion of defining criteria in Section 8.1.2.)

9.2 The auditor's written report may be accompanied by a statement from management asserting adherence to established or stated criteria. If so:

1. The auditor's written report should be accompanied by a summary of the specific management practices designed to assure adherence to established or stated criteria.

2. The auditor's written report should identify and explain any exceptions to or deviations from the established or stated criteria.

3. The auditor's written report may contain recommendations when the potential for significant improvement in environmental controls and performance is substantiated by the audit findings. The auditor should consider prioritizing the comments and recommendations to ensure that the most important findings are emphasized.

10. Quality Assurance

Organizations that conduct environmental audits should establish and maintain a quality assurance program to evaluate the operations of the environmental auditing function. The purpose of this program is to provide reasonable assurance that audit work conforms with these standards.

10.1 Supervision: Supervision of the work of environmental auditors should be carried out in a consistent and ongoing manner to assure conformance with the environmental auditing standards, and applicable policies and audit protocols.

10.2 Internal Reviews: Internal reviews should be performed periodically by members of the environmental auditing staff to appraise the quality of the audit work performed. Internal reviews must be documented in writing.

10.3 External Reviews: If the entity maintains its own environmental auditing program, such program should periodically be reviewed by an external environmental auditing firm or individual. This review may be a component of an external environmental auditing team's engagement to audit an entity's entire environmental management system. These reviews should be performed by qualified persons who are independent of the organization. On completion of the review, a formal, written report should be issued. The report should express an opinion as to the organization's compliance with this Environmental Auditing Standard and, as appropriate, should include recommendations for improvement.

11. Corrective Action

Organizations that conduct internal audits or after the completion of an external audit should establish and maintain corrective action to address environmental concerns identified from the audit. Preventive actions should be initiated to correct deficiencies, and any changes resulting from corrective action should be tracked.

12. Non-Scope Considerations

This standard does not include environmental assessments for property transactions, site compliance with environmental laws and regulations, pollution prevention program measurement, or assessments related to the cleanup of site contamination.

William P. Gulledge is a director in the Regulatory Division of the Jefferson Group, in Washington, DC. Previously, he served as senior consultant with Tillinghast, an associate director for environmental programs at the Chemical Manufacturers Association, and a program coordinator/senior environmental engineer at the U.S. Department of Energy in Pittsburgh, Pennsylvania.

10

Voluntary Standards at the Dawn of ISO 14000: Fit or Folly for TQEM?

Lynn Johannson

"There can be no improvement where there are no standards."[1]

Masaaki Imai in Kaizen

Improve or die. I mean that quite literally. Masaaki Imai's basic principle of continuous improvement holds compelling implications for anyone involved in improving the environment. Environmental standards, whether they relate to an organization's internal operations or from one country to another, establish a minimal level of acceptable performance and serve as a catalyst for improvement. However, the issue of standards, in general, is often shrouded in confusion as evidenced by discussions taking place around the globe.

Simply defined, a standard is "anything, a rule or principle, that is used as a basis for judgment, an average or normal requirement, quality, quantity, level, grade, established by authority, custom or by an individual as acceptable."[2] Standards usually imply a model or pattern for guidance, by comparison with which the quantity, excellence, or correctness of a thing or condition can be determined.

In quality circles, standards are broadly viewed as a set of policies, rules, directives, or procedures established for all major operations, which serve as guidelines that enable all employees to perform their jobs successfully.

Standardization is one of the most important pillars of total quality environmental management (TQEM—a prerequisite for management/empowered employee teams to understand where the company is vis-à-vis work and performance as shown in **Exhibit 1**. The improvement process cannot be undertaken successfully until these standards are established and understood.

Voluntary standards are created through a consensual process with experts. "Consensus" means that the experts pooled their collective knowledge to achieve the best and highest level of thought. In the North American standardization process, "consensus" means substantial but not necessarily unanimous agreement.

Standards created through this consensus process can be made mandatory. However, voluntary standards have advantages over mandatory ones, and the window of opportunity for voluntary environmental standards is widening. I will elaborate on these two points later.

Exhibit 1: Internal Standards–Environmental Standard Operating Procedures

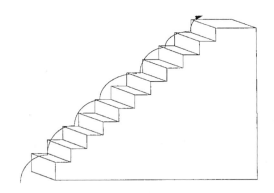

Each riser represents a documented action that the empowered employee knows, understands, and acts upon.

Standards are not, and cannot be static. In Masaaki Imai's Kaizen, the strategy is based on never-ending improvement. Standards exist only to be superseded by higher standards. Whether the standard is a physical constant (e.g., parts per billion) or a norm (e.g., referring to a technical specifications document), standards should be binding on all employees. Kaizen philosophy is based on a strategy of continuous improvement, and it is management's job to see that everyone works within that framework.

Each standard requires

- Individual authorization and responsibility,
- Transmittal of individual experience to the next generation of workers,
- Transmittal of individual experience and know–how to the organization,
- Accumulation of experience (particularly failures) within the organization,
- Deployment of know–how from one work area to another, and
- Discipline.

The development of environmental standard operating procedures (ESOPs) within an organization is an important step to maximizing management control of environmental factors. For example, clear direction on how to prevent spillage on a line producing soup enabled employees to recognize that the value of the product is in the can, not on the floor. The company estimated that in improving performance by changing handling techniques, the first benefit was an increase in revenue by $3 million. Another savings occurred when the BOD (biochemical oxygen demand) loadings on the sewer dropped enabling the company to renegotiate the sewerage charges.

Although you cannot exercise absolute control over environmental outcomes, you can effectively manage the processes that affect the ecology within your organization's work environment. Development of voluntary internal ESOPs also supports the fact that it is the cumulation of individual, incremental improvement that will make a significant difference. Organizations cannot rely on breakthrough technology as a continuous solution.

Developing effective internal ESOPs is an important step, but it is one that is not going to occur in isolation. The development of internal ESOPs is affected by global factors. Voluntary standards are referred to in Agenda 21, the reporting document that evolved around UNCED (United Nations Conference on Environment and Development). International standards for environmental management are evolving to become a key activity in many countries. ISO standards developed at this level are based on negotiation points between countries as seen in **Exhibit 2**.

An underlying goal of international standards is harmonization, recognizing that the whole earth operates as one organism, one organization, one house. This "house" is separated by natural boundaries (water, topography) and artificial boundaries (culture/language, political, and economic/monetary). Despite these artificial boundaries, the "house" functions naturally as one unit.

To assure that these resources can flow freely between nations, there must be some commonality, some basis on which we can speak a common language. Normative or written standards for environmental management systems must be applicable regardless of where you operate in the world.

Environment quality is a subject of international concern for the public and world leaders. All agree that there is substantial room for improvement in all areas of the world. (Please see **Exhibit 3**, which shares the highlights of a 1989 survey.)

In this chapter, we explore the area of voluntary environmental management

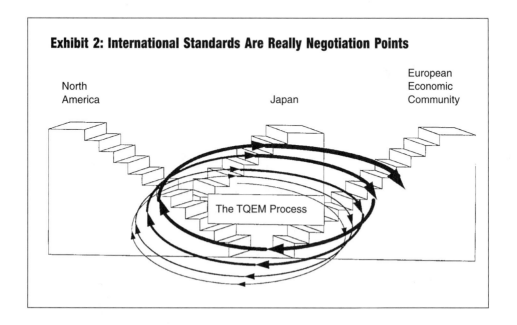

Exhibit 2: International Standards Are Really Negotiation Points

North America

Japan

European Economic Community

The TQEM Process

standards, the challenges in their development and integration, and the controversy that surrounds them by posing the question "Voluntary standards—fit or folly for TQEM?" Our first respondent is Alan Knight, Ph.D., program administrator for environmental management projects for the Canadian Standards Association.

"Coming as I do from the voluntary standards development industry, you'll understand if I say unequivocally that there is a good and essential fit here. And I don't say this simply because my mortgage is not yet paid off.

"Voluntary international standards respond to a need for greater organizational and market efficiency. They also help to define the ground rules for competition in a way that focuses creativity on valued difference rather than wasteful difference.

"An organization, whether it is providing products or services, has to compete. It can choose basic, price-based competition. Or it can choose to compete in the arena of value-added differentiation.

"If you choose to compete on price, you find out what the minimum standards are—whether regulated or voluntary—you meet them and price your product or service at a level that allows you to continue as a going concern. These minimum standards will be continually revised, usually resulting in a rise in the benchmark.

"If you choose to compete by performing at a level higher than the minimum standard, you will likely be developing and using internal standards of one sort or another, but often based on existing benchmark standards. Once again you will be continuously improving in an attempt to stay ahead of your competitors. But not just by trying to keep the price attractive; you will also be looking at innovations in design, new bells and whistles, and new products and services.

"But these types of standards, whether regulated or voluntary, whether externally or internally developed, are mostly about the attributes and performance levels of your products and services. There are also real gains to be made through improved management and organizational performance. How do you assess the needs of your stakeholders and then manage the design, development, production, evaluation, and improvement of your products and services?

"This involves more than improved process controls and operational procedures. Better management performance does allow you to increase productivity and efficiency, but it also helps you to better understand your market and its risks, what policies to put in place, and what innovations to invest in.

"The new ISO 14000 series of standards on environmental management is concerned with the attributes and performance of your products and services, but it is also concerned with the performance of your organization. They are systems standards that define and provide guidance on the management elements . . . of a well-performing organization driven by continual improvement.

"The basic premise is that the organizations sets its own policies, objectives, and targets. These may be derived from internal or external, regulated or voluntarily developed standards. The environmental management systems standards simply provide the framework for identifying, developing, and managing them. There are also, I should add, a number of other standards within the series that provide tools to help you manage certain specific attribute and performance issues (i.e., environmental labeling and life-cycle assessment). The number of these tools will undoubtedly increase in the future.

"As international, voluntary standards, they also offer the opportunity for related private sector assurance programs—whether third-party registration audits or self-declaration. Such assurance can help reduce potential liability and be used to demonstrate due diligence or the responsible management of environmental performance.

"There is a fear that third-party registration programs will create barriers for small and medium-sized enterprises and companies from lesser developed countries.

A prescriptive program might indeed create barriers. On the other hand, a system designed to encourage improvement, that is flexible in terms of assurance options and that accepts a gradualist approach to implementation, should do much to alleviate these fears and to help small and medium-sized enterprises and lesser developed countries tap into the benefits.

"The fact that these environmental management systems standards are themselves voluntary should help to ensure that they remain flexible tools of innovation and not prescriptive requirements."

Our next respondent is Hugh Ritchie, regional sales manager for A V Qualité Toronto, (AIB Vinçotte Brussels), an ISO 9000 registrar. Ritchie's insight on this issue emanates from his perspective as a registrar and how ISO 14000 compares to ISO 9000.

"There is currently a new environmental standard being developed in Europe, in a combined effort of the British Standards Institute (BSI) 7750 and the International Standards Organization (ISO) 14000 Eco-Audits. The ISO Technical Committee (TC) 207 is currently refining and improving the standard; it is expected to be implemented in 1996. The environmental standard focuses on the environmental management systems (EMS) of a company rather than the quality system (QS). ISO 14000 is somewhat like the current quality standard ISO 9000, though more general and broader in scope. Companies are going to have a considerably tougher time preparing and complying with the ISO 14000 Eco-Audit than they did for the ISO 9000 standard. This is mainly because of the breadth of scope in the new standard. ISO 14000 is very similar in structure and approach to the ISO 9000 standard. By evaluating what makes ISO 9000 tick, we can see how the ISO 14000 standard may work.

"The scope of ISO 14000 is much broader than ISO 9000, where ISO 9000 is mainly concerned with the quality system of an organization. The environmental standard is concerned with the whole company and all of its products. The standard will require companies to be concerned with everything from incoming raw material, through to the final product—a cradle-to-grave approach. The statements in the standard are more general than ISO 9000, thereby leaving a wide margin for interpretation and hence confusion. To implement and run an ISO 14000 program will require more commitment, resources, and effort than required for ISO 9000.

"It is worth evaluating the similarities to ISO 9000 and ISO 14000 to see how an environmental program may run. There are 20 sections in ISO 9001, the most comprehensive of the three ISO 9000 standards. Each section covers a different function of the standard. There are four key functions in ISO 9001 that are the heartbeat of the system. They are

- 4.1 Management responsibility,
- 4.17 Internal quality audits,

- 4.14 Corrective and preventative action, and
- 4.5 Document and data control.

From these elements we can see into to the core of the mechanism. Management responsibility and commitment is the motor that drives the gear, internal quality audits. The results of internal quality audits are corrective actions and a review that the system is functioning and improving. Document and data control is the glue that keeps everything in its place. The registrar, on the other hand, through independent verification would assess the power of the motor driving the gear, and [whether] the gear is doing its assigned task. Ultimately, the auditor would evaluate the objective evidence of how the system is working; how were the corrective actions resolved; did the solutions to the corrective actions in fact solve the problem; is the documentation in place to show the changes implemented; and are all of the requirements in the standard being met.

"In ISO 14000, the same core mechanism exists. They have slightly different names, but the intent is the same. ISO 14000 will have to have a motor:

4.2 Organization

...The organization's top management with executive responsibility for environmental affairs shall appoint specific management representatives, who, irrespective of the responsibilities, shall have defined authority and responsibility for

(a) ensuring that environmental management system requirements are established, implemented and maintained in accordance with the standard; and

(b) reporting on the performance of the environmental system to the executive management for review and a basis for improvement of the environmental system.[3]

"The gear will be:

4.8 EMS-audit (internal and external)

The organization shall establish and maintain procedures for audits to be carried out, in order to

(a) determine whether or not the environmental management system

(1) conforms to this standard, and

(2) has been properly implemented; and

(b) contribute to the determination of the continued effectiveness of the environmental management system in fulfilling the organizations's environmental policy and objectives. Audits shall be scheduled on the basis of the environmental importance of the activity concerned and the results of the previous audit.

Audit findings shall be recorded and reported to those responsible for the activity and or area audited. These persons shall take timely action on reported deficiencies.[4]

"The corrective actions are the means to track and solve problems that are identified in the system:

4.7.3 Nonconformance and corrective and preventative action
 The organization shall establish and maintain documented procedures for handling and investigation of nonconformance and for initiating corrective and preventative action, including defining responsibility and authority.
Any corrective or preventative action taken to eliminate the causes of the actual and potential non conformities shall be appropriate to the magnitude of problems and commensurate with the environmental impact encountered.
The organization shall implement and record any changes in the documented procedures resulting from corrective and preventive action.[5]

"Documentation will keep the system on track:

4.10 Documentation and records (not developed yet)
Clearly there is a mechanism in ISO 14000 that will force management to take a leading role in ISO 14000 as they must do in ISO 9000.

"Given the commitment requirements by management, and the effort to implement and run such a system, there will no doubt be similar arguments as used in the quality world to not implement ISO 14000. Many companies will take the wait-and-see approach, as they have in the case of ISO 9000.

Companies that have ISO 9000 in place already will find the implementation of ISO 14000 easier, though it will still require considerable change in focus. The organizations will already have individuals who will readily be able to adapt to understand the system. They will need to be able to understand and manage the design, manufacturing, distribution, end use, as well as the environmental impact of the product, while implementing the program. A company that waits until the last moment to implement ISO 9000 and ISO 14000 will face a daunting task that may take as long as three years to implement and achieve. The path of wait and see may be most costly in lost business, implementation, and missed opportunities."

Our next respondent is Lisa Brown of EPA, who is currently on loan to the National Institute for Standards and Technology, U.S. Department of Commerce (DOC). (The thoughts expressed are Brown's own and do not necessarily reflect the views and policies of EPA or the DOC.)

"Clearly any organization with goals of environmental improvement must have environmental standards to compare performance and work toward their goals. An informal, internal standard will already exist if a clear goal can be stated. As an organization makes improvements and comes to understand its needs better, the internal standards of the organization will change.

"By developing international standards, every organization around the world would be able to compare itself to the same metrics. While this seems laudable on the surface, there are many points that should be examined in the process of developing international environmental standards. How will the standards be set up?

Standards Applied by Industry

"Will one industry's standards be stricter than another? Can the argument be made that water polluted by one industry with the same chemicals as water polluted by another industry is just as intolerable? Yet, one industry may be able to dramatically reduce its pollution while the other the cannot. Or, a company may change its industry classification with the addition of a new process and immediately their different standards—possibly more lenient, maybe more strict.

Standards Applied to Process Improvement

"By concentrating on the process, many companies can neglect the product. It seems to be much easier and cheaper to tweak the process than to redesign the product. Products will have to be reexamined to make the next step in reducing the pollutant load on the planet.

Standards Applied to Products

"Will there be a standard for toxic raw material input? What if a reduction in toxic material input for a product compromises that product's lifetime? Will there be a standard for durability? What if a product outlives its function and/or, to obtain durability, pollution factors are increased (e.g. a longer-lasting light bulb that uses more electricity).

Standards Applied by Nation

"Will the standards be on a per-capita basis to be fair? Should they be based on some other measure such as per forest area (to encourage reforestation and utilization of CO_2). Mining is one of the most polluting processes, yet ores are not distributed evenly throughout the globe. The international standards board may abhor the practice, but non-mining countries may demand the products that utilize the ores.

"We have to take care, since—what gets measured is what gets done."

Editor's Commentary

It is clear that standards for environmental management are going to play a role in your organization's future. I believe that standards are becoming a driver of improvement for the management of environmental issues, which in my mind, is preferable to the command-and-control process centered around regulations.

Standards are not a perfect solution in and of themselves. Some of the drawbacks include the following:

- The setting of standards tends to be done by the "big" guys, large companies and developed countries.
- The interpretation of standards is subjective. As Lisa Brown pointed out there is room for manipulation. In my view, some of this results from activity that is logical for making the standards work within a local context. (Remember TGAL—think globally, act locally.) In some cases it's pure dodgeball.
- As standards are not clearly understood, in many instances because poor communications tend to surround them, the environmental special-interest community views environmental standards as a less favorable tool to command and control.

With the growth around environmental standards, no organization will be able to dismiss environmental issues because of size. From a TQEM perspective, this is positive, as it is the cumulation of individual actions that makes the difference. Environmental efforts are too often focused on acute events—crises—to the detriment of chronic or normal chaotic events. Internal standards, properly introduced as a part of an organization's TQEM process as shown in **Exhibit 4**, will be a valuable tool to correct this imbalance.

At the same time, external forces are promoting standards. Environmental standards are becoming part of procurement and vendor certification programs. If you want to supply these enlightened, competitive firms, you have to meet or exceed their environmental standards. The ability to compete on this level is not based on size, it's based on having a clear vision, knowing exactly what your customer wants and delivering it right the first time, thus lowering risk to your customer. Providing assurance means your organization must have an environmental management system (EMS) in place or be in the process of putting one into place. It also means that

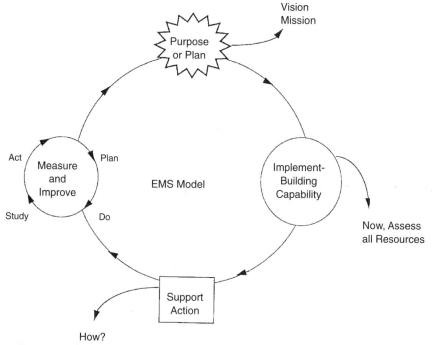

Exhibit 4: Internal Standards as Part of TQEM Process

Vision
Mission

Purpose
or Plan

Implement-
Building
Capability

EMS Model

Now, Assess
all Resources

Act Plan
Measure
and
Improve
Study Do

Support
Action

How?
Document - Internal Standards -
ESOPs, checklists; External - ISO

- A TQEM tenet is "do it with data."
- ISO is a documentation process that assures that your organization is doing what it says it is doing.
Hence, ISO and TQEM are complementary.

Can you answer these questions with confidence?
- Do you have environmental standard operating procedures?
- Do you really know what your customers need?
- Can you provide them assurance of your environmental performance?
- Is your organization ready to educate your customers?
- Is your organization ready for the competition?
- Will you set standards, or will you have to meet someone else's?

you will have to continuously improve to stay ahead. But this is no different to matching changes in the marketplace.

In today's marketplace, supply chains surround the globe. Customers in the United States may have suppliers in Ireland, Japan, and South Africa; either meet or exceed their standards or find a less demanding customer. However, the latter option just defers the supplier's need to improve until the regulated, command-and-control approach hits and /or your next customer takes a similar stance. Take note, environmental performance is moving into the arena of global competition. Are you ready?

Many thanks to Lisa Brown, Alan Knight, and Hugh Ritchie[6] for sharing their insights.

Notes

1. Imai, Masaaki, Kaizen, *the Key to Japan's Competitive Success*, New York, McGraw–Hill, 1986. Kaizen literally translates as improvement, but it means improvement in all aspects of life, not just in the workplace. Perhaps TQEM should adopt the term Kaizen over continuous improvement to reflect the ubiquitous aspects and presence of the environment.

2. Webster's Encyclopedic Unabridged *Dictionary of the English Language*, New York, Portland House, 1989.

3. Environmental Management SYSTEMS - Specifications (First Preliminary Draft), *Quality Systems Update Special supplement*, April 1994.

4. Id.

5. Id.

6. Hugh Ritchie's firm will be able to audit organizations to ISO 14000 (416–441–4535).

Lynn Johannson is the director of E2 Management Corporation in Georgetown, Ontario.

Measuring for Success:
New Quality Assessment Tools for
Environmental Managers and Auditors

Environmental Cost Accounting:
The Bottom Line for Environmental Quality Management

11

William G. Russell, Steven L. Skalak, and Gail Miller

Recent years have seen the environment emerge as one of the most pressing issues facing American business. Eventually, environmental costs will affect the bottom line of every American company. A recent study in the National Law Journal *estimates that cleanup of the nation's known hazardous wastes sites will cost $752 billion over thirty years under current environmental policies.*

Environmental legislation and regulations impose annual compliance costs estimated by the Environmental Protection Agency at more than $30 billion. In the near future, environmental expenses for cleanup, regulatory compliance, and management are anticipated to grow to between 2.5 and 3 percent of GNP. Corporations that wish to be competitive must successfully manage these costs while maintaining or improving their role as responsible corporate citizens.

Implementing a comprehensive system for identifying and managing environmental costs requires a multidisciplinary team effort. Environmental costs impact product selection, design and pricing, capital budgeting, and future strategic direction. In order to make informed and meaningful managerial decisions on environmental programs, real cost data are vital. An environmental management system (EMS) requires information to set goals and then monitor progress towards those goals over time. This chapter discusses the current cost accounting systems (CASs) available to support the myriad goals of environmental management systems.

In addition, the chapter outlines a framework for plotting the location of your current EMS on a matrix of regulatory and information requirements and evaluating whether your corporation's CAS is adequate to support the goals and objectives set by your environmental management program. By anticipating future regulatory and information requirements, flexible systems can be developed to adapt to new and more stringent regulations and more complex information requirements.

Each corporation's environmental management system will have unique goals and objectives. However, many share fundamental principles, such as Total Quality Management and internal controls, in order to develop and attain goals and objectives. The success of any EMS requires the support and participation of senior management. A strong corporate environmental policy statement, coupled with measurable goals and objectives, provides the strongest foundation for an EMS. Measurability of goals and objectives against governmental regulations and internal standards is essential to the long-term success of any program.

Proactive environmental management systems can take many forms: recycling and pollution prevention, responsible purchasing, innovative manufacturing technologies development, community involvement. However, in today's market, a company cannot expect to be considered an "environmentalist" unless it is moving beyond the law and also ahead of its industry and many of its consumers. Many of the principles and standards used as the basis for EMS goals and objectives assume corporate goals are beyond compliance. Innovative management techniques are helpful in attaining these nontraditional goals.

Total Quality Management is a management practice that seeks to improve competitiveness through a continuous process of review, analysis, and implementation. TQM principles lend themselves well to an EMS application since TQM requires that definable goals and objectives be set and progress measured on a regular basis. In order to implement environmental TQM, the corporation must have quantifiable and accurate environmental information including environmental costs.

An internal controls approach is also an excellent base for the development and improvement of an EMS. Internal control was recently defined by the National Commission on Fraudulent Financial Reporting, known as the Treadway Commission, in its 1987 report as:

> the process by which an entity's board of directors, management, and other personnel seek to obtain reasonable assurance regarding the achievement of objectives in one or more categories:
>
> - Effectiveness and efficiency of operations.
> - Reliability of financial information relating to activities.
> - Compliance with applicable laws and regulations.

The report of the Treadway Commission sets forth five components of internal control. These components can serve as a model for internal control and EMS effectiveness:

1. Control environment
2. Risk assessment
3. Control procedures
4. Information and communication
5. Monitoring and feedback

Under an internal controls approach, environmental management is geared toward achieving an entity's *goals and objectives*. Environmental management is a process; it is a means to an end, not an end in itself. Environmental management as an internal control is effected by *people;* it is not a set of policy manuals and forms, but rather a large-scale effort by people at every level of an organization. Finally, environmental management as an internal control cannot be expected to provide more than *reasonable assurance* that the objectives will be achieved.

Environmental Goals and Objectives

The key elements of a successful environmental management system are goals and objectives. An environmental management system without measurable goals and objectives is merely an environmental policy statement. Once goals and objectives are set, monitoring progress towards goals and objectives is vital if a corporation wishes to measure and communicate its environmental progress. Goals and objectives can be based entirely on internal criteria, on published external standards, or a combination of both.

Some of these external standards range from basic compliance goals, like the Toxic Release Inventory, to ambitious sustainable development objectives, as embodied in the CERES principles. Other standards driving environmental quality management include the Chemical Manufacturer's Association Responsible Care principles, EPA's industrial toxics program (33-50 program), and its Energy Star program ISO 9000, and the International Chamber of Commerce Business Charter for Sustainable Development.

Environmental Information Systems

Once environmental goals are set, timely and complete information is necessary to monitor progress towards objectives and quantify improvements. Goals and objectives cannot be set or monitored in an information vacuum. For this reason, it is essential to have an environmental information system to support the environmental management system. Information requirements range from tracking annual permit renewal deadlines to complex sustainable development cost-benefit models. Integrating a cost accounting system into the environmental information system is the key to quantifying real costs and benefits, both internal and external, of your operations.

Given management's increased attention to environmental costs, the trend is toward tighter integration among management, information, and accounting systems. Information collection, measurement, and assessment issues should be addressed by multidisciplinary teams consisting of representatives of many company functions, such as engineering, operations, accounting, environmental affairs, public relations, and planning and budgeting, together with appropriate outside experts.

The usefulness of information gathered will be dependent on the scope of the company's overall environmental information system and the sophistication of the analysis it applies to environmental issues and costs. It is estimated that as little as 5 percent of the statistics in a typical environmental report emerge from continuous measurement. Another 30 percent or so come from frequent measurements; some of the remainder may come from a single reading or from estimates. Although several companies ask independent experts to "audit" their compliance programs, few audits assess the quality of the environmental information collected. Integrating the CAS into the environmental information system provides a strong framework for continuously measured information that can enhance managerial decision making.

Environmental Cost Accounting Matrix

The remainder of this chapter will provide an approach for determining where your corporation's environmental management, environmental information, and cost accounting systems are today and where future changes may lead.

Future trends are discussed, and various types and levels of EMS and CAS are described. The framework, expressed as a grid in **Exhibit 1**, describes five examples for you to compare with your corporation. The matrix has EMS goals along the vertical axis and CAS scope along the horizontal axis. The table accompanying the matrix defines the EMS and CAS goals at each point (A-E) on the matrix. The table also defines the environmental information system (EIS) requirements that link each set of goals.

The vertical axis of the matrix represents the goals of your environmental management system. As described in the illustrative table, corporate goals may range from managing the environmental crisis of the moment to assessing your corporation's ability to achieve sustainability, adding value to society with no net loss of resources. The midrange of EMS goals is defined as a system that will achieve compliance with existing environmental regulations. The horizontal axis of the matrix represents the information requirements of your environmental management system or, interchangeably, the goals of your environmental CAS. Accounting system goals, as described in the table, may range from tracking costs for income tax and SEC reporting requirements to evaluating the economic costs of the disposal of your product by customers after consumption. The midrange of CAS goals are segregated by those systems with an internal cost focus versus a system that incorporates external costs. Internal costs are those directly controlled by and affecting the corporation and are generally subject to the principles of supply and demand. External costs or externalities are defined as costs imposed or benefits conferred by one economic agent on another without a corresponding market payment.

In addition, the matrix provides a reference for proactively anticipating the requirements of EMS and CAS in the future. One expected trend would be that of

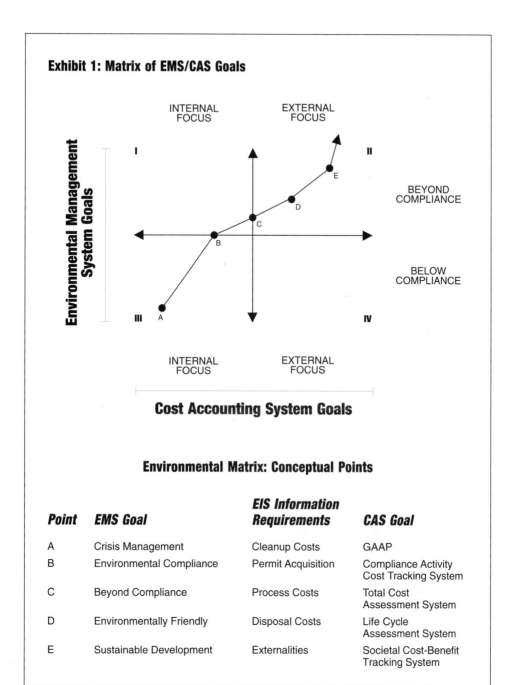

Exhibit 1: Matrix of EMS/CAS Goals

Environmental Matrix: Conceptual Points

Point	EMS Goal	EIS Information Requirements	CAS Goal
A	Crisis Management	Cleanup Costs	GAAP
B	Environmental Compliance	Permit Acquisition	Compliance Activity Cost Tracking System
C	Beyond Compliance	Process Costs	Total Cost Assessment System
D	Environmentally Friendly	Disposal Costs	Life Cycle Assessment System
E	Sustainable Development	Externalities	Societal Cost-Benefit Tracking System

more stringent environmental regulations. This trend could be visualized by sliding the horizontal axis upward, causing a corresponding increase in the need for environmental cost information. As environmental costs have a larger impact on the corporate bottom line, senior management will desire more specific cost information, sliding the vertical axis to the right. This matrix also illustrates how an EMS that merely maintains a status quo will eventually be left behind as regulatory and information requirements increase.

Environmental Cost Accounting Systems

As corporations focus more carefully on environmental costs and regulations, broader participation of a company's financial and accounting personnel is required. This is especially true from the viewpoint of the chief financial officer (CFO) and/ or controller. Most discussions and decisions concerning environmental matters are in some way decisions about cost. Further, the cost aspect is beginning to take precedence over technical, engineering, or legal issues. In our competitive business environment, the participation of accountants and other financial executives is critical to a successful EMS. Typically the financial executive brings an objective method of measuring alternatives and also provides a comprehensive view of risk. In the following sections we discuss ways to view and evaluate costs, and present a framework for assessing corporate risk.

Environmental Costs and Conventional Cost Accounting

There is little evidence to suggest that accountants have been actively participating in the development of EMS goals and objectives. Traditional accounting systems are focused on financial accounting of environmental liabilities and are of little value to environmental managers. To be in a position to manage environmental issues effectively and proactively, a corporation must have accurate information on environmental costs. Conventional cost accounting systems must at a minimum focus on whether environmental costs are capitalized or expensed, and be segregated into sufficient detail to aggregate specific costs for certain anticipated uses such as insurance recoveries and other third-party litigation, fines and penalties, and regulatory compliance costs. Also, the costs of environmental quality should be tracked.

There are three categories of environmental quality costs: failure costs, prevention costs, and appraisal costs. Examples of expenses that an organization may include in its determination of total cost of environmental quality are as follows:

- Payroll and direct expenses associated with the environmental compliance program
- Environmental audits and environmental testing
- Purchasing, calibrating, and operating environmental monitoring and control equipment
- Environmental fines, penalties, and cleanup costs
- Environmental liability insurance premiums

- Waste disposal costs
- Reserves set aside for contingent environmental liabilities
- Revenue loss because of negative public relations

Current cost accounting systems generally fail to assign environmental costs to the specific products and processes that generate them. Costs arising from emissions, effluents, and solid waste are usually treated in the same manner as overhead expenses such as utility costs and depreciation. These costs are aggregated in cost pools and then allocated to products on the basis of measures of production volume such as machine or labor hours, or, alternatively, they may be subtracted in a lump sum from operating income. Potential financial liabilities and legal costs for violations of environmental regulations often are not accounted for at all.

The system of allocation of overhead based on labor hours was developed sixty-five years ago. Since that time, advances in technology have reduced the amount of labor involved in the production of most products and have made labor hours an inappropriate and misleading cost driver for many companies. For example, a product that generates a lot of waste may require only a small amount of labor and thus be allocated only a small amount of overhead. This system can underestimate the cost of producing an item that generates a large amount of waste or overestimate the cost of an item that generates little waste. Moreover, the manager of a facility may underestimate the profitability of investments in pollution prevention when investment costs, but not the consequent savings, are charged to the facility. Under such a system, business decisions regarding product pricing, profitability comparisons and capital budgeting, and long-term strategy tend to be systematically distorted.

Activity-Based Costing

Given the shortcomings of traditional cost accounting systems, what can a company do to get more accurate and useful information about its costs? One solution would be to implement activity-based costing (ABC) to specific processes or systems that contain a large portion of the environmental risks and liabilities. ABC is a valuable concept that can be used to correct the shortcomings of overgeneralized cost accounting systems currently in use. Such a system accumulates and reports costs by activity or process, rather than by traditional budget categories, and thus gives a much more accurate picture of a company's cost of producing a product than that provided by conventional cost accounting.

ABC provides a blending of the goals and objectives of the EMS and information collection and allocation abilities of the CAS. **Exhibit 2** illustrates these two convergent views of the system. The EMS view is derived directly from the identification of environmental risks and opportunities from an operational perspective leading to

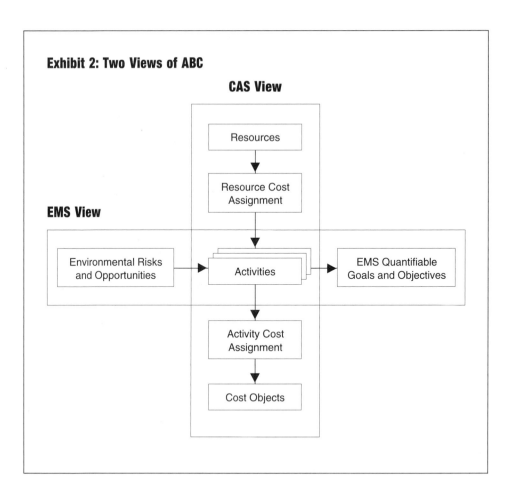

Exhibit 2: Two Views of ABC

CAS View

Resources

↓

Resource Cost Assignment

EMS View

Environmental Risks and Opportunities → Activities → EMS Quantifiable Goals and Objectives

↓

Activity Cost Assignment

↓

Cost Objects

the establishment of quantifiable goals and objectives. The CAS view must identify information required about resources, activities, and cost objects. The key step to implementing the CAS view is that of cost assignment and allocation.

One approach is to establish sub-accounts to the general ledger which can allocate to various activities in the appropriate proportion, much like traditional accounting systems, except for the added sensitivity to environmental costs. Another approach is to mirror more closely the actual flow of costs through an organization. This approach emphasizes the relationship between activities, and the relation between different cost drivers. Following this approach, costs move from incurrence to cost objects in a series of steps, all based on the relationship of cause and effect.

The World Resources Institute (WRI) has launched a project aimed at "developing a revised cost accounting system that more effectively captures all product costs and risks, including environmental ones, and assigns them to their proper source within the firm," i.e., an activity-based costing system. WRI is embarking on a series of approximately six case studies of production units in different industries. Confirmed participants include Dow Chemical, Ciba-Geigy, 3M, Amoco, and S.C. Johnson Wax. A report on this project is pending final review and comments by the participants but is anticipated to enhance the credibility of applying ABC systems to environmental costs.

Total Cost Assessment and Full Cost Accounting

Total cost assessment (TCA) is the next level of analysis that a corporation can perform above activity-based costing. It includes managerial accounting systems and investment analysis/capital budgeting. Under TCA, a corporation's assessment of its environmental costs would include not only information from its CAS but also analysis of investment and capital budgeting information. For example, what environmental cost savings will the corporation forego by not making an investment in a certain pollution prevention technology?

The EPA has selected the TCA approach to environmental cost accounting as the preferred system for evaluating pollution prevention activities. An initial program, Design for the Environment, outlined two long-term goals pertaining to financial analysis and accounting: First, stimulate the development of improved corporate accounting systems and financial analysis tools to evaluate the quantitative and qualitative aspects of pollution prevention projects. Second, stimulate interest in capital budgeting and managerial accounting for environmental expenses. The two financial analysis definitions applied to these goals are total cost assessment and full cost accounting (FCA). TCA is a generic term for long-term comprehensive financial analysis of the full range of internal costs and savings of an investment. FCA is a method of managerial cost accounting that allocates environmental costs (direct and indirect) to a product, product line, process, service, or activity.

Recently, EPA cosponsored a three-day workshop on accounting and capital budgeting for environmental costs. The workshop was extremely successful in accomplishing its objectives of stimulating ongoing dialogue, identifying and discussing key issues and needs, and developing a "stakeholder's action agenda" for improving environmental accounting and capital budgeting. Although the action agenda was not finalized, some key points were formulated:

- Developing systems for environmental capital budgeting and accounting is a multidisciplinary effort.
- It requires the full support of senior management to be successful.
- Proactive environmental corporations will ultimately become the low-cost providers of their products and maximize value and profits due to their ability to make the correct investment decisions for allocating corporate resources.

Life Cycle Assessment

The three cost accounting systems discussed to this point all have had an internal corporate focus. We will now discuss the first of two levels of analysis whose focus extends beyond the corporation, namely life cycle assessment (LCA). Life cycle thinking has been defined by Carl Henn in *The New Economics of Life Style Thinking* as

> a way of looking at life on earth. . . .The life cycle approach is a holistic understanding of the long term continuity, bioregeneration and perpetual trade-offs in the integrated support of all forms of life, natural resources and socio-economic systems....Life cycle decision-making aims for productive and efficient stewardship of human, material and energy resources. It starts *before* the cradle (R&D, design) and goes *beyond* the grave (recycling, re-use). It evaluates *all* the short term and long term costs, benefits and risks involved in assuring the continued success and survival of any enterprise in performing its socio-economic mission....A life cycle analysis can be a simplified judgment matrix, a comprehensive systems analysis, or something in between. The method chosen depends on the analytical resources available and/or the nature of the problem(s) to be solved. It is a process for planning (life cycle planning), management (life cycle management), industrial design (life cycle engineering, costing and design to specified performance criteria) and environment and health protection (life cycle assessment).

Life cycle assessment has its roots in the 1960s, when concerns about a decreasing supply of raw materials and energy resources led the Coca-Cola Company to develop the concept of life cycle inventory analysis. During the late 1970s and early 1980s, interest in life cycle inventory analysis faded as resource and energy concerns eased and hazardous waste management became a growing problem. As solid waste moved to the forefront of world-wide environmental concerns in the late 1980s, life cycle analysis resurfaced as a tool for analyzing environmental problems.

According to the Society of Environmental Toxicology and Chemistry, a complete life cycle assessment consists of three separate, but interrelated, components:

1. *Life Cycle Inventory.* An objective, data-based process of quantifying energy and raw material requirements, air and water emissions, solid waste, and other environmental releases incurred throughout the life cycle of a product, process, or activity.
2. *Life Cycle Impact Analysis.* A technical, quantitative, and/or qualitative process to characterize and assess the environmental effects of energy, materi-

als, and emissions identified in the life cycle inventory. The assessment should include both environmental and human health considerations.

3. *Life Cycle Improvement Analysis.* A systematic evaluation of opportunities to reduce the environmental impact associated with energy and raw materials use and emissions throughout the entire life of a product, process, or activity.

External Costs and Benefits

A cost accounting system designed to support an EMS based on making decisions incorporating LCA must be able to capture and integrate external costs and benefits, or externalities, related to their specific production or service activities. Environmental externalities arise when an environmental impact is conferred by one economic agent on another without a corresponding market payment. Examples of externality costs and benefits are

- Acid rain deposition from combustion of fossil fuels
- Noise pollution from airports or highways
- Reduced landfill utilization due to the use of cogeneration facilities
- Ozone depletion caused by aerosol cans containing CFCs

Efforts to develop LCA-based environmental cost accounting systems build on prior experience valuing externality cost-benefits developed for use in other contexts. One regulation requiring federal agencies to perform a regulatory impact analysis on all new significant rulemakings was Executive Order 12291, enacted in 1981. Regulations having environmental impacts were required to monetize such costs whenever possible. Another regulation requiring the estimation of environmental economic impact values was the Comprehensive Environmental Response, Compensation, and Liability Act (CERCLA). The economic damage from such events as oil spills or hazardous substance releases must be evaluated as part of a natural resource damage assessment. Recently, much work in this area has been performed by the utility industry as a result of investment decisions being made to comply with the Clean Air Act (CAA). One development from the CAA that directly relates to valuing externalities is the concept of emissions offset trading.

Currently, most cost accounting systems have incorporated LCA objectives into their systems by creating formulas that effectively internalize the externality costs. When an externality is internalized, the incrementally added environmental cost is the amount where the marginal environmental damage cost avoided is equal to the marginal abatement or mitigation cost. As a result of internalizing hazardous waste landfill disposal contingent liability costs into its waste disposal investment decisions, General Motors centralized disposal from 100 local disposal sites to 2 national disposal sites. Internalizing external costs is one way to ensure that decision makers provide the right mix of competing uses of scarce resources.

Sustainable Development

The most comprehensive and abstract environmental management doctrine is that of "sustainable development." Sustainable development has been defined by the World Commission on Environment and Development as development that "meets the needs of the present without compromising the ability of future generations to meet their own needs." At the level of a corporation, sustainable development could mean adding value without simultaneously causing environmental and other consequences damaging to world development.

On a macro level, it is widely perceived that the world cannot continue the course followed in the post-World War II era indefinitely, given current trends in population growth, environmental damage, and natural resource depletion. According to Tom Gladwin's *Managing for Environmental Excellence: The Next Business Frontier*:

> There are obviously no quick and easy answers for solving a world problematique [sic] of environment and development which is global in scale, unequal in distribution, transgenerational in effects, uncertain in prediction, complex in system dynamics, accelerating in pace, interconnected in structure, systemic in causation, consequential in survival terms, and urgent in need of corrective action. . . .The doctrine of sustainable development, however, may offer the greatest promise for guiding and organizing this transformation.

Some corporations, in particular large western European firms, have been pursuing the idea of sustainable development. Stephan Schmidheiny, chairman of the Business Council for Sustainable Development (BCSD) and head of a large Swiss multinational, claims that:

> All over the world business is involved. Business is a major force behind the huge development revolution taking place in many Latin American countries. Malaysian business people have set up their own BCSD. In Thailand, business is working with the government and environmentalists on some of the developing world's more innovative economic instruments. We have just finished collecting, from all over Africa, case studies of businesses working toward sustainable development. Our members have also generated other BCSD reports on Latin America, Africa and parts of Asia.

Closer to home, sustainable development is already on the minds of executives in several industries such as oil and gas, mining, utilities, and water supply. Many water supply companies are evaluating the benefits of creating completely recyclable water supply systems. Cost accounting systems with a sustainable development goal orientation will more quickly justify paying the higher cost of water treatment in order to achieve the goal of a sustainable water supply.

Implementing a New CAS

Implementing new cost accounting systems is an organizationwide effort and requires the support of senior management as well as a formal implementation plan. An implementation plan should anticipate requirements such as employee training, assignment of responsibility for providing input for and ownership of the system, and likely effects of the new information on current operations. Utilizing more sophisticated environmental management accounting systems such as ABC or LCA may lead to management decisions that contradict fundamental principles previously thought indisputable. For example, Ontario Hydro is utilizing a combination of investment decision outcomes comparing normal capital investment returns against the returns obtained from TCA and LCA models.

Given the flexibility of today's relational database-oriented accounting systems, a fully integrated system is desirable for accounting for environmental costs. Environmental cost accounting systems can become a primary source of information for improving business processes and future planning while eliminating non-value-adding activities. Conversion of any CAS must be shown to be cost-effective, just like any other investment. The superior information provided by an enhanced cost accounting system usually justifies the cost of its implementation.

Conclusion

Given the magnitude of environmental costs and their impact on a corporation's bottom line, most firms recognize the need to have sound environmental management systems in place to manage these issues effectively and proactively. This can only be achieved if management has clear and accurate information. We have reviewed the various levels of thinking that a company can apply to environmental questions, ranging from the largely inadequate traditional cost accounting systems to the all-encompassing doctrine of sustainable development. The CAS utilized to make environmental investment decisions must be consistent with the corresponding environmental management system goals and objectives.

A multidisciplinary team is required to determine the appropriate methods to establish and monitor progress toward achieving the goals of the environmental management system. Accountants can play a valuable role in converting environmental units such as pounds, kilos, and units sold into cash.

References

Desvousges, William H., et al. December 1991. "Accounting for Externality Costs in Electric Utility Planning in Wisconsin," Center for Economics Research, Research Triangle Institute, RTI Project Number 35U-5198-01 FR.

Gladwin, T. *Managing for Environmental Excellence: The Next Business Frontier.* New York: University Working Paper.

Greenberg, R. and C. Unger. Winter 1991/92. "TQM and the Cost of Environmental Quality." *TQEM.*

Hawken, P. April 1992. "The Ecology of Commerce." *INC.*

Henn, C., *The New Economics of Life Cycle Thinking.*

Lavell. Jan. 20, 1992. "Superfund Studies Begin to Fill Hole in Data-Dry Field." *Nat'l L.J.*

Price Waterhouse. 1992. "Accounting for Environmental Compliance: Crossroad of GAAP, Engineering, and Government" (second in series).

Research Triangle Institute. February 1993. "Life Cycle Impact Assessment. Part 1: Issues." Draft final report.

Schmidheiny, S. Fall/Winter 1992. "The Business Logic of Sustainable Development." *Columbia J. of World Business.*

SETAC Foundation for Environmental Education. September 1991. "SETAC Product LCA Advisory Group Mission Statement." Pensacola, FL.

World Commission on Employment & Development. 1987. *Our Common Future.* New York: Oxford University Press.

World Resources Institute. March 1993. "Corporate Accounting for Environmental Costs and Risks: Prospectus for Case Study Phase."

William G. Russell is a director in the Environmental Services Practice of Coopers & Lybrand; **Steven L. Skalak** is a partner in the Litigation and Environmental Services Practice of C&L; and **Gail Miller** is an associate in the Environmental Services Practice.

120

Council of Great Lakes Industries' Framework and Assessment Tool for Implementing TQEM

12

Grace H. Wever and George F. Vorhauer

Total Quality Management provides a powerful management foundation and framework to implement an organization's environmental vision and principles. The elements of TQM include customer/stakeholder focus, a high degree of senior management commitment, a long-term focus, and tools such as continuous improvement, empowerment, and a prevention-based approach. This chapter describes a matrix developed by major U.S. and Canadian firms that serves as (1) a guide to organizations implementing TQEM from the ground floor up and (2) an assessment tool that can be used internally or externally to measure progress toward environmental management excellence and to identify opportunities for improvement. The matrix is based on categories adapted from those used in the Malcolm Baldrige National Quality Award process. The relationship between individual matrix cell criteria and key concepts such as pollution prevention and sustainability is also described.

This article focuses on the management foundation and framework needed to implement an organization's environmental vision, principles, and goals. While there are many vehicles that can move an organization toward these ends, some are more effective than others. A unit can choose a meandering path that leads to mediocrity in management style and performance. Or it can commit to a structured framework that ensures that its environmental performance will be ranked as world-class or best-in-class by peers, customers, and stakeholders alike and that its economic performance will also be highly competitive.

TQM emerged as a widely used management approach in Japan following the Second World War. Although its earlier and certainly less auspicious origins were in the United States, it has become much better known here since the Malcolm Baldrige National Quality Award was launched. Few are aware that TQM was also first applied to environmental management during the late 1970s by Japanese industry. Only during the past few years did the term Total Quality *Environmental* Management (or TQEM) become familiar within business circles.

There are a number of reasons why TQM is the management framework of choice to translate basic environmental principles (for example, Responsible Care, the International Chamber of Commerce's Sustainable Development principles, or principles that the unit itself establishes) into action. These elements include

- A strong customer and stakeholder focus
- Senior management commitment to meeting stakeholder/customer needs
- A "tool kit" that includes teamwork, empowerment, continuous improvement, and a prevention-based approach

The highly detailed criteria associated with the Baldrige categories provide yet another tool: a structured measurement approach. This "tool kit" has become fundamental to improving management systems of all types within business, government, and academia.

Although there is a growing literature on TQEM, it consists for the most part of anecdotal, case study-oriented materials. In 1990, the Council of Great Lakes Industries began a project to fill the need for a more highly structured approach to TQEM. This project began with a partnership between this binational industry group and the Council of Great Lakes Governors to develop a regional TQEM award.

A binational, multi-industry work group formed by the Council of Great Lakes Industries began to develop criteria to assess environmental management systems. The work group found that a self-assessment matrix approach developed by Eastman Kodak Company for TQM offered a unique model on which to build a quantitative measurement tool for excellence in environmental management. At Kodak, the original rating system provides a clear indication of an organization's strengths, weaknesses, and improvement opportunities. It is also very concise, thus scoring can be done directly on the matrix itself.

The team involved in this project spent nearly a year adapting the original TQM matrix to the area of environmental management. A primer was published in June 1993 that describes the basic elements of TQEM and provides a set of assessment questions based on each of the individual cells in the matrix, as well as a case study of a model firm applying TQEM.

Roadmap for TQEM Implementation

The matrix is not just a self-assessment tool; for, unlike such tools, it actually provides a roadmap to implement TQEM. That is, the corporate unit begins with the bottom cell and moves up toward the top cells in each category as its TQEM program grows and matures. The matrix thus describes the sequence of steps that one would follow in building such a program from the ground floor up. The matrix then can be used to

- Rank an organization or unit within any of the Baldrige categories
- Use that ranking as an initial assessment
- Use the continuous improvement process to move up further in each column to improve the overall score

Headings at the top of the matrix correspond to the Baldrige award criteria. The relationships between these categories, shown in **Exhibit 1**, are easily understood:

- TQEM begins and ends with the *customer/stakeholder*. Knowing what stakeholders expect leads a unit to develop systems that improve its performance in ways that better satisfy their needs.
- To do this, the unit needs to begin with *leadership* from senior management itself. Without that leadership, it can never obtain commitment to resources needed to get the job done, and it can never speak with one voice.
- Once the unit has that commitment, it can then begin to gather *information and analyze* it, and funnel that information into *strategic planning*.
- Throughout planning, goals and objectives are set, and measures for success selected.
- None of this can be done without the appropriate involvement of people (*human resources*), who need to work effectively together using teamwork and consensus.
- The unit will also need a system of checks and balances, or what we call *quality assurance* systems. These review or feedback loops help to continuously improve the overall system.
- This approach then brings us to *environmental results* that *satisfy customer/ stakeholder needs*.

Like the Baldrige award, each of the categories is also weighted differently to reflect the relative importance of different categories. For example, Environmental Results was given the highest overall rating (30 percent). The matrix is scored as follows:

- If the activity shown in a given cell is fully in place, the cell receives a 1.
- If no activity is underway, the cell receives a 0.
- If some activity is underway, the cell is rated 0.5.

No score is assigned for higher cells once a cell is reached that has no activity (undeployed, or 0). The philosophy behind this approach is that activities in lower cells need to be in place because they are fundamental to the success of higher-ranked cells. During the process of creating the TQEM case study, we also learned that flaws in one category can also create, or arise from, flaws in other categories. That is, the root cause of a deficiency can lie elsewhere and will need to be identified.

Exhibit 1: Total Quality Environmental Management Implementation Guide and Assessment Matrix

Category:	Leadership	Information & Analysis	Strategic Planning
Weighting:	15.0%	7.5%	7.5%

Level	Rank			
Maturing	10	Benchmarking indicates unit is "Best-in-Class" in leadership area.	Benchmarking indicates unit is "Best-in-Class" in area of information and analysis.	Benchmarking indicates unit is "Best-in-Class" in area of strategic planning.
	9	Top management proactively participates in public policy decision-making processes in environmental area.	Environmental data/analysis directly affect behavior and lead to improved environmental performance of products, operations, services (results).	Environmental improvement plans for processes, products & services are totally integrated into long-term and short-term business plans.
	8	Top management's external actions reflect commitment to unit's environmental principles; management encourages employees to do the same.	Environmental data/analysis used in strategic decision making.	Improvement plans in place at all organization levels support unit's key environmental objectives.
	7	Top management has completed at least one full continuous improvement cycle; management performance measures based on meeting key environmental objectives; decisions based on vision.	Process in place to use environmental data to plan/design for new products/operations/services.	Strategic planning process is supported by a system of rewards and consequences based on both behavior and results.
	6	Management uses reward/consequence system in all areas to reinforce commitment to environmental management.	Process in place to continuously improve environmental data collection/analysis/dissemination.	Process in place to include stakeholder contributions to strategic planning.

Human Resource Development	QA of Environmental Performance	Environmental Results	Customer/ Stakeholder Satisfaction
10.0%	15.0%	30.0%	15.0%
Benchmarking indicates unit is "Best-in-Class" in levels of employee morale and attitudes toward environmental management.	Benchmarking indicates unit is "Best-in-Class" in level of QA of environmental performance.	Benchmarking indicates unit is "Best-in-Class" in environmental results.	Benchmarking indicates unit is "Best-in-Class" in customer/ stakeholder satisfaction with respect to environmental quality.
Career development and education opportunities in environmental management are widely available.	Processes in place in all areas to continuously improve environmental performance of products, processes, and services.	Sustained improvement in environmental performance of processes, products, and services is evident in all areas.	Active customer/ stakeholder involvement contributes to sustained improvement in environmental performance of processes, products, services.
Education and career development plans exist and are linked to environmental management goals, tactics, and strategies.	Formal process used to consider all stakeholder input to environmental performance improvement.	Benchmarking measures identified; benchmarking initiated.	Customers/stakeholders are actively involved in environmental problem solving.
Environmental management is an essential element of reward and consequences systems.	Environmental expertise included in cross-functional teams involved in development cycle for new and existing products, processes, and services.	Rewards/consequences are used to reinforce environmental performance improvement.	Customers/stakeholder involvement contributes to sustained improvement in environmental performance of processes, products, services.
Environmental management training is evaluated for improvement.	Process in place to obtain/use stakeholder input to develop environmental objectives for products, processes, services.	Measures are reviewed and updated at least annually to reflect all stakeholder input.	Customer/stakeholder satisfaction data are integrated into the continuous improvement cycle for all aspects of the unit's functions.

Exhibit 1: (continued)

Category:	Leadership	Information & Analysis	Strategic Planning
Weighting:	**15.0%**	**7.5%**	**7.5%**

Level	Rank			
Growing	5	At least half of top management are using environmental considerations as part of decision-making process.	Environmental data routinely used to improve current products, operations, services, focused on prevention.	Long- and short-term plans that include environmental management are reviewed and improved at least annually.
	4	Dialogue occurs between top management and customers/stakeholders regarding your environmental principles.	Environmental data analyzed for trends.	Resource allocation is consistent with environmental plan implementation needs.
	3	Unitwide plan in place to implement environmental programs including necessary resources.	Environmental data inventory and management process established; some external environmental data collected.	Consistency exists at all levels for environmental management planning and implementation.
	2	Management directly involved in environmental quality management processes as leader/role model. Employee empowerment framework established.	Processes in place to assure validity (Quality Assurance/Quality Control) of basic environmental data.	Quality management process links existing and anticipated environmental regulatory requirements with the planning process.
Beginning	1	Environmental mission, vision, principles defined, published, and understood internally.	Basic internal environmental data identified and gathered.	A long-term (2-5 years) and short-term (1-2 years) planning process addresses environmental needs; annual operating plan includes environmental management needs.

Human Resource Development	QA of Environmental Performance	Environmental Results	Customer/ Stakeholder Satisfaction
10.0%	15.0%	30.0%	15.0%
Measures and trends of employee attitudes toward environmental performance exist.	Evidence exists that quantitative measures of environmental performance extend fully into all aspects of unit's operations.	Improving trends of environmental performance in major areas.	Customer/stakeholder satisfaction measures indicate positive trends.
All employees have completed appropriate environmental training. Employees are empowered. System in place for periodic retraining.	Evidence exists for prevention focus, rather than reaction (e.g., pollution prevention); root-cause analysis used for problem solving. Audit systems used to assure continuous improvement.	Improving trends of environmental performance in some areas.	Measures of customer/ stakeholder satisfaction exist with respect to environmental considerations.
Appropriate environmental awareness and training/education programs developed and scheduled for all employees.	Process in place to assure goals/objectives followed for modification/production of current products, processes, services. Document control process in place and used.	Management system in place for improving environmental performance; major areas for environmental improvement identified.	Proactive process exists to identify customers/stakeholders and environmental considerations beyond measurement of questions, complaints.
Resources are allocated for developing/implementing environmental training and education.	Process in place to assure environmental principles translated into policies, practices; environmental objectives followed to develop new products, processes, services.	Baselines for environmental performance established.	Process exists to respond to customer/ stakeholder environmental questions/ concerns.
Clear assignment of environmental responsibility exists.	Processes in place for ensuring precision and accuracy of measurement systems; internal standards are in place.	Measures of environmental performance are identified.	Process exists to meet existing environmental regulatory requirements for customer/stakeholder information about products, services, and operations.

Now that the matrix scoring approach has been briefly described, it will be useful to review each of the Baldrige categories to show how the TQEM framework works, and how it facilitates application of key principles such as pollution prevention or sustainability.

Leadership

Adopting TQM requires a fundamental change in the way an organization does business. Therefore, a conscious choice, or buy-in, is required from its senior management to create a culture change within the organization.

To make this more dramatic, instead of viewing these matrix elements as a set of management criteria, we can illustrate them instead as a series of choices. For example, in the category of Leadership:

- Management can choose to create a vision or mission, and adopt a set of environmental principles—or it can try to operate without a clear sense of where it is going.

  It can include concepts such as sustainability among the environmental principles it adopts—or it can leave to others the difficulties inherent in wrestling with such concepts. (If it chooses the latter, it will never become a full partner in shaping policy in this area or setting agendas for the future.)
- Management can create a framework that will empower its work force—or it can retain a style of management where decisions are made without worker input (this is particularly important in a unit where improvement opportunities are best identified by workers on the shop floor or staff).
- Management can choose to integrate environmental management and concepts such as pollution prevention or sustainability directly into the unit's decision-making processes and planning—or it can deal with them as an afterthought.
- Senior managers can choose to be role models and leaders in the environmental arena—or relegate this task to a staff function. (This can include, for example, encouraging others to adopt environmental standards and principles, such as suppliers or downstream users of products.)
- Management can actively engage stakeholders, and can become involved in the public policy process—or let staff "take the heat."
- And finally, senior management can benchmark its environmental leadership against others to identify improvement opportunities—or it can remain unpersuaded about the value of information on strengths and weaknesses of peers and competitors.

These are the major elements described in the TQEM matrix under the leadership category. Up to this point, leadership criteria were presented in the form of choices, to give the reader a sense of the potential risks associated with adopting such a fundamental change in corporate culture. By now it should be equally apparent that there are also many benefits attainable from a management system based on TQM. The following discussion will examine matrix criteria associated with the remaining six Baldrige categories and how they relate to implementing the unit's vision and key environmental principles.

Information and Analysis

Once the unit has a firm commitment from its senior management to an environmental vision and a set of principles, it should begin

- Determining what information it needs for environmental management (matrix cells 1 and 3)
- Making certain that this information is useful to those who need it (for example, is it valid, timely, and relevant?) (matrix cells 2, 3, and 6)
- Using the information in a way that ensures excellence in environmental performance while supporting competitiveness (matrix cells 5, 7, 8, and 9)

In the case of different management issues such as compliance, pollution prevention, or sustainability, there is an enormous list of basic information needs. Only a few are listed below to give you a sense of their diversity.

- Who are the unit's key customers and stakeholders, and what are their needs, concerns, and expectations? Clearly today, a unit is accountable to more than just its traditional customers.
- What are the greatest risks associated with operations? products? services? What are the greatest *perceived* risks?
- What are the most toxic or highest volume chemicals used, and which create the highest exposure potential?
- What regulatory drivers exist?
- How well trained/educated are employees and managers on environmental issues? What guidance do they have in the area of sustainability?
- Is valid life cycle analysis information available for products or processes to aid in redesign or reformulation?
- Are risk, cost, and benefit data available for alternatives? Are factors such as future liabilities or risk considered? Are comprehensive data on waste treatment and other environmental management costs provided to managers for decision making? Does the unit understand the concept of full

cost accounting (and external pressures to adopt such methods) with respect to the resources it uses?

- What efficiencies can be gained by adopting different alternatives, and do these approaches create competitive advantage? What are competitors and peers in other fields doing in these areas, and what can be learned from them?
- What are the needs of government for public policy input on new legislative or voluntary approaches in the areas of pollution prevention, product stewardship, or sustainability?

This is also an excellent point at which to gather information on whether the organization's definition of stewardship or sustainability is very different from that of other stakeholders and how that might affect decision making, planning, and goal setting by different groups. In other words, will these groups and the unit be at cross-purposes? A two-way dialogue may be required to resolve such issues.

Once it is clear what types of data are needed, systems should be established for data collection and analysis, as well as to determine trends. It is also critical to identify the types of trend data required for decision making. (For example, in R&D, the development staff needs to know whether proposed process/product changes are consistent with the unit's environmental principles.)

Matrix cells 1 through 5 in this category focus on the *process* of gathering data and managing its quality and usefulness. Matrix cells 5 through 9 in this category focus on *how* data are used. Do the data gather dust on a shelf, or is a process in place to apply it to improve processes, products, or services so that they support the principles of sustainability? And do the data influence both behavior and results? Certainly, the influence of data on behavior was eloquently illustrated a few years ago in the United States when the Toxics Release Inventory data were first released and provided additional impetus to industry's waste reduction programs.

During the process of gathering information and analyzing it, the unit will identify gaps. Significant gaps exist in the area of life cycle analysis, which in many ways is still in its infancy. Perhaps a unit can decide whether to use simple paper or plastic products, but how does it make decisions relating to more complex products or operations? How does it, for example, factor in site-specific effects for which formulas are not available and data are uncertain? Yet without such guidance, managers, R&D staff, and workers will not be able to make well-informed decisions. It is clear that such gaps in the unit's knowledge must be identified and addressed in planning so that resources can be committed to fill those gaps. In some cases, it is clear that partnership with others is required to develop such information, and these resource needs should also be addressed during planning.

Strategic Planning

This leads us to a discussion of strategic planning, where the unit's vision is translated into goals and long- and short-term plans, resources are prioritized and committed, and a framework for implementation is created. The quality of the unit's goals and plans will be only as good as the information provided in the planning process. TQEM ensures the quality of such data. It also ensures that the Pareto process will be used to select the best alternatives. The strategic planning process helps ensure the following:

- Environmental issues will become an integral part of planning.
- Goals will be consistent with the environmental vision and principles the organization adopts.
- Resources will be committed at a level that will realize the unit's improvement plans.
- Processes to improve plans will be adopted that maintain long-term momentum toward the organization's goals, while providing short-term flexibility.
- A process will be in place to communicate with customers and stakeholders and include their input in planning.
- Goals set will be prevention-based (rather than oriented to the quick-fix) and will focus on the long-term good of both the organization and society.

Human Resource Development

Best results can be obtained only when there is a high level of commitment from people. The first matrix cell in the Human Resource Development category requires that responsibility is clearly assigned throughout the organization. The definition of responsibility is much broader today. For example, if an individual has responsibility for a process or product, that person "owns" not only the product the unit makes, but its waste streams, its compliance-related problems, and even, in a sense, its basic design framework. And he or she may also own responsibility for improving every aspect of that process or product, such as anticipating and preventing future problems and finding the best ways to minimize waste, costs, and risks and to maximize product output and other benefits (for example, protection of health and environment).

Empowerment is essential to make that ownership real. The framework for empowerment begins with moving decision making downward in the organization into the hands of those closest to process, product, or service, thus allowing workers to contribute most effectively. The quality of their decisions will only be as good as the training the unit provides through its formal training programs and job assignments. But workers will also gain knowledge from informal associations with environmental specialists assigned to the organization to participate in quality circles or design and development teams.

An effective framework for empowerment also requires that management provides a climate, culture, and the needed vehicles to stimulate voluntary contributions from employees.

In the area of human resource development, it is important to provide an empowerment framework for action, but it's also important to determine what workers think. This determines how motivated they will be to act. As the unit progressively implements its TQEM program, it should ask about worker attitudes toward their organization's environmental management and performance as well as the commitment and leadership of management. Employee perceptions and attitudes should be communicated to management so that productive use can be made of such data. Another key element in moving toward excellence is a consistent system of rewards and recognition that recognizes both individuals and teams for their contributions.

The higher cells in this category examine the extent to which career development plans are linked to the overall environmental improvement goals of the organization. Clearly, managers who have had some personal experience with environmental management will have a different mindset toward environmental issues and toward risk management. They will also be more willing and able to integrate environmental priorities into business plans.

Quality Assurance

The category of Quality Assurance (QA) addresses the system of checks and balances mentioned earlier. For example, QA includes assuring the quality of measurement systems, and the extent to which the unit documents what it *should do*, and what it *actually does*. It includes establishing systems that ensure consistency throughout the unit with respect to its vision, principles, goals and objectives, and implementation plans. Thus, systems are needed to ensure that environmental objectives set during planning are actually followed when products, processes, or services are developed or modified. It also includes tying environmental staff tightly into operations so that no modifications are made without their agreement that those changes reflect the unit's environmental vision and principles and are consistent with its objectives.

Perhaps the most important element in the entire QA category is the concept of a prevention *mindset*. The principles of sustainability require that the needs of future generations are considered, even while the unit is going about the business of today. Thus its operating policies and its practices should not only *prevent* deterioration of the natural resource base but enhance its quality. The unit also needs to use other quality-based "tools" from this category including Pareto processes, root-cause analysis, and continuous improvement. These techniques are fundamental to identify and prioritize issues, identify alternative approaches, construct practicable plans, and allocate increasingly scarce resources. These tools are used to determine which processes and waste streams to address, which products to redesign, and which alternatives to adopt. Without this "tool kit," the evolution of business toward more sustainable approaches will be impeded.

Environmental Results

This brings us now to the category of Environmental Results, or the bottom line in the eyes of customers and stakeholders. The first requirement in the matrix is to identify how success *will be measured*. This is relatively easy in areas such as compliance or waste reduction but assumes new dimensions in areas such as satisfying customer and stakeholder needs for greener (more sustainable) products and processes. Once the unit has decided what those measures will be and has established performance baselines, it should be ready to use the continuous improvement process to move toward its goals. It will also have to track its progress, communicate successes, and provide positive reinforcement for performance excellence. If its improvement plans were based on the end goal of sustainability, then the unit's performance should move closer to that goal with each increment of improvement.

As the unit reaches higher performance levels, its level of excellence should be comparable to best-in-class. It is at this point that benchmarking pays off. During benchmarking, a narrow area is selected and other units are chosen for comparison (including peers and others outside the unit's industry sector). This allows the unit to identify opportunities for improvement that it may not have discovered by internal assessment or benchmarking efforts.

Customer/Stakeholder Satisfaction

This last category completes the circle, bringing us back to where we began: the customer and stakeholder. The matrix begins at the lowest level with the simple requirement that response systems have been established to handle customers' simplest concerns or requirements. At higher performance levels, it requires that the unit become proactive, anticipating customer/stakeholder expectations or problems. The unit also has to measure whether it has actually satisfied customers and stakeholders. If *their* measure of success is sustainability, then the unit needs to understand what sustainability means to them.

Just measuring satisfaction is not enough. Above matrix cell 5, something needs to be done with those measurements. For example, customer/stakeholder-based data should actually be used in continuous improvement cycles, in decision making, and in planning. Information about environmental performance improvements (and other data) should be clearly communicated to stakeholders. If the unit chooses to do this through an annual report or newsletter, it will need to supplement its one-way communications with vehicles that permit two-way dialogue. Active involvement of stakeholders, required at higher matrix levels, is obviously not without risk. Business, for example, may be concerned about confidentiality issues when involving stakeholders directly in the "greening" process (that is, protecting confidential information on new "green" products or processes).

If the unit uses the data it gathers effectively (that is, as the basis for its continuous improvement process), then it should find improvements not only in its overall environmental performance, but also in the extent to which that performance satisfies customers and stakeholders.

That is how our approach to TQEM works. The criteria described for each Baldrige category build from the ground floor (level 1) up to the midpoint (level 5), creating a sound management system, then guide the organization in its progress toward world-class or best-in-class performance.

Conclusion

To summarize the value of the approach presented here:

- The matrix provides a guide for implementing TQEM, including a continuous improvement process and a framework to implement key principles such as pollution prevention, compliance, or sustainability.
- It sets standards for excellence.
- It provides a tool for economic improvement through the integration of environmental goals into strategic business planning.
- It reinforces partnerships, and encourages sharing information and technologies, in ways that foster pollution prevention and sustainability.
- It fosters consensus among business, government, and the public that the right priorities have been set and that resources are being used in a way that does not compromise the needs of future generations.
- And lastly, it promotes a high level of environmental awareness and stewardship.

After the CGLI TQEM work group completed development of the matrix, it went on to develop other tools, including a TQEM primer, that includes

- A description of the key elements of TQEM
- An extensive list of assessment questions based on individual matrix cell criteria
- A case study of a hypothetical manufacturing firm that adopted TQEM, which translates the abstract terms of the matrix into more concrete examples

We are convinced that these will be useful tools for environmental managers as TQEM becomes the management system of choice within industry. Indeed, the matrix was recently used as the basis for a major environmental conference, Globescope '93, to examine the effectiveness of a number of "processes for sustainability." We have also used TQM as a tool to analyze public policy development and implementation cycles and to evaluate how firms can be more effective in shaping public policy.

To obtain a copy of CGLI's TQEM *primer and assessment matrix*, please contact: Evelyn Strader, Council of Great Lakes Industries, Suite 275, 151 W. Jefferson, Detroit, MI 48226; or phone 313-259-1166.

Grace H. Wever, Ph.D, is vice president of environmental affairs for the Council of Great Lakes Industries (CGLI), a public policy body. She also serves as director and corporate liaison to the Council for Eastman Kodak Company in Rochester, New York. **George F. Vorhauer** is director of corporate quality initiatives in the Corporate Quality Office at Eastman Kodak Company and is an ad hoc member of the Corporate Quality Breakthrough Council. He is a 1993 Malcolm Baldrige National Quality Award examiner.

The authors acknowledge the contributions of the Council of Great Lakes Industries TQEM work group to matrix development. The authors gratefully recognize the ongoing guidance and personal support of Dr. Ronald Heidke, vice president and director of corporate quality, Eastman Kodak Company, and thank Dr. Alan Monahan, vice president of worldwide manufacturing at Xerox Corporation, for his encouragement as CGLI's Board sponsor of the project.

Selecting Measures for Corporate Environmental Quality: Examples from TQEM Companies

13

Chris FitzGerald

Companies undertaking TQEM programs must decide how to measure continuous improvement in the environmental field at the outset of their implementation activities. In the past three years, the leading TQEM companies have made these tough choices and have begun to share their findings with the larger professional community. The author proposes a model for classifying environmental measurement data and presents examples of approaches adopted by TQEM companies.

The Challenge of Appropriate Measures

Identifying appropriate measures of quality has been one of the principal challenges for companies applying total quality management (TQM) principles to their environmental programs. TQM systems rely in part on appropriate statistical procedures applied to appropriate, accurate measurements, yet at the program level most of the environmental manager's professional practice tools are almost exclusively qualitative rather than quantitative. Selection of appropriate measures is critical, because systems tend to optimize around their key measures. Inappropriate measures will produce inappropriate results; in other words, watch out, because you might get what you ask for. In TQM terms the traditional site compliance audit is a qualitative, after-the-fact inspection for defects. There are reams of qualitative data items produced for reports mandated by regulations, but meaningful measures tend to get obscured rather than enlightened by production of these huge quantities of data points.

Computers are not helpful in selecting *what* to measure. The availability of large data bases can be a temptation to substitute volume for meaning, much as vague request for proposal (RFP) specifications for big projects can lead to consultant proposals that are intended to be weighed rather than read. Environmental professionals more often serve their information systems than are served by them. Deming Prize-winner Florida Power & Light (FPL) recognized this by "banning" the term *environmental information management systems*, because that term reflected the need to service these potential data-hungry monster systems. Information systems must demonstrate and justify their value to the management goal at FPL, where the acceptable term is *environmental management information systems (EMIS)*.

137

Who Is Measuring What?—Classifying Environmental Information Functions

What measures are meaningful in our TQEM program? The answer will vary according to who is doing the measuring. In general, the selection of an appropriate measure will be more straightforward as you get closer to the *task-level engineering function* (see **Exhibit 1**). If your job is to run a water treatment plant (source monitoring), you know that timely reporting and minimizing the concentrations and quantities of target pollutants are likely to be among your principal measures of quality and of continuous improvement potential. There are many data points (results), but the parameters are consistent and comparable.

For the manager with *plant-level, cross-media* responsibilities, there are many more data sources and more complex data relationships involved. Reduction of stack or wastewater emissions is no longer a pure benefit if it increases shipment of wastes to landfills; the full life cycle of hazardous components within the plant must be identified and to some extent quantified. Although dedicated environmental emissions data bases are useful for source monitoring, at the material management level data must be captured from a wide range of operational sources, such as purchasing, distribution, personnel, material planning, process management, and shipping. The meaningful integration of these data in a time- and cost-effective manner is a significant challenge at this level, and without prioritizing key measures it is impossible to identify performance levels and opportunities for continuous improvement.

Exhibit 1: A Hierarchy of Environmental Management Information Requirements

Responsibility	Orientation	Typical Data Sources	Data Characteristics
Environmental Performance; Compliance/Risk Management	Corporate Environmental Policy & Programs Internal Compliance	Auditing Permit Management Facility Reports Surveys	Highest Integration Summary & Exception Relatively Lower Volume
Materials Management	Plant-Level Processes	Chemical Inventory Waste Tracking Material & Emissions Balances	High Integration High Volume
Source Monitoring	Engineering Task	Air & Water Reporting Tank Testing Exposure Monitoring Groundwater & Soils'	Low Integration High Volume

At the *corporate or divisional program level,* it becomes even more difficult to identify quantitative measures that associate program goals with hard, measurable data. If the source management and material management level data collection analysis is being done properly and consistently, there are many millions of data points available, but which measures are meaningful within the context of a corporate-level program? On one level there is a need to assure that the functions are being carried out properly, and compliance-oriented measures are an obvious choice. These measures typically focus on the number and timeliness of audits conducted, reports submitted, and notice of violations, releases, incidences, and noncompliance occurrences. But compliance in itself is assumed to be a basic performance standard for TQEM firms and not much of a rallying cry for excellence and continuous improvement. What other quantitative measures are being applied to corporate environmental performance?

Reports from the Measurement Front

This discussion will focus on the attempts to create measurement systems to be employed and promoted companywide to help implement corporate environmental policy statements. All of the TQEM firms discussed here also employ a variety of other measurement systems to track improvement at other function levels (e.g., source management and materials management).

Apart from a few pioneering companies, most firms are still in the first few years of implementing TQEM programs. Measurement systems rely on several years' data to become meaningful, because TQEM measures gauge progress rather than absolute levels of quality. TQEM companies are still devising, implementing, or calibrating their corporate measurement systems, but are now beginning to share their findings in the environmental management community. At two recent TQEM conferences, twenty speakers addressed measurement strategies in their presentations. The Total Quality Environmental Management Conference was held in San Francisco on March 9-10, 1992, and was sponsored by Executive Enterprises. The Corporate Quality Environmental Management II: Measurements and Communications Conference took place on March 16-18, 1992, in Arlington, VA, and was sponsored by GEMI: The Global Environmental Management Initiative. We will summarize eight of the measurement programs that represent the different approaches presented here (see **Exhibit 2**). In referring to the papers presented, we will abbreviate the conferences as TQEM-SF and GEMI '92.

AT&T/Intel Joint Benchmarking[1]

In 1991 AT&T and Intel joined forces to identify the "best-in-class" corporate pollution prevention (PP) programs and develop benchmarks for targeting their own firms' efforts at continuous improvement in PP. The proposed benchmarks

Exhibit 2: Selected TQEM Measurement Systems

Company	Purpose of Measures	Parameters
AT&T/Intel Joint Project	Develop benchmarks for corporate pollution prevention (PP) programs	• Weightings of program elements • Evaluations of "best of class" • Design of generic PP program • Gap analysis
Sandoz Corporation	Plant and corporate S & E (safety and environmental) performance	Key indices reported at all facilities: • Lost time & workday accident rates • Totals: energy, water, waste • S & E investments, expenses, personnel • Total production, personnel
Niagara Mohawk	Track effectiveness of corporate environmental protection programs	• Weighted index comprised of: — Compliance incidents (NOV's etc.) — Emissions and wastes — Enhancements (dollar value)
Green Environment	Track effectiveness of corporate environmental protection programs	Score sheet of program implementation: 25 questions, 0-2 pts. each. Categories: • PLAN • DO • ACT • CHECK
Xerox Corporation	Integrate environmental issues to core company values	Economic Incentives • Gain market share via positioning • Cost savings reporting • Reduce risks, future costs
3M Company	Track continuous improvement in Pollution Prevention Pays (3P) and production efficiency	Waste quantities reflect 3P, efficiency • Absolute values • Reductions over time • As percentage of inputs
US EPA	• Publicize polluters • Economic incentives • Recognize "good citizens"	• SARA 313/TRIS • Clean Air Act 1990 pollution market • 33/50 • Green Lights

were needed to serve PP participants by: 1) encouraging them to "look outside the box" of existing practices for new PP opportunities; 2) providing comparative data to help convince management of the need for improvement; and 3) developing momentum for the PP efforts at every level of the company.

The project team used scoring systems to weigh PP quality parameters, select the best-in-class companies, and again to weight the factors that would determine level of PP quality. Quality parameters were selected in brainstorming sessions in which environmental and safety work areas were categorized (i.e., Superfund management, audit process, smoke detection, paper recycling, etc.) and then scored on the basis of relative importance and self-evaluation of their own company's progress and process status:

- Importance   1= Very important   to   5 = Not important
- Self-Grading   A = Excellent   to   F = Poor
- Process Status   E = Emerging   or   M = Mature

After voting on scores, the team created a weighted evaluation template, brainstormed a list of potential best-of-class companies, then conducted high-level searches to provide data for scoring companies on the weighted template. This process narrowed the list to eight companies for evaluation, five of which were visited for face-to-face structured interviews. After the interviews the team assembled to evaluate which program elements of successful PP systems were (1) critical, (2) important, (3) nice to do, or (4) not relevant.

As a result of the research, the team developed a "generic pollution prevention program" synthesizing the weighted program elements and performed gap analyses to determine what their own companies needed to do to implement the generic program.

Sandoz Corporation[2]

Sandoz Corporation decided that relatively simple, straightforward parameters were the best choice from the standpoint of comparability and easy access to data, allowing for immediate implementation. All of Sandoz's 350 facilities worldwide now report these ten safety and environmental data items on a regular basis:

1. Lost time accident rate
2. Lost workday rate
3. Total energy consumption
4. Total water consumption
5. Total liquid and solid waste

6. Total S & E investments
7. Total S & E expenses
8. Total S & E personnel
9. Total production
10. Total personnel

The advantage of this approach is that almost all of the data items can be provided from existing data sources. Items 1 and 2 are already required for US OSHA reporting, and the remaining items can be summarized from existing production and personnel systems. The measures are primarily useful for comparisons over time for individual facilities, but additional inter-plant comparisons can be made for similar operations by creating ratios, such as waste per ton of product.

Xerox Corporation[3]

While Xerox Corporation employs many other measurement systems to monitor environmental quality, economic indicators are emerging as key incentives to integrate environmental values with the corporation's core values. Laws and regulations, which were originally the driving forces for environmental improvements, are external drivers. By identifying environmental improvement with values of internal customers (employees, customers, and management), TQEM can become an integral aspect of company operations. While maintaining other environmental quality measurement systems, Xerox is emphasizing data which illustrate opportunities to

- Gain market share by positioning environmental quality as an aspect of total quality management;
- Treat pollution at the source via redesign; and
- Reduce risks and future costs.

Even though Xerox has implemented and maintains many other qualitative and quantitative measures of environmental progress, Xerox will emphasize its commitment to environmental leadership by explicitly stating the economic benefits of each program element. Thus proactive compliance is justified as an opportunity to reduce future costs; packaging reuse produces both costs savings and cost avoidance; energy programs are quantified both as conservation improvement and cost savings. In every instance, the environmental initiatives produce results that are visible on balance sheets in the company's mainstream financial reporting, rather than just in special environmental reports.

Niagara Mohawk Power Corporation (NMPC)[4]

At Niagara Mohawk an interdisciplinary task force was formed to develop an index to measure progress in achieving a new corporate policy for environmental protection. Five options were considered:

1. A compliance-oriented index modeled on another utility's environmental index
2. External benchmarking of selected utilities
3. A three-category "weighting and rating" index
4. An index based on air emissions
5. A social welfare index based on weighting emissions and waste parameters

The task force selected the third option and developed parameters to measure and weigh corporate environmental performance based on compliance, waste emissions, and environmental enhancements. Benchmarks for current performance are being established, and future performance will be weighed on a -2 to +2 scale representing lower or higher performance against the benchmark.

The *compliance* parameters weigh notices of violations and fine paid the highest, followed by audits performed and then nonconforming discharges and emissions. The *emissions and wastes* parameters apply half the weight to emissions/MWhr of SO_2, NO_x, and CO_2, and the remainder to solid wastes, hazardous wastes, LLRW, and discharges of heavy metals. *Environmental enhancements* are rated based on NMPC's dollar investment in each enhancement. Niagara Mohawk recognizes that the index is measuring widely disparate parameters, and doesn't assign significance to the actual score on the index. The real value of the index is to measure relative improvement over time.

Green Environment, Inc.[5]

Environmental consultant Mark Green has developed an ambitious tool for measuring corporate environmental, called TQEMPE: total quality environmental management performance evaluations. TQEMPE is patterned on the Baldrige Award criteria and reflects aspects of the Deming, Crosby, Juran, and Harwood methodologies. Green identifies seven essential criteria for an evaluation tool:

1. Instrument must be accurate.
2. Instrument must be precise.
3. Measurement must be powerful.
4. Instrument cost and cost of measurement must be economical.
5. Instrument must be adaptable.
6. Instrument must be simple to use.
7. Instrument must be effective.

TQEMPE attempts to meet these criteria through a twenty-five question evaluation tool in which each question can be scored from zero to two, for a potential perfect score of fifty (nonapplicable questions are scored two). The questionnaire is divided into four topical areas: PLAN (five questions); DO (seven questions); CHECK (seven questions); and ACT (four questions). A sample question from the DO section asks:

B. Are all levels of management involved in and accountable for achieving environmental objectives?

- All levels of company management have a role in and are accountable for achieving company environmental objectives. (2 points)

- Some levels of company management have a role in and are accountable for achieving company environmental objectives. (1 point)
- Company management roles for achieving company environmental objectives are not defined, or an accountability mechanism does not exist. (0 points)

TQEMPE can be applied as an assessment tool at the plant, division, and/or corporate level. Green stresses that the tool is intended to provide a common language and metric system for comparison over time and between operations, and that the scores are not intended as absolute values for one-time ratings.

3M Company[6]

3M Company's pioneering and influential *Pollution Prevention Pays* (3P) program employs the simplest measurement approach of all; absolute data for waste produced are reported companywide and are expected to show improvement each year. Every plant measures all of the wastes being generated from that facility, including all facility wastes that go to the air or water, or are generated as hazardous or solid wastes. Waste measurements are taken before the wastes are subjected to any treatment measures, to assure that any reductions that are achieved have been accomplished by pure pollution prevention rather than by improvements in pollution control efficiency. These waste values are normalized to production levels so that increases or decreases in production levels are removed from the evaluation.

Tom Zosel, manager of 3M's pollution prevention programs, says that this approach to measuring improvement is consistent with 3M's engineering orientation and commitment to placing responsibility for 3P in the operating divisions:

> If we really look at what we are measuring, it is the efficiency in our total use in raw materials. We believe that 3M is one of the first companies that can quantitatively determine on a percentage basis exactly how much of our raw materials goes into product, how much goes into productive recycling or secondary uses, and how much ends up as waste. This takes into account all materials used at product facilities including packaging supplies, quality control materials, maintenance materials, and clean-up supplies.

The success of 3P is well-documented. Established in 1975, the program has reduced 3M's pollution by an estimated 50 percent and has saved the company over $500 million.

U.S. EPA

We'll ask you to suspend skepticism for a moment and look at recent EPA program initiatives as efforts to serve the corporate customer sector by providing simpler, comparable measures as both carrots and sticks. On the stick side, the SARA 313 Form R can be seen as a reporting burden and a community embarrassment when TRIS reports make the local front pages. But many firms also report that the Form R reports have provided operational data that they never had available before, allowing comparisons both among plants within a company and between companies utilizing comparable production processes. In his address to the GEMI conference, EPA Administrator William Reilly posed TRIS-type disclosure as the single most effective first step Eastern European countries can take in the effort to clean up the massive pollution legacies of the old Eastern bloc regimes:

> My answer is to begin with the disclosure of emissions . . . , that the data be published in local newspapers. They support a healthy nongovernmental, environmental movement. At that point a fascinating dynamic will begin to occur: the community will interact with plant managers, workers and government to reduce pollution levels. Such is the power of information.[7]

On the carrot side, the 33/50 and Green Light programs offer industry quantitative goals, quantitative information on progress, and the opportunity for companies to demonstrate leadership and good citizenship. Although the Clean Air Act Amendments have many proscriptive provisions, they also encourage continuous improvement by developing benchmarks for emissions per unit of production for many processes and rewarding the top 12.5 percent of companies for performance in this arena. Finally, by encouraging the development of markets for surplus emission credits, EPA and regional agencies such as California's South Coast Air Quality Management District are supporting the coin of the realm (dollars) as the most basic, comparable measure of improvement.

Conclusions

Although even the pioneering companies described here will caution that the development of measurement systems is still in its infancy, a number of consistent trends are emerging:

- Measurement systems are essential to give meaning to corporate environmental policy statements; without measures they are platitudes.
- No measurement system has value as a one-time exercise; meaning emerges only as data are reported over time to track improvement.
- Deciding what to measure is only one aspect of the measurement challenge. Measurement programs must be implemented to encourage ownership and provide useful feedback at the levels where improvement can be implemented.

- You can't keep the measures in the corporate closet; results must be widely distributed in order to be effective. Documenting accomplishments is critical to encouraging pride of ownership and momentum to the people who are ultimately accomplishing continuous improvement.
- The right measures will draw data from mainstream business data systems rather than exclusively from specialized, isolated environmental applications. The better the measure reflects the core values and goals of the company, the more the environmental functions will be integrated into everyone's job.
- Make the measures as lean and clean as possible. The more complex, fuzzy, and data-hungry the measure, the less likely you will be to achieve wide-scale, meaningful reporting. There is a definite need for qualitative evaluation as well as quantitative measures, but people understand and respond to success that can be plotted.

Finally, the degree of cooperation and open information sharing in the measurements field is remarkable. There are strong disincentives to sharing company information about pollution issues with other companies, and one can imagine that a lot of corporate counsel time has been engaged in examining how much can be disclosed. But the constructive, open disclosure of methods and the devotion of time to intercompany benchmarking, publishing, and speaking reflect the real enthusiasm and value that the leading TQEM firms are deriving from seeing the results of measurement systems.

Notes

1. GEMI '92: Klafter, Brenda A. (AT&T), "Case Study: AT&T and Intel Pollution Prevention Benchmarking."
2. GEMI '92: Ankers, Ray, "Measuring Safety and Environmental Performance and Risk."
3. TQEM-SF: Bhushan, Abhay K. (Xerox Corporation), "Economic Incentives for TQEM: How Will It Improve Your Bottom Line?"
4. GEMI-92: Miakisz, Joseph A., "Developing A Composite Index for Measuring and Communicating Environmental Performance."
5. TQEM-SF: Green, Mark (Green Environment, Inc.), "Total Quality Environmental Management Performance Evaluations Using TQEMPE."
6. TQEM-SF: Zosel, Thomas W., "Pollution Prevention from a TQM Perspective."
7. GEMI '92: Reilly, William K., "The Power of Information."

Chris FitzGerald, the editor-in-chief of *Total Quality* Environmental *Management*, is a consultant in environmental information management and teaches courses on environmental software selection and implementation.

Quality Metrics in Design for Environment

14

Joseph Fiksel

There is a growing commitment by manufacturers, both in the United States and abroad, to assure environmental responsibility for all of their operations. This trend is driven partly by market demands for "green" products and partly by changes in international standards and regulations. In response, leading companies are demonstrating that environmental improvement can actually increase profitability, and design for environment (DFE) is emerging as an important business practice.

The ability to evaluate environmental quality in objective, measurable terms is a key component of an effective DFE capability. In particular, environmental quality metrics are essential to support goal setting, monitoring, and continuous improvement in the design of products and processes. This chapter describes environmental quality measurement tools and procedures, particularly as they relate to DFE. One of the challenges of performance measurement is to incorporate a life-cycle view of environmental performance into measurement tools that can be easily computed and tracked.

In recent years, there has been a fundamental change in the way that manufacturing firms view environmental, health, and safety management. The traditional approach to environmental issues was based on the notions of regulatory compliance and risk management, in other words, "staying out of trouble." Today, most leading companies are abandoning this traditional, passive posture and engaging in voluntary initiatives to improve the environmental performance of their products and processes. Most manufacturing firms have adopted policies that embrace a commitment to environmental responsibility, and many have made efforts to communicate this commitment to customers and stockholders through glossy environmental reports (printed on recycled paper, of course). These changes are evident in virtually every major industry, including chemicals, electronics, motor vehicles, consumer products, food and beverages, pharmaceuticals, pulp and paper, petroleum, and electric power, and have led to the flourishing of consortia such as the Global Environmental Management Initiative (GEMI) and the Business Council for Sustainable Development, as well as EPA-sponsored programs such as Green Lights and 33/50.

There are a number of motivating factors that have contributed to this remarkable trend:

- **Customer consciousness**—retail customers are increasingly concerned about the environmental quality of the products they use, and major corporations are beginning to systematically review the environmental performance of their suppliers. Moreover, product "eco-labeling" regarding environmental sensitivity is becoming common.
- **Competitive differentiation**—product designs that consider environmental issues will generally be superior in terms of elegance, energy-efficiency, and cost of ownership and can frequently sway a purchase decision if price and performance are comparable.
- **Profitability improvement**—a green approach to the design of products and processes can have a significant impact on product line profitability through savings in manufacturing and other operating costs, as well as through increased market share.
- **Regulatory pressures**—both in the United States and abroad, government regulations regarding the environmental impacts of products and production processes are becoming more stringent, especially as regards the disposal and recycling of products at the end of their useful life.
- **International standards**—many leading U.S. manufacturers are participating in a worldwide effort, coordinated by the International Standards Organization (ISO), to establish standards for environmental stewardship over the full product life cycle.
- **Employee satisfaction**—employees and their families are increasingly conscious of their responsibility to the environment, and incorporation of such values into business activities contributes to their positive feelings about their workplace.

Perhaps the most important factor in changing industry attitudes has been the realization that paying attention to environmental responsibility can actually increase profitability. Reducing pollution at the source and designing products and processes in ways that enhance environmental quality will generally result in increased efficiency and reduced operating costs.

This potential for profitability through environmental improvements was demonstrated recently by several industry projects which were sponsored by the President's Commission on Environmental Quality. For example, AT&T's telecommunications equipment manufacturing plant in Ohio eliminated the use of a known toxic chemical (1,1,1-trichloroethane, or TCA) while achieving a projected annual savings of $200,000. A DuPont chemical plant in Texas reduced ammonium sulfate emissions due to acrylonitrile manufacturing from 100 million to 40 million pounds a year and cut annual manufacturing costs by $1 million with no capital investment required. Most impressively, a Procter & Gamble plant in Pennsylvania that produces tissue, paper towels, and diapers implemented a comprehensive waste minimization program resulting in annual estimated savings of $25 million.

The Need for Quality Measurement Tools

While there are many success stories similar to the above both in the United States and abroad, it is fair to say that environmental quality improvement has not yet matured into a systematic business practice. Companies that have launched such efforts cite a number of barriers, including resource limitations, organizational inertia, and lack of understanding of environmental issues. A recent survey of key environmental executives, conducted by Decision Focus Incorporated, explored how leading companies are addressing these challenges. The twenty companies surveyed ranged from those for which manufacturing is primarily a *continuous process* operation, including 3M, Amoco, DuPont, Merck, Intel, and Shell, to those for which manufacturing is primarily a *discrete assembly* operation, including Boeing, Chrysler, Compaq, DEC, IBM and Polaroid. Each executive was asked whether their company:

- Has a policy or mission statement regarding environmental responsibility
- Establishes quantitative targets or objectives for environmental improvement
- Rewards individuals and groups based on environmental performance
- Uses environmental auditing and review procedures for facilities and products
- Employs environmental metrics in design, engineering, and quality management
- Integrates environmental awareness into business strategy and decision making

The survey revealed a strong commitment on the part of these companies to achieving environmental excellence. However, a striking finding was that while 55 percent of them claim to have integrated environmental awareness into their business strategy and decision-making, only 30 percent of them have actually included environmental metrics in their design engineering and quality management processes (see **Exhibit 1**).

The lack of implementation of quality metrics among 70 percent of the respondents presents a paradox—without quality measurement it is difficult or impossible to achieve continuous improvement in environmental performance. Broad objectives, such as "50 percent reduction in total waste generated by 1995," are certainly commendable, but it is difficult to achieve such objectives without operational metrics, accountability, and reward systems at the level of individual and

Exhibit 1: Environmental Management Practices at 20 Major U.S. Companies

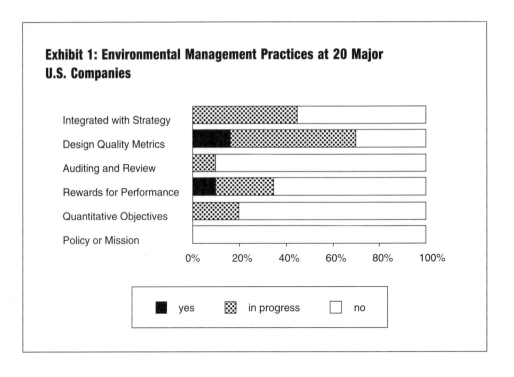

team functional responsibilities. In particular, without a quantitative basis for understanding the relative contribution of environmental quality to profitability and customer satisfaction, it is difficult to make meaningful trade-off decisions in the development of new products. These results suggest that, while many of these companies have introduced environmental awareness into their business strategies in a *qualitative* sense, they may still lack the analytical tools to evaluate the costs and benefits of business decisions from an environmental perspective.

The Emergence of Design for Environment

A common theme among the companies mentioned above is the recognition that *environmental quality is just one aspect of total quality*. While seemingly obvious, this simple statement reflects a radical change in attitude and has profound implications in terms of a company's business processes. Instead of viewing environmental management as an unavoidable cost of doing business and treating it as an overhead expense, these companies view environmental management as an essential core function associated with enterprise management and allocate funds to this function based on its contribution to corporate value. The implied business process changes include integrating environmental quality metrics and assessment tools into engineering practices, as well as developing accounting systems that recognize environmental costs and benefits.

This modern view of environmental quality has led many companies to adopt the concept of design for environment (DFE), defined as *systematic consideration during new product and process development of design issues associated with environmental safety and health over the full product life cycle*. DFE can be seen as the convergence of two worldwide thrusts:

Enterprise integration—the reengineering of business processes and information systems to improve teamwork and coordination across organizational boundaries. The establishment of cross-functional teams for *integrated product development* has been widely adopted as a strategy for agile manufacturing, allowing companies to release higher quality products while reducing time to market. In this approach, DFE is one of many design practices addressing different aspects of quality throughout the product life cycle, e.g., design for testability, manufacturability, reliability, and maintainability.

Sustainable development—economic progress that, as defined in *Our Common Future*, "meets the needs of the present without compromising the ability of future generations to meet their own needs." This notion that industrial growth and environmental quality are mutually reinforcing, rather than conflicting, is a logical outgrowth of environmental stewardship and pollution prevention practices that have been going on for years. Leading manufacturing firms have begun to replace end-of-pipe pollution control strategies with more cost-effective DFE strategies such as reducing energy use, recycling process water, and eliminating waste.

The scope of DFE encompasses many overlapping disciplines, including environmental risk management, product safety, occupational health and safety, pollution prevention, ecology and resource conservation, accident prevention, and waste management. **Exhibit 2** shows a hierarchical breakdown of DFE disciplines that are reflected in the practices of many manufacturing firms. There are a variety of specific DFE practices that have emerged, which often address several different areas of concern. For example, reducing the mass of a product can result in both energy and material conservation, which contributes to sustainability, and reduced pollutant emissions, which contributes to health and safety. The following are some of the more common DFE practices in industry today:

- **Material substitution**—replacing product constituents with substitute materials that are superior in terms of increased recyclability, reduced energy content, or other metrics.
- **Waste source reduction**—reducing the mass of the product or of its packaging, thus reducing the resulting quantity of waste matter per product unit.
- **Toxic use reduction**—reducing or eliminating the types and amounts of

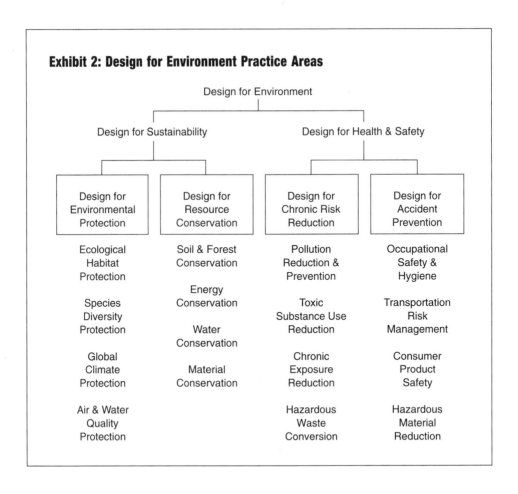

Exhibit 2: Design for Environment Practice Areas

Design for Environment

Design for Sustainability — Design for Health & Safety

Design for Environmental Protection	Design for Resource Conservation	Design for Chronic Risk Reduction	Design for Accident Prevention
Ecological Habitat Protection	Soil & Forest Conservation	Pollution Reduction & Prevention	Occupational Safety & Hygiene
Species Diversity Protection	Energy Conservation	Toxic Substance Use Reduction	Transportation Risk Management
Global Climate Protection	Water Conservation	Chronic Exposure Reduction	Consumer Product Safety
Air & Water Quality Protection	Material Conservation	Hazardous Waste Conversion	Hazardous Material Reduction

toxic chemicals incorporated into the product or used in its manufacturing process.

- **Energy use reduction**—reducing the energy required to produce, transport, store, maintain, use, recycle, or dispose of the product and its packaging.

- **Life extension**—prolonging the useful life of a product or its components, thus reducing the associated waste stream.

- **Design for separability and disassembly**—using techniques such as snap fastening of components and color-coding of plastics.

- **Design for disposability**—assuring that all nonrecyclable materials and components can be safely and efficiently disposed.

- **Design for recyclability**—ensuring both a high recycled content in products and a high degree of product recycling at end of life.

- **Design for refurbishment**—enabling certain components of a product to be reclaimed, refurbished, and reused.

- **Design for remanufacturing**—enabling the recovery and reprocessing of used products or materials and their recycling as inputs to the manufacture of new products.
- **Design for energy recovery**—extracting energy from waste materials through incineration or other processes.
- **System-oriented design changes**—decreasing the life-cycle cost or increasing the life-cycle efficiency of the product in terms of resource usage or waste generation (for example, encouragement of recycling through supplier partnerships that enable conversion of waste streams into useful materials).

One well-known application of DFE techniques is Xerox's worldwide asset recycling program, which reclaims and recycles finished piece parts worth approximately $200 million each year.

There are a number of existing tools that contribute to the practice of DFE. For example, *risk analysis* techniques such as exposure assessment, probabilistic simulation, and cost-benefit analysis are important tools for managing environmental quality. Traditionally these tools were applied to existing products and processes in order to identify potential hazards, quantify their significance, and determine how they might be mitigated. DFE provides an opportunity to apply these techniques during the design process, as a means of evaluating alternative design concepts and technologies. Today, most risk management groups are moving beyond compliance with government regulations toward proactively anticipating and minimizing risks.

Another important technique is *life-cycle analysis*, which has become an accepted practice for quantifying the total environmental emissions associated with each stage of a product's life cycle, including extraction, transport, manufacture, end use, disposal, and recycling. To perform a full life-cycle impact assessment for a given set of industrial activities requires inventory data regarding materials and energy consumed and released at various life-cycle stages, analytic methodologies for assessing the actual or potential environmental impacts implied by the inventory data, and technical assumptions to support the application of these methodologies in cases where empirical data are either incomplete or subject to uncertainty.

Environmental Quality Metrics

In the context of DFE, environmental quality *metrics* are parameters used to measure design improvement with respect to environmental goals. Because of their fundamental role in the development process, quality metrics clearly are essential to the successful practice of DFE. Examples of environmental quality metrics that can be used to establish design objectives include

- Total energy consumed during the product life cycle
- Renewable energy consumed during the product life cycle
- Power used during operation (for electrical products)
- Useful operating life (for discrete products)
- Toxic or hazardous materials used in production
- Total industrial waste generated during production
- Hazardous waste generated during production or use
- Air emissions and water effluents generated during production
- Greenhouse gases and ozone-depleting substances released over life cycle
- Product disassembly and recovery time (for discrete products)
- Percentage of recycled materials used as input to the product
- Percentage of recyclable materials available at end-of-life
- Percentage of product recovered and reused
- Purity of recyclable materials recovered
- Percentage of product disposed or incinerated
- Average life-cycle cost incurred by the manufacturer
- Purchase and operating cost incurred by the customer
- Fraction of packaging or containers recycled

At the top level, these metrics typically are driven either by a fundamental customer need or by important internal constraints (e.g., process capability). These are often called *primary metrics*, and their relationship to product goals is illustrated in **Exhibit 3**. Primary metrics can be used to establish measurable overall objectives for a product team.

Primary metrics generally need to be decomposed into *derived metrics*, which represent measurable and controllable parameters of the product or process design. The derived metrics become operational when they are associated with a specific feature, module, or component of a design and can therefore be estimated, tested, and verified. **Exhibit 4** illustrates the relationship between primary and derived metrics.

Categories of Metrics

Environmental quality metrics can be classified according to the following three distinctions.

Qualitative versus Quantitative

Qualitative metrics are those that rely on semantic distinctions based on observation and judgment. An example is the GEMI Environmental Self-Assessment Program (ESAP), which allows companies to assess the characteristics of their environmental management systems based on a generic rating system. While it is possible

Exhibit 3: Environmental Goals and Corresponding Metrics

Goals	Examples of Metrics	Examples of Specific Objectives
Reduce or eliminate waste	• lbs. of emissions over the life cycle • % of product weight disposed in landfills	• Reduce life-cycle emissions by 30% annually • Reduce solid waste disposed to 1 lb. per product unit
Develop "green" recyclable products	• % of product weight recovered and recycled • solid waste emissions	• Achieve 95% recycling • Eliminate end-of-life waste disposal
Reduce life-cycle cost of product	• manufacturing cost • distribution and support cost • end-of-life cost	• Reduce total life-cycle to $7,500 per product unit • Reduce end-of-life cost (or increase value) by 20%
Cost of ownership for customers	• annualized purchase and operating cost ($)	• Must be less than $500 per year
Conserve energy consumption over the life cycle	• total energy (BTUs) to produce one unit • average power use	• Reduce to 1000 BTUs • Reduce by 10% annually • Power less than 30 watts
Conserve natural resources by raising the recycled content	• % by weight of product materials that is recycled	• Achieve 20% or greater total recycled content • Achieve 30% recycled plastics

to assign numerical values (or scores) to qualitative metrics, such numbers have no intrinsic significance. An advantage of qualitative metrics is that they impose a relatively small data collection burden and are easy to implement. However, a disadvantage is that they implicitly incorporate subjective information and therefore are difficult to validate.

Quantitative metrics are those that rely on empirical data and derive numerical results that characterize performance in physical, financial, or other meaningful terms. An example is the Toxic Release Inventory (TRI) system mandated by the U.S. EPA. Quantitative metrics are objective, meaningful, and verifiable; however, a potential disadvantage is that the required data may be burdensome to gather or simply unavailable.

Absolute versus Relative

Absolute metrics are those that are defined with respect to a fixed measurement scale. An example is "total annual hazardous waste generated." *Relative* metrics are

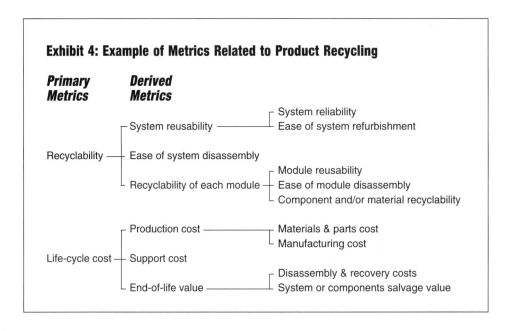

Exhibit 4: Example of Metrics Related to Product Recycling

Primary Metrics — *Derived Metrics*

Recyclability
- System reusability
  - System reliability
  - Ease of system refurbishment
- Ease of system disassembly
- Recyclability of each module
  - Module reusability
  - Ease of module disassembly
  - Component and/or material recyclability

Life-cycle cost
- Production cost
  - Materials & parts cost
  - Manufacturing cost
- Support cost
- End-of-life value
  - Disassembly & recovery costs
  - System or components salvage value

those that are defined with respect to another metric or variable. An example is "total hazardous waste generated per unit produced." A common approach is to use *time-based relative metrics*, i.e., those that compute the change in a particular quantitative metric over a given time period; for example, "percent reduction from 1992 to 1993 in total hazardous waste generated per unit produced."

The use of absolute metrics may lead to inappropriate comparisons of performance among two or more organizations, whereas relative metrics are generally less biased by differences of organizational characteristics. This potential for abuse of information has made many companies wary of reporting their environmental performance results.

Source versus Impact

With regard to environmental performance, *source* metrics are those that address the presumed root causes or origins of environmental consequences associated with an organization's activities. An example is the TRI, which measures the quantity of toxic materials released at a given site. An advantage of source metrics is that they are both readily observable and controllable. A disadvantage is that they are an indirect indicator of potential impacts and generally ignore differences in fate, transport, exposure, and effect pathways among different organizations.

Impact metrics are those that address the actual environmental consequences that may result from an organization's activities. An example is the calculation of "increased cancer risk in the exposed population." While impact metrics have the obvious advantage of directly addressing the impacts of concern, the development of environmental impact metrics is generally challenging because of the technical and statistical uncertainties involved in assessing impacts and attributing them to specific sources.

In practice, the most efficient means of quality measurement is to select company-specific indicators (typically source-oriented) that are believed to be correlated with broad categories of environmental impacts. A common example is the measurement of total emissions of ozone-depleting substances, which are believed to be related to global climate change. Even though the magnitude (or even existence) of the relationship may be speculative, the use of a source metric allows companies and regulatory agencies to establish clear targets for improvement.

Aggregation and Weighting Schemes

A common practice in environmental quality assessment is to use scaling or weighting techniques to aggregate various specific performance measures. For example, a frequently used approach to circumvent the challenges of environmental impact analysis is to rely on source measures but to assign them priorities or weights based on an assessment of their relative importance, taking into consideration the available information about environmental impact pathways. Weighting schemes may be adopted to reflect a variety of different considerations, including

- Values of different stakeholder groups (e.g., customers versus community)
- Relative importance of environmental impacts (e.g., human health versus ecology)
- Internal business priorities (e.g., strategic advantage)

While the aggregation of quality metrics may be desirable for purposes of simplifying decision making, there are a number of problematic aspects to the use of weighting schemes for environmental metrics:

- There are usually implicit policies and value judgments embedded in the weighting system which are not apparent, yet may skew the results in unintended ways.
- Performance metrics are much more meaningful when considered separately, whereas the significance of improvement in an aggregated score is unclear.
- Aggregated measures invite comparisons among dissimilar products or facilities while concealing important differences between such organizations.

By applying good practices, it is possible to avoid some of the above abuses or pitfalls; for example, a measurement system that captures the sources and rationales for all aggregated scores will allow later exploration and decomposition of the results, if necessary. A hierarchical approach toward decomposition, as illustrated in Exhibit 1, would fulfill this need. In general, there is no universal weighting scheme that will suit the needs of diverse organizations, and each company should develop a scheme that suits its business characteristics and priorities.

Conclusion

Environmental quality metrics are useful in two ways: as an indicator of environmental performance for purposes of external communication, and as a basis for setting internal design objectives related to new products and processes. The latter use of metrics is more important to business success and is also more challenging. Specifically, in the practice of design for environment, the availability of credible tools for quality measurement is a critical need.

To introduce environmental metrics into its product and process development activities, a company should establish a systematic program of environmental quality measurement, involving the following steps:

Development of metrics
- Identify key company goals and objectives relevant to environmental performance.
- Select a reasonably small set of primary metrics that reflect the environmental goals.
- Derive corresponding operational metrics that are measurable and controllable.

Implementation of metrics
- Establish systematic measurement tools for each of the DFE metrics selected.
- Develop an appropriate aggregation and weighting scheme.
- Assess the baseline environmental quality of existing products and processes.
- Track environmental quality improvements relative to the baseline.

Continuous improvement
- Institutionalize the metrics and associated tools using computer support as appropriate.
- Benchmark environmental quality progress against competitors.
- Periodically establish new objectives for improvement.

Once environmental quality metrics are seamlessly integrated into the Total Quality Management process, the practice of DFE will become a familiar, natural part of product and process development.

References

Berko-Boateng, V., J. Azar, E. DeJong, and G.A. Yander. "Asset Recycle Management—A Total Approach to Product Design for the Environment." In *Proc. IEEE Symposium on Electronics and the Environment*, Washington, DC, May 1993.

Fava, J.A., R. Denison, B. Jones, M.A. Curran, B. Vigon, S. Selke, and J. Barnum (eds). *A Technical Framework for Life Cycle Assessments*. Washington, DC: Society of Environmental Toxicology and Chemistry, 1991.

Fiksel, J. "Design for Environment: An Integrated Systems Approach." In *Proc. IEEE Symposium on Electronics and the Environment*. Washington, DC, May 1993.

Global Environmental Management Initiative, "Environmental Self-Assessment Program." Washington, DC, September 1992.

Peet, W.J. and K.J. Hladik. "Organizing for Global Product Development." *Electronic Business*, March 6, 1989, pp. 62-64.

President's Commission on Environmental Quality. "Total Quality Management: A Framework for Pollution Prevention." Washington, DC: GPO, January 1993.

World Commission on Environment and Development. *Our Common Future*. Oxford U., 1987.

Joseph Fiksel is principal and vice president at Decision Focus Incorporated, a management consulting firm in Mountain View, California, where he directs the company's work in design for environment. He is an active member of the U.S. Technical Advisory Group to ISO TC207 and is the author of a forthcoming book on DFE to be published by McGraw-Hill.

Planning Quality Management Audits

Benchmarking Environmental Audit Programs: Best Practices and Biggest Challenges

15

Lawrence B. Cahill

As Total Quality Management (TQM) has become an important concept in learning how to manage environmental (health and safety) audit programs more effectively, an especially useful TQM tool has been competitive benchmarking. Companies are using benchmarking studies to identify "best practices" that could be incorporated into their programs. In conducting benchmarking studies, evaluators often also identify the biggest common challenges facing audit program managers.

This chapter discusses these best practices and biggest challenges associated with environmental audit programs. The conclusions are based on a number of benchmarking studies and third-party evaluations of corporate audit programs. As the sources are necessarily limited to the author's own experiences, there are no doubt many other specific best practices that are not discussed in this chapter. These will surface over time.

The concept of competitive benchmarking has received considerable attention in the literature in the past few years.[1] As defined by the Xerox Corporation in its Leadership Through Quality Program, competitive benchmarking is defined as "the continuous process of measuring company products, services and practices against the toughest competitors or those companies recognized as leaders." The steps used in a benchmarking study are relatively straightforward and are shown in **Exhibit 1**. It is not the intent of this chapter to provide a discourse on each of the steps involved in the benchmarking process. That is better handled through other sources. However, based on previous environmental audit program benchmarking experiences, there are five issues that are key to conducting a successful study. They are:

1. Precisely Define the Scope. One can benchmark any and all components of an audit program. For example, one chemical company that was in the midst of a reorganization, wished to determine the best reporting relationship for its audit program. Thus, their goal in a benchmarking study was to determine just that; among a dozen targeted companies, to whom did the corporate audit program manager typically report?

More broad-based studies can help as well. However, there are many components to an audit program and it is probably best to define and analyze only those

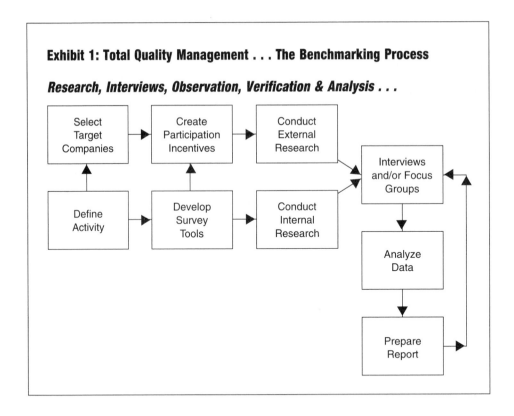

Exhibit 1: Total Quality Management . . . The Benchmarking Process

Research, Interviews, Observation, Verification & Analysis . . .

that are most crucial (e.g., use of attorney-client privilege, frequency of audits, follow-up systems).

2. **Select Target Companies Using a Variety of Techniques**. One can select among companies in similar businesses, industry in general, or companies with known best-in-class audit programs. Any of these approaches would suffice, depending on the ob-jectives of the study. An example of one type of technique that can be used is shown in **Exhibit 2**. In this exhibit, fourteen companies are evaluated against one another using three criteria: company size, return on equity and the percent of the company's sales that are in service businesses. Other criteria can be used as well (e.g., percent of business that is outside the U.S.), but the idea is to possibly find groupings of companies that are similar based on key financial criteria against which to benchmark.

3. **Create Participation Incentives**. Benchmarking has become a common business analysis technique, so quite often it is not difficult to identify willing participants. Usually, however, some incentive will be required. This can be a report summarizing the results of the study. In order for a participant to receive the full analysis, some financial participation in the study is usually expected.

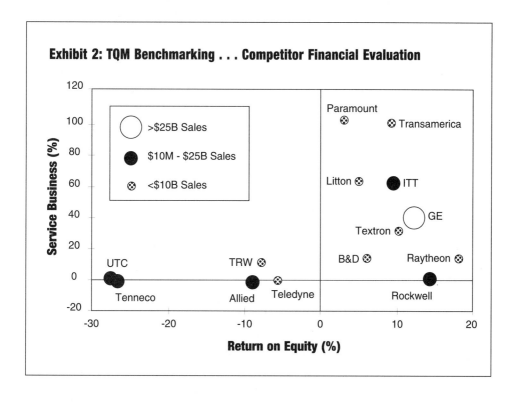

Exhibit 2: TQM Benchmarking . . . Competitor Financial Evaluation

4. Develop Measurable Criteria. This can be a difficult challenge, especially if one is evaluating the "softer" components of a program. However, developing measurable criteria in advance is crucial to comparing results from disparate companies. These criteria might include:

- Frequency of audits for major facilities
- Type of report, if any, left with site staff at the close of the field audit
- Draft and final audit report types (e.g., exception reporting only) and schedules
- Frequency and type of follow-up system
- Use of legal protections
- Frequency and type of reporting to management
- Organizational levels between the audit program manager and the chief executive officer
- Budget for audit program per unit of company sales

Each of the above criteria is generally quite measurable and requires short responses. The evaluator can then make broad conclusions based on the results (e.g., 50 percent of the benchmarked companies use attorney-client privilege protections to protect their audit reports).

5. Utilize Focus-Group Sessions. Bringing together the participants of a benchmarking study for a day can be an extremely useful exercise. It can help to assure that individuals are not discussing "apples and oranges" when addressing complex program issues. The technique can also help to identify subtle nuances in programs that otherwise might not surface during a one-on-one interview. Where participants have difficulty assembling in one location, teleconferencing can be a suitable substitute.

Best Practices

In benchmarking audit programs over the past few years, a number of best practices have surfaced. Not all of these might be applied effectively to a given audit program. But using them selectively should result in an improved program that meets the ever increasing expectations of stakeholders. This section describes a number of those practices.

Reports to Management

Reporting health and safety statistics to executive management has been a common practice in U.S. industry for many years. More recently, overall environmental, health and safety performance is being reported not only to executives but to the public as well. Annual environmental reports are becoming commonplace among progressive companies.[2] Within these reports, environmental audit programs are occasionally, but increasingly, addressed. For example, DuPont in its *1992 Corporate Environmentalism Report*[3] provided the Executive Summary, along with DuPont's response, from a third-party evaluation of the company's Corporate Environmental Audit Program.

For environmental audit programs to be successful, some form of reporting to the company's executives is paramount. In a few companies, like Hoechst Celanese, the chief executive has shown enough interest that he reviews every report and calls are made to line managers where it is perceived that individual issues are not being resolved quickly enough. This demonstrates the top management commitment that the U.S. Environmental Protection Agency calls for in its Environmental Auditing Policy Statement.[4] More commonly, senior management might receive a quarterly or semi-annual briefing on issues identified by the audits. These issues might be: non-compliance problems that cut across the corporation and are in need of a systemic remedy, statistics among business units on timely resolution of findings, or instances where the audit program saved the company money through, for example, the avoidance of fines or substitution of less toxic materials.

Relationship to Compensation

In order to assure support for an environmental audit program, many companies will factor audit results into the bonus equation used for plant and/or environmental managers. This usually gets the attention of the individuals principally responsible for remedying problems. Some caveats, however, are in order.

First, managers should be held more accountable for fixing identified problems than for the results of the first audit at a given facility. This first audit usually sets the baseline and should not be a pejorative exercise. How well the site staff respond after the audit is really what should be evaluated.

Second, one has to be careful of getting into the trap of numerically scoring the results of an audit in order to apportion compensation. For one thing, it is difficult to compare facilities and their audit performance. There are many factors beyond the plant manager's control, such as the regulatory stringency of the state in which the plant is located, the type, age and size of the facility, the toxicity of the materials used and the nature of the property (e.g., the presence of wetlands). Using a scoring system tied to compensation also can heighten the tension of an audit as the plant staff will typically be more argumentative about the number and significance of findings.

Use of "Spill Drills"

One of the most important EH&S compliance areas to audit is emergency response. A good response program can save both money and lives. Moreover, emergency response is now an integral component of regulations promulgated under a variety of statutes:

- Spill Prevention Control and Countermeasure Plans under the Clean Water Act
- Contingency Plans under the Resource Conservation and Recovery Act
- Hazardous Waste Operations Emergency Response Planning (HAZWOPER) under the Occupational Safety and Health Act
- Hazard Identification and Release Reporting under the Emergency Planning and Community Right-to-Know Act
- Risk Management Planning under the Clean Air Act Amendments.

This has made developing an effective emergency response program a complex exercise. The more progressive audit programs will not only verify that the emergency response program meets regulatory requirements but, more importantly, that the program will work when needed. To provide these assurances, firms like Safety Kleen actually conduct spill drills during their audits and many of these take place in the early hours of the morning. As a suitable but less direct alternative, some audit programs will review the results of spill drills conducted during the year. Either way, emergency response programs should include drills and audit programs should assess the results of those drills.

"Red Tag" Shutdowns

This is an interesting approach used by a West Coast aerospace company. Essentially, their auditors carried with them red equipment tags that could be attached to an individual unit to shut the operation down if observed non-compliance issues seemed to warrant it. Obviously, the technique proved to be very powerful. It was used once and only once. Subsequently, the mere threat of its use provided sufficient leverage to obtain adequate responses.

Community Participation

In 1992, DuPont initiated a demonstration program in which a community member participates on a select number of audits each year. This program appears to be unique among U.S. corporations. The rationale is as follows: "As one element of our efforts to understand and respond to community concerns, drive improved environmental performance, build trust, and continue to achieve this consent, we will consider community participation in each corporate environmental review."[5] Selected audit team members must come from the local Community Advisory Panel (CAP) and their participation does not typically extend to employee interviews because such participation "might inhibit the free flow of information essential for an environmental review and compromise employee rights."[6] The demonstration program is continuing through 1994.

Next Site Participation

One way to reduce the anxiety of being audited is to have a site environmental manager participate on an audit, as a team member, directly prior to the audit of his or her site. Some companies use this technique to help the individual better understand the process and prepare effectively for the audit of his or her site.

Use of Portable Computers

Use of portable computers is becoming almost mandatory on audits. Computers are used in a variety of ways. Some companies, BFGoodrich for example, use commercially-available automated checklists in a Windows® environment in order to directly insert findings generated from a review of the checklists into a report skeleton written in Word Perfect®. The checklists also contain regulatory digests so that the multi-volume Code of Federal Regulations does not have to be carried to every audit. In general, computers are used for three purposes on audits: (1) access to an on-line, CD ROM or floppy-disk based regulatory data base, (2) generation of reports prior to leaving the site, and (3) use of automated checklists in the field. The ability to leave a draft report with the site, in particular, is especially valuable in that it helps to maintain the momentum of the audit. Computers are also helpful in keeping in touch with the home office through electronic mail.

Assessment of Ancillary Operations

Most audits rightfully focus on the site's line operations. However, the better programs address certain ancillary operations as well. These include:

- **Off-site hazardous waste treatment, storage and disposal (TSD) facilities.** This is an especially important area to review. Audit teams typically are not expected to visit off-site TSD facilities. At a minimum, however, the audit team should check to assure that only corporate-approved facilities are being used by the site and/or the facilities have been visited at a frequency consistent with corporate guidance.

- **Purchasing.** Purchasing staff should be interviewed to determine if they use any environmental guidelines in procuring materials. For example, one company's policy requires the purchasing of materials in fifty-five-gallon drums on an exception basis only. Other companies have a similar policy for chlorinated solvents. The two relevant audit questions are: Is purchasing required to meet any environmental guidelines and, if so, are they being followed consistently?

- **Maintenance.** This function is almost always audited. However, the depth of the audit can at times be quite shallow. Key environmental issues to address include the use and disposal of maintenance chemicals. The safety of the maintenance equipment (e.g., grinders, lathes, drill presses) should also be reviewed. An area often overlooked is the storage and application of pesticides.

- **On-site contractors.** Temporary and permanent on-site contractors, such as asbestos removal companies, should be reviewed by the audit team. Their contracts should be reviewed to verify that appropriate EH&S provisions are included and that they are being followed.

- **Nearby warehouses used by the site.** Off-site owned or leased warehouses can create liabilities for companies and, therefore, should be audited on occasion. If the warehouse is nearby, many audit programs include them in the site audit.

- **Local publicly-owned treatment works (POTWs).** Quite often a site will discharge some or all of its wastewater into a local sewer system. Visiting the local POTW can provide the audit team insight on the municipality's view of the company's compliance status and if there is any likelihood of forthcoming changes in the effluent standards or surcharges.

Addressing these ancillary areas does add time to the audit. However, many companies believe that this is time well spent.

Use of Verification Audits

One of the biggest challenges associated with audit programs is assuring that findings are corrected in a timely fashion. Companies typically set up sophisticated data bases to track the status of corrective actions. How data are input into these data bases, however, is the real challenge. Typically, sites send quarterly status reports to a central location and the data are entered. This approach works reasonably well except in the instance where site management's perception of a "fix" diverges from that of the audit team.

One interesting approach, used by Hoechst Celanese, is to conduct verification audits of a select number (e.g., 10 to 20 percent) of sites with outstanding corrective actions. The audits would involve only one to two auditors on site for one to two days. Their sole objective is to review the status of completed and outstanding corrective actions from the previous audit report. These audits help to "verify" the accuracy of the quarterly data being submitted and assists in resolving any problems the site might be having with interpretation of a finding. They also help to "keep the responses honest" because sites recognize that there is some possibility each year that they will be the recipient of a verification audit.

Site-Satisfaction Questionnaire

One way for the audit program manager to assure that the program is achieving its objectives is to have the site staff being audited complete a questionnaire evaluating the audit team's performance. This questionnaire is typically given to the site management at the close of the audit and it is mailed back to the audit program manager, not the team leader. Survey topics include: the competency and reasonableness of the team, the adequacy of the interpersonal skills of the team, the depth of the audit, the perceived value of the audit, and any improvements that could be made.

Companies like Hoechst Celanese keep extensive statistics on the returned questionnaires, which are used to make adjustments to the program. It should be noted, however, that the completed questionnaires must be reviewed very carefully. One has to be careful if the site responses are overly positive. While this might be a good result, it could also mean that the audit team was quite lenient in its dealings with the site management. While site management should respect the audit team, they should not necessarily be pleased with their results.

Periodic Third-Party Evaluations

Consistent with good TQM practices, many companies are now having outside consultants (i.e., third parties) or their internal audit departments (i.e., second parties) evaluate their environmental audit programs on a periodic basis. The annual or biennial studies help the companies meet their "continuous improvement" objectives and the increasing pressure by stakeholders to provide assurances that the company is identifying and remedying its EH&S issues. In Europe these third-party reviews will be much more prevalent and formalized once the European Community Eco-Management and Audit Scheme (CEMAS) becomes effective in March of 1995. This program requires site environmental statements and audits to be validated through an external environmental verifier. Although the CEMAS is voluntary, companies like DuPont have committed to implementing the Scheme for all facilities in the European Community.

The third-party evaluations conducted in the U.S. usually include a review of program documentation, including audit reports and corrective action plans, interviews with key program participants and observation of a select number of audits. Programs typically are compared with the Elements of Effective Environmental Auditing Programs provided as an Appendix in U.S. EPA's 1986 Auditing Policy Statement,[7] other companies' programs and internally developed standards and policies.

Development of a Program Newsletter

There should be no secrets about the objectives, implementation, and operation of an environmental audit program. Most programs have guidance manuals that describe the workings of the audit process. The manuals provide a needed program constancy should the audit program manager be reassigned. Rohm & Haas has taken this one step further by developing a Program Newsletter in 1993. This attractive single-sheet, two-sided document is produced quarterly and among other items, includes: remarks from managers who have been audited, a discussion of exceptional EH&S programs identified on audits, profiles of auditors; upcoming audit training seminars for those who might want to become part of the auditor pool; and entertaining EH&S facts. The newsletter can do much to advertise the program in a very positive light and to communicate important information, such as the exceptional EH&S programs, which might otherwise go unrecognized.

There are surely other best practices among audit programs that have not been identified in this chapter. If one is interested in identifying other techniques that are being used, these could be identified, surprisingly enough, through a benchmarking study.

Biggest Challenges

Benchmarking studies and third-party evaluations identify not only best practices but usually the biggest challenges as well. Listed below are a few items that seem to recur time and again as deficiencies in environmental audit programs.

The Program Manual

Putting together an Environmental Audit Program Manual can be an onerous task and quite often, as a result, it is not done formally. Some programs will have no written guidance document whatsoever while others might have a presentation package describing the program that is used in the opening conferences on audits. The lack of a program manual does not necessarily mean that a given program is not operating well. However, a manual does help document and communicate the program's objectives and procedures. Further, it is difficult to assess the relative successes or failures of a program without some written guidelines against which this evaluation can be made. Consistent with TQM principles, all programs should be evaluated on a periodic basis. Finally, a manual helps to guide the program during the transition if the program manager were to vacate the position.

Protocol Updating

The problem with audit checklists or protocols is that they are typically out-of-date once they are reproduced. This poses a problem as auditors may not be evaluating a site based on the most recently applicable requirements. Many audit program managers have a difficult time allocating the resources or the time to update protocols more than once every couple of years. An update at least annually is consistent with good audit practices.

Use of commercially available automated checklists[8] can help to avoid the problem of outdated program documents. These checklists are updated automatically by the company providing the product. The initial investment in the checklists may seem high but this update service can be very cost effective.

State Regulatory Review

It is imperative that audit teams independently evaluate a site's compliance against both federal and state requirements. The federal government establishes only a regulatory floor from which state agencies can and do develop more stringent requirements. These state requirements are not always addressed appropriately on audits. Because many audit checklists and protocols emphasize only the federal requirements, too often the auditors rely on the site EH&S manager's knowledge of the applicable state requirements; this is clearly not an independent assessment. There are now several regulatory data bases available that allow for an independent review of state regulations prior to an audit.[9] Rohm & Haas uses these sources to actually develop a state checklist prior to any audit. State requirements must be addressed, and addressed independently.

Misleading Closing Conferences

The closing conference is one of the most difficult elements of the audit process. There is a strong tendency to "sugar coat" the findings in order not to antagonize site management and to make the meeting go smoothly. All too many closing conferences begin with an extended discourse on how wonderful the site staff are and how well the site is operated. I observed one audit, in particular, where the team leader opened with the statement that the large chemical plant "was found to be in compliance" whereupon the plant manager left the meeting, leaving the EH&S manager to deal with the forty or so findings that the audit team subsequently raised. Audit team leaders must have the fortitude to make sure that plant management gets the right message. If there are significant findings they should be raised early in the meeting and be given their rightful emphasis.

Report Timeliness and Quality

As much emphasis as most companies place on the audit report, one would think that there would be few problems in this area. However, this is not the case. With established programs, there are generally more problems with late reports than anything else. Late reports can destroy the momentum gained by the audit and can create liabilities for the organization. Quality is always an issue with any program, yet after a few reports have been developed there are typically adequate models to follow. A good technique that is used by many companies is to develop an Audit Program Writing Manual, which provides general guidance and samples of acceptable findings and complete reports. Eastman Kodak has developed one of these manuals and gone one step further. The company has a data base containing hundreds of findings, taken from previous reports, that auditors have access to in the field. Finally, any audit training that is conducted as part of the program should stress the written report as much as anything else.

Insufficient Follow-up

This is a chronic problem in many programs. Audit reports are developed. Corrective action plans follow and then many systems break down. There are no systematic assurances that findings are being corrected in a timely fashion. This, of course, can create major liabilities for the organization. Development of a sound data base, which allows periodic (e.g., quarterly) tracking of corrective action status can help to alleviate this problem. Verification audits, as practiced by Hoechst Celanese and discussed earlier in this chapter, are another useful technique. One should not wait until the next scheduled audit, which might be three or more years later, to verify completion of corrective actions. The closure of findings from a previous audit should be a formal part of any audit.

Notes

1. For example, see: Leibfried, K.H.J. and C.J. McNair, *Benchmarking: A Tool for Continuous Improvement,* The Coopers & Lybrand Performance Solutions Series, HarperCollins Publishers, Inc., New York, NY, 1992.

2. For example, see: Deloitte Touche Tohmatsu International, The International Institute for Sustainable Development, and SustainAbility, *Coming Clean: Corporate Environmental Reporting,* 1993.

3. DuPont External Affairs, *Corporate Environmentalism: 1992 Progress Report,* H-44712, December, 1992, Wilmington, DE.

4. U.S. Environmental Protection Agency, *Environmental Auditing Policy Statement,* FR25003, Vol. 51, No. 131, July 9, 1986.

5. *DuPont Environmental Auditing: Corporate Guidelines,* Appendix B, Community Participation in Corporate Environmental Reviews, June 4, 1992.

6. *Ibid.,* Appendix B.

7. *Op.Cit.,* EPA Policy Statement, pp. 25008-25010.

8. As of early 1994, there were two principal automated checklist offerings: Audit Master® by Utilicom, Inc., Rochester, NY and CompQuest Pro+® by Semcor, Inc., Mount Laurel, NJ. Each provides semi-annual updates as part of the maintenance contract.

9. Two on-line regulatory data bases that cover both federal and state requirements are Earthlaw by Infodata Systems Inc., Falls Church, VA and the Computer-Aided Environmental Legislative Data System (CELDS) by the U.S. Army Corps of Engineers through the University of Illinois, Champaign, IL.

Lawrence B. Cahill is a senior program director with ERM, Inc., and the author of *Environmental Audits,* now in its sixth edition, published by Government Institutes, Inc. *Note:* Any discussion of a company's individual environmental audit program approaches in this paper is based on information provided to the public at large through technical papers, presentations, and the like. Any discussion of a commercially available audit product does not imply an endorsement of that product.

16

Audits and Root Cause Analysis

Randy A. Roig and Peter Schneider

Many current audit programs are very good at determining the compliance issues at a site, but are less successful in developing long-term compliance solutions. One method for addressing these issues is the use of root cause analysis techniques. These techniques allow the facility to identify and focus on permanent solutions to compliance issues. We note the following:

Conducting a root cause analysis is not a substantial burden on the audit team or the facility. Most information is already collected during the audit, but is not being used.

Looking at the overview pattern of the root cause analysis can provide a picture of the maturity of your audit program.

Pareto charts are excellent methods to convey the results of your analysis. They show both the trends of analysis and help highlight the most significant root causes.

In the last few years, many corporations have developed environmental, health, and safety (EHS) audit programs in their efforts to increase the level of regulatory compliance at their facilities. In spite of these efforts, however, many companies have discovered that they quickly reach a plateau in their compliance efforts—repeat audits continue to find the same compliance issues at the same facilities. Notwithstanding this increasingly exacting and intensive scrutiny, the facilities appear to be stuck at a certain level of compliance. The intensive audit programs serve only to document this level of non-compliance.

Typically, a facility's initial reaction to findings of non-compliance is to increase accountability through use of internal sign-offs designed to ensure that findings are corrected. Others develop elaborate scoring systems or tracking systems in an attempt to monitor progress. Often, the problems will persist, leading to frustration on the part of corporate and plant management alike. We have been party to another typical result of this initial reaction—the facilities hire outside consultants to perform audits and get their sites into compliance before the corporate auditors arrive.

The key to solving the "compliance plateau" problem is to understand not only what the site is doing wrong, but also to understand *why* the deficiency occurred in the first place. In this chapter, one method of reaching such an understanding is discussed: the application of root cause analysis. Root cause analysis is a technique that identifies the underlying causes of your compliance findings, determines why the problem occurred, and allows the site to focus on permanent solutions to compliance issues.

How Root Cause Analysis Is Applied

The technique of root cause analysis has been developed and used successfully in a variety of applications: accident investigation, safety analysis, and, most recently, in many total quality management (TQM) programs.

By using a common environmental audit finding as an example, the utility of root cause analysis can be demonstrated. In this example, the label on a 55-gallon drum used for accumulating hazardous waste was found to be missing during an audit.

A standard audit report would probably state that the drum's label was missing, would cite the regulation that applied, and might recommend that the site develop a correct drum-labeling procedure. In our experience, the facility will often respond by labeling the offending drum and, perhaps, telling the person in charge of the main accumulation area that "the label needs to be put on the drums." This action corrects the problem with the existing drum, but would it solve the problem for the next drum or for drums generated six months from now?

By contrast, let's examine the potential root causes behind the improper date on the drum. Here are a few possibilities:

- The site environmental coordinator doesn't understand the details of labeling regulations, including the need to label the drum as soon as it is used to store waste.
- The site environmental coordinator understands the regulations, but has not communicated these requirements to the operator of the storage area, either verbally or through a written labeling procedure. The storage area operator thinks that the drum requires labeling only after the drum is filled.
- The site has developed a labeling procedure for drums and communicated it, but the label supply had run out.
- The label had been put on the drum, but the label was not waterproof and fell off after exposure to rainfall.

There are many other possibilities. However, without knowing the cause of the problem, the "solution" selected by the facility may be entirely inappropriate. In the example discussed above, the facility had purchased labels that were not waterproof. Since the drums were stored outside and exposed to the rain, it is highly likely that the problem will recur in the future unless the type of label used at the site is changed. By analyzing root causes, the facility can determine what is required to develop a permanent solution instead of simply applying the temporary band-aid of labeling the offending drum.

Methods of Root Cause Analysis

Applying root cause analysis to audits requires the collection of more information—in addition to identifying the problem, the auditor must also identify the "why" behind the problem. Generally, this is not a substantial additional burden—most auditors already identify this information during the course of their interviews and inspections, but fail to use it when reporting their findings. For example, to collect audit evidence for the drum-labeling issue, the auditor would have had to conduct a physical inspection, review records in the accumulation areas, and probably interview the environmental coordinator, the satellite area operator, and the accumulation manager. During this process, it is highly likely that the reason(s) for the incorrect label would or could be determined.

How does one conduct root cause analysis? In our efforts to apply this technique consistently across many sites, we have used the following approach:

Step 1   Develop a starting *a priori* list of potential root causes, perhaps grouped by type of cause. This list can be added to as new causes are found. An example of our *a priori* list for equipment is shown in **Exhibit 1**. Typical

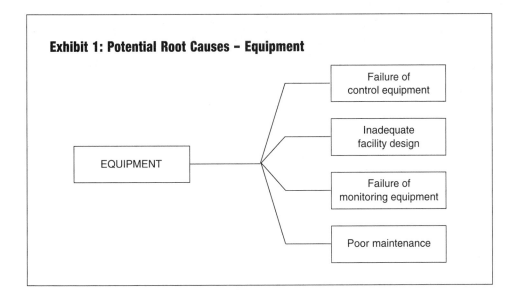

Exhibit 1: Potential Root Causes – Equipment

EQUIPMENT

- Failure of control equipment
- Inadequate facility design
- Failure of monitoring equipment
- Poor maintenance

other causal groups are materials, procedures, and personnel.

Step 2 For each deficiency found during the audit, assign the two root causes that most describe the problem.

Step 3 Gather the findings in a "Pareto diagram" for the site (**Exhibit 2**). A Pareto diagram is simply a bar graph that summarizes the root causes for the audit in order of frequency of occurrence.

Exhibit 1 is often referred to in quality circles as a "fishbone diagram." This type of diagram was developed in 1953 by Professor Kaoru Ishikawa to summarize the opinions of engineers on quality problems in a steel plant. The diagram serves to summarize the types of potential conditions that might create a defect in production or operations.

The list of potential conditions can be developed by a variety of means—brainstorming, using lists developed by others, or by working with facility EHS personnel to review likely causes. However, it is important that both the facility and, if appropriate, corporate personnel "buy into"

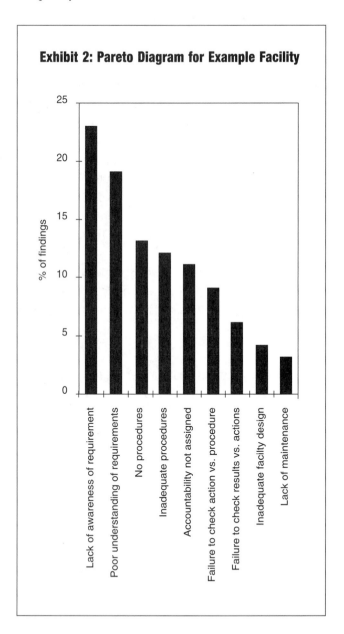

Exhibit 2: Pareto Diagram for Example Facility

the list and agree that the categories are appropriate. Because the categories must be interpreted consistently by all involved, we strongly suggest preparation of a formal list of definitions. Otherwise, each auditor will independently interpret the difference between causes such as "Accountability not assigned" and "Failure to check results versus actions."

In our work, we have discovered that most findings are rarely explained by one single root cause. By contrast, we have found that two causes usually explain the majority of the issues involved. By listing both causes, we are better able to develop permanent solutions to the problem that was identified.

The causes can be used to address both individual findings and to understand management systems at the site. Below, we discuss interpretation of the findings.

Interpreting the Pareto Diagram

In the Pareto diagram for a typical site shown in Exhibit 2, the most common cause, "poor understanding of the requirements," is typical of many sites that have not fully developed their compliance programs.

By applying the root cause analysis technique to many audits, we have seen the emergence of a clear pattern that parallels the development of compli-

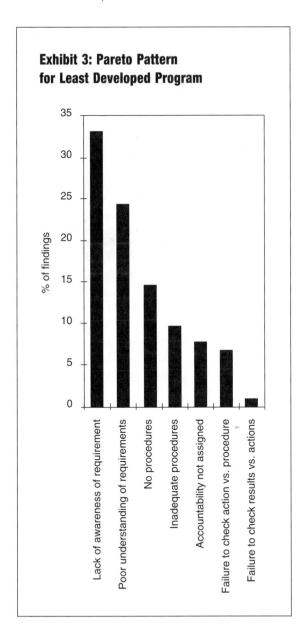

Exhibit 3: Pareto Pattern for Least Developed Program

ance management systems at a facility.

First-Stage EHS System

At sites with poorly developed compliance systems, the majority of the root causes involve either a lack of understanding of the requirements (leading to the complete absence of a required plan or program) or a poor understanding of the requirements (leading to major deficiencies in the plans or programs). Sites often experience two separate versions of this stage, one as the environmental or safety coordinator learns the regulatory requirements, then another as the plant operations personnel are trained. This first stage in the development of compliance management systems is typified by the Pareto profile shown in **Exhibit 3**.

Second-Stage EHS System

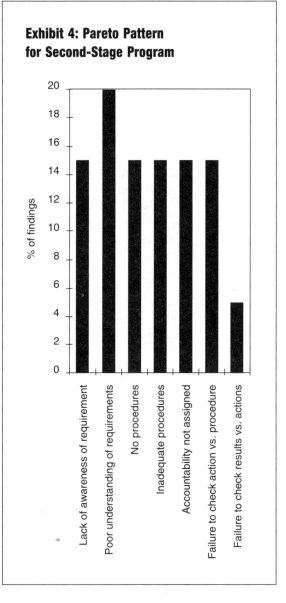

Exhibit 4: Pareto Pattern for Second-Stage Program

As facilities learn the regulatory requirements, they start to develop procedures, either written or verbal, and communicate these procedures to their operations personnel. Often such procedures initially contain significant deficiencies, or they fail to recognize the need to accommodate exceptions or uncommon events. While facilities at this stage still face issues related to understanding the regulatory requirements, the number and significance of these omissions begin to decrease relative to other issues. This second stage is typified by the Pareto profile shown in Exhibit 4.

Third-Stage EHS System

At the third stage, the site has generally recognized the requirements that apply to its operations and has developed compliance procedures. The majority of the deficiencies occur because of errors in the procedures (usually related to uncommon events) or to the failure of personnel to recognize the applicability of a procedure and to follow it (**Exhibit 5**). By this stage, the severity of the audit findings has been significantly reduced.

Fourth-Stage EHS System

In the final stage, the facility has recognized the applicable regulatory requirements and developed good procedures. Personnel issues related to accountability and responsibility still lead to a number of minor findings, but this number has been reduced. The pattern for this stage is shown in **Exhibit 6**.

From Root Cause to Solutions

Root cause findings can be interpreted for individual findings, as an overview for a specific site, grouped by regulatory area, or summarized across sites. In our original example, an au-

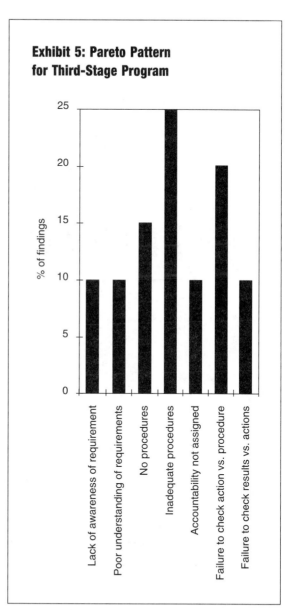

Exhibit 5: Pareto Pattern for Third-Stage Program

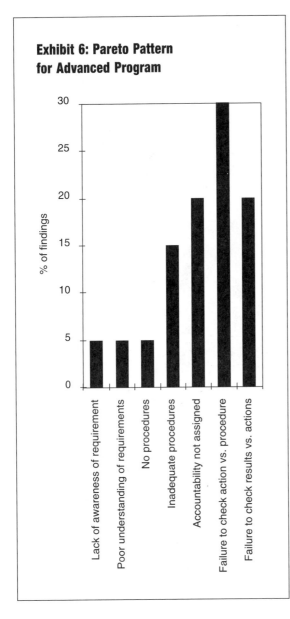

Exhibit 6: Pareto Pattern for Advanced Program

ditor might recommend both a short-term and a long-term solution for the individual drum labeling problem:

> We recommend that the site (1) label the drums that are now without labels and (2) start the purchase and use of waterproof labels for all drums stored outside.

In **Exhibit 7**, we show the overall Pareto diagram for a site and the individual diagrams for hazardous waste and air quality issues. Clearly, the site profiled in Exhibit 7 is in Stage 1 in its ability to comply with air quality issues, while it is near Stage 3 in terms of hazardous waste compliance. If we were auditing the site shown in Exhibit 7, our recommendation might include a training program for the site coordinator in air quality while the hazardous waste program coordinator would be advised to review his or her compliance procedures. By contrast, the overview summary of root cause findings (**Exhibit 8**) for a group of hospital and medical facilities shows that this group of facilities is in the early stages of developing a compliance program.

Randy A. Roig, Ph.D., REA, is a principal at ERM-West. **Peter Schneider**, CEP, is a principal at ERM-New England.

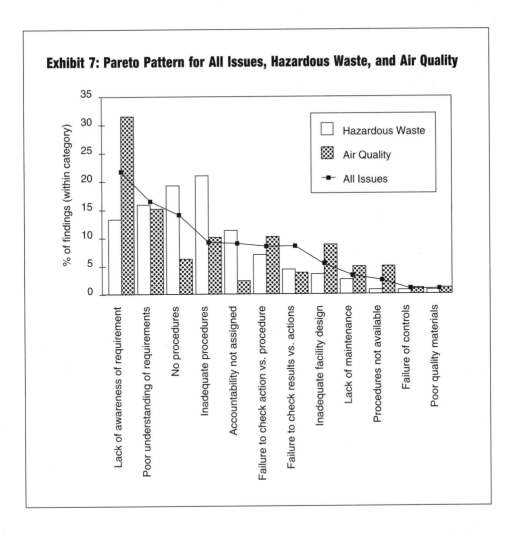

Exhibit 7: Pareto Pattern for All Issues, Hazardous Waste, and Air Quality

Legend:
- Hazardous Waste
- Air Quality
- All Issues

Y-axis: % of findings (within category)

Categories:
- Lack of awareness of requirement
- Poor understanding of requirements
- No procedures
- Inadequate procedures
- Accountability not assigned
- Failure to check action vs. procedure
- Failure to check results vs. actions
- Inadequate facility design
- Lack of maintenance
- Procedures not available
- Failure of controls
- Poor quality materials

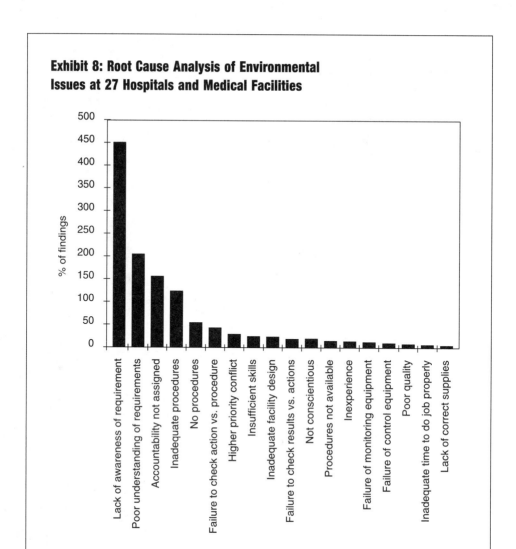

Exhibit 8: Root Cause Analysis of Environmental Issues at 27 Hospitals and Medical Facilities

184

Environmental Auditor Qualifications: Meeting New, Rigorous Demands for Quality Audits

17

Lawrence B. Cahill

"Ah, Mr. Cahill, I wonder if you could come back to the auditor's team room. It seems one of your auditors has fallen asleep for the second time this week. I know you had a grueling trip getting here, but this is embarrassing to everyone."

So went an audit I led some time ago. It was not a fun experience, and it has left some scars.

There has been much discussion lately in the profession about certifying environmental (health and safety) auditors against certain performance criteria. But how does one evaluate for such important measures as physical stamina?

This chapter discusses the qualifications that environmental auditors should have if they are to lead or conduct a quality audit. It becomes evident after reviewing these expectations that certifying auditors through a traditional written examination might ignore some of the most important skills an auditor should possess, especially in working with managers throughout an organization. Before certifying organizations progress too far down the restrictive written-exam road, they should determine how these other skills are to be assessed. No amount of book learning can overcome the drawbacks of a poor or combative interviewer or even an exhausted auditor.

I am reminded of the case some years ago where an exceptional auditor with a master's degree in regional planning could not become a registered environmental assessor in California because she did not have a degree in engineering, science, or law. Thankfully, this restriction has been relaxed. Environmental auditing is a demanding profession requiring a multitude of skills, and these such arbitrary restrictions do not improve professional standards.

The Core Skills

There are certain core skills that every auditor should have. Some of these can be easily learned; others are more inherent to the individual's makeup.

The Learned Skills

The essential learned skills include a working knowledge of the regulations, a familiarity with the facilities being audited, and, more recently a necessity, computer literacy.

Auditors should have a working knowledge of the applicable regulations. This knowledge can be acquired in several ways; through courses, textbooks, and the review and application of audit checklists or protocols. However, regulations do not have to be, and more importantly, cannot be committed to memory. As of 1992, there were over 11,000 pages of federal environmental regulations in Title 40 of the Code of Federal Regulations and another 3,000 pages of health and safety regulations in Title 29. Therefore, the term "working knowledge" is just that. Auditors should be familiar enough with the regulations to be able to use a protocol effectively. And the protocols need to be detailed enough to support the auditor's efforts.

There is a secondary issue related to regulatory knowledge. Auditors too often limit themselves to their very defined area of expertise. It is important that over time auditors "stretch the envelope" and become comfortable reviewing areas related to those in which they are expert. This makes them more valuable and flexible as team members and would allow them to pinch-hit should one of the team members become indisposed during an audit.

The auditor should also be familiar with the facilities being audited and should be comfortable in a plant setting. This does not mean, however, that to be effective every auditor of a chemical plant must be a chemical engineer with twenty years of plant experience, as some people would have you believe. In fact, a good, solid, smart professional with an unabashed, natural curiosity and some familiarity with the facility being audited is probably your best candidate to do a quality audit. Further, there is no one particular educational background that is best suited for auditing. Engineers, scientists, lawyers, managers and, yes, even financial auditors can bring valuable skills to the table.

More recently, auditors are finding that computer literacy is also a necessary core skill and for several reasons. First, it has become routinely expected that a working draft report (using a laptop computer) will be prepared before the team leaves the site. Also, some companies are now using automated checklists and/or protocols loaded onto laptops. Further, computerized regulatory databases are providing additional field support to audit teams. Finally, plant data files (e.g., training records and discharge monitoring reports) are now more frequently automated. Thus, it is now difficult to get by on an audit without some familiarity with computers.

The Inherent Skills

All of the above skills can be acquired with a little effort and dedication. However, there are other core skills that are more difficult to attain unless there are existing, fundamental building blocks within the auditor's personality. The two that come to mind are interpersonal traits and physical stamina.

Good interpersonal skills go a long way in conducting quality audits. Of all the core skills required, this is clearly the most important. Skills include being able to interview people effectively, having a high degree of curiosity, adjusting smoothly to changes in schedule, responding professionally to challenges made to your verbal and written statements, working well under pressure, and generally keeping a cool head when those around you are panicking.

The bottom line is that an auditor must be both a good communicator and an excellent listener. This takes sincerity, patience, and, at times, a great sense of humor.

While these attributes can be learned through experience, many individuals will never attain the skills at a sufficient level to work effectively as an environmental auditor. We must remember that audits, unlike regulatory agency inspections, are meant to be a supportive exercise; therefore, individuals who are inherently brusque, volatile, argumentative, and overly egocentric will not be successful.

It may sound silly to place a strong emphasis on physical stamina as an important trait for auditors. However, any one who has participated on audits knows how important this can be. I have been on audits where team members have fallen asleep on the job; been stung by a bee, developed an allergic reaction, and have been out of commission for two days; contracted the flu and spent two days in their hotel room; and so on. Although many of these problems can neither be anticipated nor prevented, auditors should realize that a typical audit trip is not for the faint of heart.

Physical stamina also comes into play when considering the pace of an audit. Auditors are often traveling on the weekends or late at night. Climbing towers and buildings all day can be exhausting. There is a constant pressure to perform and to assure that we are diligent and thorough in the investigation.

And the most taxing tasks of all are the daily late-night team meetings discussing observations and findings. Where a draft report is to be prepared prior to leaving the site (a general trend these days), the last night before the closing conference can last into the early hours of the morning if one is not careful about ending the data-gathering phase sufficiently early. Attempting to craft an articulate, accurate, and precise finding at 1:00 AM is no simple feat.

Observations in the Field

How do these skills and attributes actually contribute to or hinder the quality of an audit? As an audit team leader or program manager, what should I be looking for or watching out for in an auditor? Examples of the worst and best behaviors are discussed below.

The Worst Attributes

These are behaviors that are commonly exhibited but should be avoided.

Insufficient records review. When starting an audit, too many auditors immediately want to perform a field inspection. Records must be reviewed first to determine the applicable requirements. This problem is often a result of a lack of familiarity with the regulations. Take the time early on to determine the requirements.

Too much records review. This often occurs when the auditor is intimidated by the size or complexity of the site and just doesn't know where to begin. He or she will become buried in the records and not come up for air. First get a "windshield" tour of the facility, and then conceptualize the operation into discrete parts and visit appropriate locations in a modular fashion.

Identification of symptoms. This problem commonly arises when the auditor becomes captive to the checklist. Auditors add value when they address underlying causes. Take some time to think through what really might be happening at the site to cause the identified problems.

Jumping to conclusions. This is the opposite problem of the one discussed above. Some auditors have a tendency to draw broad conclusions even before the evidence is in. Auditors let their egos get in the way of doing a thorough analysis and verifying their findings. They've seen it all before, and they simply *know* what is causing the problem. This results in statements such as, "the hazardous waste management system at the site is deficient"—not a very articulate or helpful finding. Take a step back, and make sure that evidence supports the conclusion.

Poor time management. There are auditors who never seem to finish on time. This often occurs when they are given more than one compliance area to cover and spend 90 percent of their time on the area with which they feel the most comfortable. Make sure that auditors attack compliance areas in parallel not in series. It is risky to leave one area for the last day of the audit.

"In-my-state" syndrome. Nothing annoys site staff more than having auditors preaching to them about how things are done in their state. Auditors should research the appropriate state regulations for the site, audit the site against those regulations, and leave the preaching for Sunday unless what is being done at their site might be helpful.

Too easy/too tough. Audits must strike a fine balance between being supportive and providing an honest assessment of the site's performance. Over the years, programs do have a tendency to swing back and forth between the "good cop, bad cop" scenarios. When the plants scream that the program is becoming punitive, then the "white hats" go in and the reports become so vague that management can't tell if there's a problem or not. There is no easy solution here; nor should there be. Auditors should not, however, pull any punches in the closing conference or report. Site management needs to understand the true implications of their actions.

188

The Best Attributes

What is it that makes an individual a good auditor? Communication skills, certainly. Other attributes contribute as well.

A good, even disposition. Volatile personalities do not make good auditors. It is a very stressful occupation and requires a level head and an ability to adjust to new people and constant change.

Flexibility. Audits never go quite as planned. An auditor needs to be flexible to adjust to changing dates, schedules, situations, and the like.

Natural curiosity. Mentioned previously, this is an important trait. Some would say that the better descriptor would be a "healthy skepticism." In either case a natural inquisitiveness is important.

High energy level. There is no time to relax on an audit. Days typically start at 7:00 AM with a breakfast meeting and end at 9:00 PM with a discussion of findings. This can be very taxing. One has to enter into the process understanding that.

Poise under fire. Auditors are constantly challenged by site staff during an audit. It is simply the nature of the process. Auditors must be able to handle this with professionalism. This is especially true during the closing conference where those doing the challenging are likely more senior.

Under-control ego. A healthy ego is probably an asset for an auditor. But megalomaniacs need not apply.

Making Good Things Happen

How does one assure that auditors do indeed have the appropriate skills? Most firms accomplish this through a variety of techniques. First, there are certain individuals that can be weeded out based on their personalities. This does not necessarily mean that they are not good performers but they could well be ill-suited to be an auditor.

Second, most firms require that auditors attend a formal training program. These programs can be tailored to the issues deemed most in need of attention. Some companies have both basic and refresher seminars. The best basic programs usually include a "mock audit" of an actual plant so that auditor candidates can get a true feel for the experience. The program would include simulated opening and closing conferences, and actual interviews, records reviews, and facility inspections. Improving communication skills through role playing and group exercises is usually an essential element of the program.

The refresher programs can be tailored to historical problems experienced in the field by the audit teams. How does one identify these problems? Usually through several techniques. Audit team leaders can and do critique the process and the auditors. They should be confident enough to do this during the audit, as well as after it is complete. On the spot *constructive* feedback is one of the best ways to improve performance. Further, as part of a quality assurance program, some companies will have an oversight auditor participate on a select number of audits during the year to evaluate the process. And lastly, site feedback questionnaires are used to identify problems from a customer perspective.

Conclusion

Attaining and maintaining good auditor skills is a challenging and never-ending task. Auditors need more than just a knowledge of the regulations to be effective. The challenge is to assure that auditors are trained properly and receive continuous feedback. Third-party certifying organizations must assure that the auditors they certify as competent have the full arsenal of skills necessary to conduct a quality audit.

Lawrence B. Cahill is a vice president with McLaren/Hart, a subsidiary of the Sandoz Corporation. He is the author of *Environmental Audits*, now in its sixth edition, published by Government Institutes, Inc. Mr. Cahill has over fifteen years of experience in all aspects of environmental auditing and has trained people worldwide in auditing skills.

Evaluating Auditor Characteristics Essential for Environmental, Health, and Safety Management Systems Assessments

J. Richard Pooler, Esq. and Debora L. Jones, RN, COHN
The Darien Group, Ltd.

Historically, when one mentioned an environmental audit, the universally agreed-upon context was of compliance evaluation. Nowadays, the word "audit" carries with it many different connotations, interpretations, permutations, and purposes. Broadly speaking, audits include (1) Phase I environmental assessments, (2) acquisition/divestiture studies, (3) compliance audits, (4) management systems assessments, and (5) specialty audits. These audits, assessments, and studies may also envelop various aspects of integrated environmental, health, and safety (EHS) management. This chapter discusses the different auditor characteristics required to perform environmental, health, and safety (EHS) management systems assessments, and set forth some ideas relative to identifying the personal and fundamental preferences supportive or indicative of such characteristics.

Before delving into the detail of the characteristics, attributes, and functional preferences required of auditors in environmental, health and safety management systems assessments, it is important to distinguish between compliance audits and management systems assessments.

Compliance Audits are very detailed process and operations-oriented regulatory reviews. Such an audit is used to determine the actual compliance of an operation or organization vis-a-vis individual regulatory programs, and can serve three purposes: (1) management evaluation of actual compliance conditions and the costs to achieve compliance, (2) learning tool, and (3) performance evaluation.

Compliance audits are driven by regulations, are based upon adherence to specific regulatory requirements, and deal in extreme detail. The intent is to assure that all compliance aspects of each regulatory program are being followed. Standard tasks in performing these projects include meetings, interviews, records review, physical inspections, and the like. Results are presented in the form of findings of noncompliance, which identify the specific regulatory requirement and citation. Action plans are designed to address deficiencies on a prioritized basis.

The inter-relationship of compliance programs to the overall management system may also be considered. Often a compliance audit action plan is implemented concomitantly with an evaluation of the management system. The purpose of such linkage is to determine if noncompliance is related to lack of people performance or management system failure. Short-term, non-programmatic solutions rarely achieve long-term compliance.

Management Systems Assessments (MSAs) are generally performed for senior management within an organization to assure that the environmental management system can operate and respond effectively to meet the complex requirements of integrated EHS management. When evaluating the management structure of an organization, the focus is on **people** and **systems**. The following broad-based questions are the focus of an MSA: (1) Are people effectively communicating? (2) Are people working together in an efficient manner toward common identified goals? (3) Do the current management systems help or hinder the workforce in meeting such goals? These studies are performed to evaluate and improve overall organizational EHS efficiency and assure that regulatory requirements are anticipated and complied with. The ultimate result will be reduced EHS liabilities.

In order to achieve the above stated goals, the following systems are evaluated, relying heavily on extensive interviews with key management and line personnel.

- **Policies and procedures**—Adequacy of policies and procedures, with proactive support
- **Roles and responsibilities**—Integration throughout operations and line management (vertically and horizontally, across organization boundaries)
- **Communication**—Ability of internal and external communication to ensure effective understanding of issues; reporting systems; proactive response mechanisms
- **Organization, structure, and staffing**—Number and experience of staff; effectiveness in working together; integration of EHS functions
- **Business planning and strategy**—Integration of EHS concerns into business planning; identification and impact assessment of strategic issues; coordination and enactment of response strategies
- **Project/program planning**—Incorporation of EHS factors into development plans
- **Performance standards and indicators**—Measurement and continuous improvement consistent with the Total Quality Management approach
- **Regulatory tracking**—Identification of strategic issues; performance of impact assessments; notice and comment strategies
- **Liability and risk management**—Ability of programs to identify, integrate, and mitigate risks and liabilities on both an objective and subjective basis
- **Compliance management**—Adequacy of compliance systems, programs, and procedures

- **Management reporting systems**—Ability of reporting and networking systems to ensure communication and action on issues
- **Special program implementation**—Identification and implementation of specific issues, strategies, or programs

Findings generally will identify organizational dysfunctions and recommend policy, procedural, operational, and/or structural changes to correct problems.

The assessment team should consist of broad-based interdisciplinary individuals with overlapping experience and knowledge in the following fields:

- Environmental affairs
- Occupational health
- Industrial hygiene
- Occupational safety/process safety
- Crisis management
- Regulatory affairs
- Governmental and public relations
- Site operations
- Management systems

The primary emphasis is on personal interviews, which are generally two-on-one (two interviewers, one interviewee) in nature. Interviews are usually one to two hours in duration. If a question or an issue arises with regard to a certain management area, the interviewer may ask to see appropriate supporting documents. Equipment and facilities should also be observed.

Specific steps to be executed to implement this type of assessment include:

- Identify preliminary information
- Review information and background documents
- Identify interview candidates
- Walk-through facility observation
- Interview key employees
- Review additional supporting files and documents, if necessary
- Close-out briefing session with site and headquarter management
- Prepare reports (draft and final)

As one may glean from the immediately preceding discussion, compliance audits are basically objective exercises, while MSAs are more subjective in nature. MSAs are much more complicated and abstract, and are comparatively free-wheeling, open ended, constantly evolving projects. Also, the amount and type of person-to-person interaction in each type of audit is vastly different. Therefore, a much different set of skills is required for people who perform MSA projects. The basic auditor characteristic and attribute differences relate to the level of flexibility and intuition needed to effectively execute the given tasks, and the comfort level in dealing with subjective abstract concepts and ambiguity.

Auditor Characteristics and Attributes

While creativity, intuition, and people skills are important in performing a compliance audit, such skills are *unequivocally critical* to the successful completion of an MSA.

In any audit scenario, paper and physical data are relatively easy to unearth, manipulate, and evaluate. When performing MSAs, the challenge is to pull together disparate nuggets of information, through the interview process, in order to create an accurate depiction of the way the organization actually functions. This depiction is then compared to senior management's perception as to the way the organization should function. The critical nuggets of information relative to the way an organization actually functions are predominantly gained via interviews. Conventional compliance auditor characteristics must be augmented in order to obtain these nuggets of information. The critical characteristics for MSAs include common sense, empathy, goal-guidedness, non-judgmentality, listening skills, and intuition.

Empathy. Since MSAs are heavily interview dependent, the person-to-person interface is the key point of knowledge/data transfer. However, if the interviewee does not trust the interviewer, a limited amount of useful information will be shared. An important initial basis in establishing trust is empathy. By exhibiting a positive attitude, respectful curiosity, and a professional yet friendly demeanor, the trust of the interviewee is gained. The interviewee must believe that the interviewer understands and appreciates the interviewee's position, and will accurately and fairly represent and interpret a given situation. If an interviewer can do this, trust is inevitable, and the person-to-person informational floodgates open.

Common Sense. Common sense is an important characteristic for all auditing (and all aspects of one's life, for that matter). However, in MSAs, common sense is especially necessary to force the creative process through a reality check. Ultimately, the results of the MSA will be presented to senior management, who will demand more than intuitive gut feelings as to the status of their organization. A hearty dose of common sense is necessary to counterbalance the creative side of the audit team, and make sure the findings and recommendations are grounded in fact and reality.

Goal-guidedness. One way in which to maximize information flow during an interview is to be goal-guided. Keep the ultimate project objective in mind, but don't over-impose your specific agenda or schedule on the interviewee. Usually, an interviewee will initially discuss the items they are most comfortable with, and do so in an open and honest manner. Therefore, it is much better to use those items as a starting point. After the initial interview pleasantries, cues taken from the interviewee help guide the flow of the interview. It also helps if the interviewer doesn't strictly direct the interview according to a checklist or protocol. This is why two interviewers are important to the process. The lead interviewer asks questions and ushers this "go with the flow" process, while the support interviewer monitors each topic discussed to assure completeness as the interview meanders from topic to topic. The result is a natural and comfortable interview process (more like a discussion) and a high probability of discovering useful informational nuggets.

Non-judgmentality. An interviewee must be convinced that the interviewer will not unfairly judge him or her. The interviewer must be perceived as an impartial neutral arbiter who will keep an open mind and consider the circumstances of a given situation in an empathetic manner.

Listening skills. A key talent in keeping the information floodgate open is listening. The interviewee both consciously and unconsciously responds to eye contact, body language, and verbal acknowledgment. The interviewer must concentrate, analyze the information received from the interviewee, and then probe and respond, pushing the conversation in the desired direction.

Intuition. In order to piece together the multidimensional MSA jigsaw puzzle, a certain amount of intuitive blind faith is helpful. Many data pieces may well be missing at the end of the field work. Therefore, an intuitive assembly of such limited data is often needed so that the project can be completed in a cost effective manner. More discussion of the intuitive process will be presented below.

Identification of Personality and Functional Preference

It is one thing to identify the characteristics preferred for MSA auditors, but how do you determine if a certain individual possesses such characteristics and, more importantly, whether they can effectively apply such characteristics in an audit context? One potential methodology is application of the Myers-Briggs Type Indicator. This technique is the most widely used personality profile testing method, and is based on Carl Jung's theory on functional/psychological preferences. It is important to note that the authors do not profess deep understanding of or expertise relative to either Jung or Myers-Briggs. However, each of us has taken the test, participated in the post-testing discussion and evaluation process, and applied the acquired knowledge in the workplace dynamic. It is with that admittedly low level of knowledge that we herein set forth some of our practical experiences in applying this methodology.

The Myers-Briggs Type Indicator divides the functional preferences into four categories:

- Extroversion vs. Introversion
- Sensing vs. Intuitive
- Thinking vs. Feeling
- Judging vs. Perceiving

The following paragraphs describe the key functional preferences exhibited by each preference pair, as we feel relates to MSA auditing. Please be advised that we are not proposing that there is a right or wrong functional preference for MSA auditors. Indeed, a healthy balance of functional preferences should be maintained among team members. However, we do think that certain preferences are linked to the characteristics discussed above that lead to audit success. When assembling an MSA audit team, thought should be given to each team member's functional preference, so that the team leader can effectively orchestrate task assignments and roles.

Extroversion/Introversion

Extroverts are more comfortable dealing with people and things, while introverts are more comfortable in dealing with ideas, concepts, and impressions. Since an MSA is interview dependent, extroverts are typically more at ease with this process. However, extroverts may have difficulty with the listening process. Thus, extroverts may not obtain complete information from the interviewee. Since introverts are more comfortable dealing with ideas, concepts and impressions, they can assist in piecing together the abstract concepts which will ultimately describe the overall management system. Introverts may find it difficult to relate to other people in an interview setting.

Sensing/Intuitive

Sensors tend to rely on fact, are practical, look for specific answers to specific questions, concentrate on the moment, look for tangible results, and enjoy the status quo. These individuals bring a hearty dose of "common sense" to the MSA process. This input is necessary as the audit team develops findings and conclusions. However, sensors are prone to narrowly focusing on detail at the expense of overall MSA goals.

Intuitors, on the other hand, seek connections, are comfortable in dealing with several things at once, think ahead, enjoy solving new problems, do not like to deal with details, look for patterns, meanings, possibilities, and generally focus on overall strategic goals. An intuitor is a necessary audit team member in order to strategically assemble the complex people and organizational relationships evaluated in an MSA. Intuitors are comfortable and skilled at drawing accurate conclusions from limited data. Intuitors and sensors can work well together if each is sensitive to the other's viewpoint. Intuitors frequently see and understand relationships and patterns without necessarily knowing how or why such is the case. A sensor can help the MSA team articulate and refine the facts surrounding an issue. Proper balance of the sensing/intuitive preference will result in defensible findings and conclusions.

Thinking/Feeling

Thinkers are analytical and value truth over tact. One key task in executing an MSA is the analysis of interview data in order to determine the truth of a given situation or scenario as presented by the interviewees. Thinkers excel at this task. Feelers value tact over truth, and are very skilled at the interpersonal element relative to an interview. Feelers easily exude empathy, making an interviewee feel comfortable and communicative. However, a feeler can be taken advantage of if thinking skills are not kept in balance. On the other hand, a thinker, if not tactful, may antagonize an interviewee, possibly losing nuggets of information in the process.

Judging/Perceiving

Judgers like to make decisions, need closure, and are goal-oriented. This strong focus can sometimes conflict with the goal-guided principle discussed earlier. Perceivers crave information and data, are curious and open minded, and resist closure. Therefore, the judging/perceiving dynamic on the MSA audit team must be balanced. In performing an MSA, there is never enough time to gather all of the data; however, enough data must be collected so that defensible findings and conclusions result. Proper balance of the judging/perceiving dynamic will allow the audit team to achieve such results within the given time and budget constraints of the project.

Conclusion

It is important to note that with all of these preference pairs, very few people are extreme and only able to exhibit one preference. Everyone exhibits a certain opposing level of each preference pair. When assembling an MSA audit team, one must balance those opposing preference pairs among the team members, or ensure that certain team members are able to apply their non-dominant preference for the purposes of team balance. In contrasting your typical compliance audit versus an MSA audit, we would propose that one of the primary differences relative to the four preference categories would be sensing versus intuitive. More specifically, the sensing preference is more important in a compliance audit, while the intuitive preference is more important to the success of an MSA. On a secondary level, people who can apply both the feeling and thinking preferences are important in performing an MSA, due to the heavy reliance on the interview process.

J. Richard Pooler, Esq., and **Debora L. Jones**, RN, MPH, are executive officers of The Darien Group, Ltd., specializing in integrated health, safety, and environmental management consulting services. Mr. Pooler has over 15 years of experience as an attorney/engineer in consulting, private industry, and government. He has designed, managed, and conducted over 400 compliance, acquisition, divestiture, and specialty performance audits for a variety of industries, including several multiple-site, fast-track assessments for multimillion dollar transactions. He has also evaluated the environmental management structure for companies and assisted in implementing improvements. Mr. Pooler brings an integrated legal, technical, and managerial perspective to client assignments, and specializes in developing strategic approaches to health, safety, and environmental management issues. Ms. Jones has over 15 years of health care experience, including 10 years working in occupational health and safety. Ms. Jones has completed several hundred audits of health and safety programs with emphasis on compliance and risk management. As a health and safety consultant, she has designed and managed on-site occupational health programs. Her work with industry has included management consultation on issues of loss control, risk management, and OSHA compliance.

Applying TQM to Environmental Site Assessments under the ASTM Standard

19

Howard N. Apsan

Total Quality Management was initially developed to facilitate an ethos of continuous improvement of the production process. It entails both an internal and external focus. The former depends on a cooperative effort among employees at all levels of the organization to analyze work processes, minimize process variance, and thereby maximize productivity. The latter requires close collaboration with suppliers to ensure that raw or processed materials can be readily and efficiently integrated into the production process and constant communication with the end user—the customer—to ensure that the process generates the expected level of quality.

Applying TQM to service industry processes is a bit more complex. In addition to having to tailor the TQM approach to the specific service industry, the processes are seldom identical and tend not to lend themselves to the same type of statistical variance analysis that is considered a hallmark of TQM. Nevertheless, numerous case studies have shown that TQM is applicable to the service industry and can help to generate a culture of continuous improvement and enhance customer satisfaction.

Environmental site assessments provide a unique challenge to proponents of TQM. Construction, geological, and hydrological characteristics are unique at each site; regulatory requirements differ by jurisdiction; access to historical information is inconsistent; auditors have varying backgrounds; and client needs and expectations differ. Nevertheless, as the American Society for Testing and Materials (ASTM) standard practice gains acceptance as a benchmark for environmental site assessments, the application of TQM practices to this service process becomes more practicable.

Total Quality Management can be applied to all organizational endeavors provided the applications are tailored to specific organizational and functional needs. An automobile manufacturer, a police department, a bank, and a law firm can all benefit from proper application of TQM.[1] The method of application, however, varies for each setting.

TQM consists of three basic elements. The first is continuous improvement of the organization and its processes. This notion, which assumes that methods and operations can always be improved just a little bit more, must become an intrinsic part of the organization's ethos. Improvement can assume the form of minimizing

199

statistical variance, enhancing productivity, or simply instilling a quality-focused organizational culture.

The second element of TQM is developing a quality-driven integrated relationship with suppliers. If your product requires raw or processed materials (and virtually all do), the ultimate quality of the product shipped to your customer depends on the raw or processed supplies. A faulty cathodic protection system for an underground storage tank can result in a leaking tank, which, in turn, will result in a dissatisfied customer. An analytical laboratory that delivers one-week turnaround results in ten days will also make your client unhappy. A faulty data entry can result in an inaccurate regulatory data search report, which may result in an inaccurate assessment of environmental exposure. Again, you are likely to have a dissatisfied customer. If you are not demanding and receiving quality work from your suppliers and subcontractors, it will be difficult for you to provide a quality product to your customers. TQM requires that the production process be based on cooperation and coordination between supplier and producer to maximize the benefits of the relationship.

The third element of TQM is customer satisfaction. The ultimate test of any product is whether the customer will come back a second, third, or fourth time. Repeat business (assuming a competitive marketplace, and there are few more competitive than today's environmental assessment market) will happen only when the customer perceives that the product is of the highest quality and that it meets his or her specific needs.

As the previous examples suggest, there are many opportunities for applying TQM to environmental support processes. They range from the harder side of the industry, hazardous waste handling and site remediation, to the softer side, life cycle studies, pollution prevention, and site assessment. The following analysis will explore the possible application of TQM to the Phase I environmental site assessment process and examine how the site assessment may be improved when subjected to the rigors of TQM.

This analysis is particularly timely because of a number of developments in the industry, particularly the effort to standardize the substance and method of environmental management processes. One of the milestones of the effort has been the drafting of an American Society for Testing and Materials (ASTM) standard for Phase I environmental site assessments.[2] This standard, if it continues to be seen as a benchmark, will provide a valuable tool in the application of TQM to the environmental assessment process.

What Is a Phase I Environmental Site Assessment?

The Phase I environmental site assessment—also known as a site assessment, environmental assessment, site investigations, environmental audit,[3] Phase I, property transaction environmental assessment, environmental due diligence—is the process by which a property owner or a prospective buyer surveys a property to determine any potential environmental concerns associated with it. This activity is performed primarily to assess potential value impairment associated with environmental contamination. Most commonly, site assessments are conducted in conjunction with a property transaction, whether the sale of a single parcel, an asset with multiple parcels, a portfolio of assets, or a foreclosure.

The site assessment is usually conducted as part of the overall due diligence process associated with that transaction. Just as a lawyer is retained to review and negotiate contractual issues, an accountant to review the financial details, and a surveyor to ensure the accuracy of the property boundaries, an environmental professional is retained to assess potential environmental impairment. Although the role of the environmental professional has been evolving over the past few years, it is rare for a commercial transaction of any substance to be consummated without an environmental site assessment in the due diligence process.

Over time, consulting firms and other environmental professionals have established forms, checklists, and protocols for conducting these assessments. These protocols have been derived from regulatory agency documents,[4] various environmental auditing texts,[5] and more recently from formats established by specific clients. Although most checklists and protocols cover much of the same ground, a disparity in quality, range, and depth remains. As a result, standardization of the language and content of environmental site assessments has been an ongoing concern of the industry.

In recent years, the effort toward standardization has been aided by a marked increase in the number of government agencies, private entities (primarily major lending institutions with large real estate portfolios), and professional associations developing their own site assessment criteria. In addition to the various EPA protocols and guidelines, some states have developed programs that mandate the implementation of rigorous environmental site assessments—which ultimately must be approved by the state agency—before certain types of commercial properties may be transferred. One of the more established and best known state programs is the New Jersey Environmental Cleanup Responsibility Act (ECRA). ECRA established a standard procedure for reviewing property transactions, including a general information submission, a more thorough site evaluation submission, and if needed a sampling plan to assess areas of environmental concern more definitively. Other states, such as Connecticut, Massachusetts, and Minnesota, have or are developing statutory programs requiring specific site assessment procedures.

Lending institutions have also assumed leadership responsibility for establishing standardized criteria. Private institutions, including commercial banks, investment banks, insurance carriers, and asset managers, have standard protocols that all environmental site assessments must follow. Quasi-public institutions, such as Fannie Mae, RTC, and FDIC, have also established protocols. Because of the large portfolios of questionable assets associated with the savings and loan and bank difficulties, these protocols have become particularly prevalent.

Professional associations have also grappled with this issue of standardization. Among the organizations pursuing this issue are the Air and Waste Management Association, the Environmental Auditing Roundtable, the American Society of Civil Engineers, and the National Groundwater Association. In addition to focusing on the standardization of assessment criteria, professional associations have been particularly concerned with addressing auditor training and professional qualifications.

Applying TQM to the Environmental Site Assessment Process

For any professional, the notion of continuous improvement should be part and parcel of the professional ethic. Most professions have formal continuing education requirements to ensure that their members stay current with new developments. The environmental professions are no different. Any firm that intends to pursue an environmental site assessment practice must ensure that its professional staff is current, keeping abreast of the constantly changing regulations that vary from jurisdiction to jurisdiction, and in the evolution of generally accepted practices.

Part of the continuous improvement process is to ensure that the assessor is always qualified to conduct the specific site assessment and is knowledgeable of the appropriate protocols. In most cases, the consulting firm will have a standardized site assessment protocol for conducting the survey and will send out an assessor with the appropriate level and type of expertise to implement that protocol. Today, in many instances, that approach is no longer adequate. The protocols appropriate for any given assessment will have to account for the specific guidance required by the parties involved in the transaction. For example, if an investor is considering acquiring an RTC portfolio of assets, the consultant performing the assessment would have to ensure that the protocols of all parties are at least being integrated into the process. In addition, most environmental assessments being performed today have also started to incorporate the language, form, and structure of the ASTM standard practice. To keep abreast of these different requirements demands ongoing training and a serious effort at continuous improvement.

Finally, the internal process has to be continually reviewed and reassessed. Every aspect of the process—the original proposal, the engagement process, the site-visit scheduling, the acquisition of a computerized data base search, the records review, the historical assessment, the site reconnaissance, the report writing and review, the project management and the follow-up with client—can be streamlined and fine-tuned.

TQM Companies Require TQM Suppliers

In an industrial setting, the notion of integrating suppliers into the TQM structure has been fairly well established. One often cited example is the way that some companies have managed to reduce inventory maintenance costs dramatically by working directly with suppliers to ensure that materials can be provided on a just-in-time basis. Those savings can then be passed along to the ultimate consumer. In an environmental consulting setting, the relationships with suppliers—or, more often, subcontractors—may be different but the principle remains the same. This is particularly true of the time and cost constraints associated with the transfer of real property.

An example of a common supplier of the "raw materials" that go into an environmental assessment is the industry that provides the data base searches and related support, such as topographical maps, Sanborn (historical fire insurance) maps, and aerial photographs. This industry has been revitalized as it has become a necessary part of the environmental site assessment process. This industry has developed because it provides a service that is inefficient for a consulting firm to provide for each site assessment. It would be inefficient and expensive for an environmental consulting firm to download, review, and cross-check the data bases, plot the radius maps, and order and integrate the Sanborn maps, topographical maps, and aerial photographs.

Some firms in this industry provide a serendipitous example of TQM in action. First, they have been particularly attentive to their client's needs—providing environmental consulting firms with a high-quality, timely, and inexpensive service. Second, they focus on continuous improvement by using state-of-the-art information technology to organize the volumes of data generated by regulatory agencies, and to establish quality assurance and quality control measures that cross-check data, minimize data entry error, and independently verify the data from the agencies. Third, they work closely with their clients to ensure that the final product is designed and presented to meet the specific needs of the project or the ultimate end user. To this end, many data base search firms have already integrated the ASTM standards, such as the search distance radii, into their report formats.

Other types of suppliers that service the site assessment process include the contractors that perform the analytical and intrusive work associated with an extended assessment program (commonly referred to as Phase II), such as analytical laboratories, tank tightness testers, and asbestos survey firms. In most cases, the suppliers that are most effective in the site assessment process are those who have endeavored to understand the time constraints, financial limitations, and legal and regulatory requirements, under which the consultants and their clients must work.

Customer Satisfaction

Who are the customers (or clients) of an environmental site assessment and what needs must be satisfied? The client is not necessarily the owner, the buyer, or even the person or entity that signed the engagement letter or contract. In many cases, a law firm handling a transaction for its client or an asset management firm evaluating a portfolio for its principals may be the entity signing the contract.

To quote from Tom Peters and Nancy Austin's *A Passion for Excellence*, "A market has never been observed paying a bill. Customers do that."[6] Who is the customer that must be satisfied? If a company is purchasing a new plant, for example, the customers involved in the assessment will be the plant engineer, the company's lawyer, the company's financial staff, and the company's health, safety, and environmental officer. From a TQM standpoint, all four of those individuals and any others who may be involved in the process should be considered customers, and their needs must be satisfied.

When does the concept of customer satisfaction begin and end? It begins well before the consultant is engaged to perform the work. It begins with the initial contact between the consultant and the customer, when the latter develops an impression of competence and confidence. That impression must be reinforced through every step of the environmental site assessment: as such, the concept of customer satisfaction never ends. Site assessments and client relationships are both dynamic processes. The life of a specific site assessment may extend well beyond the actual closing: Freedom of Information Act (FOIA) letters keep filtering in months after the work is done, remediation questions continue to crop up, and liability for ongoing or preexisting conditions are always with us. Presumably, the satisfied customer relationship will also continue well beyond the submission of the final report.

Why ASTM?

Of all the efforts to standardize the environmental site assessment process, none seems to be having the impact of the ASTM standard. Although it is clear that the industry has been searching for a vehicle to promote uniformity among environmental site assessments, why has the ASTM standard had such a dramatic impact? Some points about the ASTM standard and its development may help to explain this phenomenon.

First, because the ASTM has been setting standards for a broad array of commercial and industrial activities since the nineteenth century, it has the stature that other organizations may be lacking. Second, because the process elicits participation from a vast constituency and requires consensus in discussion and unanimity in balloting, it has a reputation for comprehensiveness and objectivity. Finally, and perhaps most compelling, ASTM standards are recognized by the courts. In an industry that seems to be fraught with more than its fair share of litigiousness, having a standard on which to rely during a lawsuit is very appealing, particularly to a defendant being challenged for failing to exercise due diligence.

The ASTM standard, unlike other protocols for environmental site assessments, is focused specifically on minimizing CERCLA liability and providing grounds for the innocent landowner defense. As a result, the ASTM standard focuses on hazardous wastes and petroleum wastes but does not address what are referred to as "non-scope considerations."[7] These include asbestos, radon, lead-based paint, lead in drinking water, and wetlands. In addition, it explicitly avoids addressing sampling or other Phase II activities. Finally, while the ASTM standard attempts to establish a common language for environmental site assessments, it is unable to provide clear definitions for some of the more nebulous terms such as "actual knowledge," "appropriate inquiry," and "environmental professional."[8]

These qualifications notwithstanding, the ASTM standard appears to be establishing the benchmark by which to measure the quality of an environmental site assessment. For the purposes of TQM, this helps in developing a measure for internal continuous improvement, providing a mechanism around which to integrate critical suppliers into the TQM structure, and establishing a formal system through which customers are better able to assess the ultimate quality of the product.

Differentiating the Site Assessment

One of the hallmarks of quality organizations is that they refuse to treat their products as commodities. However, as the apparent industry trend toward standardization and uniformity progresses, it seems that the environmental site assessment is threatened with becoming just such an undifferentiated product. What, then, distinguishes one environmental assessment from another? How can quality be recognized in this arena?

Every site assessment consultant claims that its product (the survey and the report) is superior to that of the competition. In the cases where this is true, what makes one assessment better than another? The ASTM standard divides the environmental site assessment into four parts: records review, site reconnaissance, interviews, and a report. Following this format, it may be possible to distinguish the superior site assessment from an average one.

Records Review

The more energy and diligence put into the records review, which includes regulatory, cartographic, and historical information, the better the results will be. Most site assessment records reviews consist of collecting and reviewing the on-site files provided by the site owner or manager, reviewing and evaluating the data base search, sending FOIA letters to the appropriate regulatory agencies and perhaps calling them on the telephone, and reviewing other source materials, such as topographical maps, Sanborn maps, and aerial photographs. A firm that performs these activities has probably exercised due diligence in meeting the letter and spirit of the ASTM standard. It may not, however, meet the TQM standard.

A TQM assessment might include cross-referencing and confirming all data provided by the property owner to ensure its completeness, accuracy, and objectivity. This may also include an independent review of all files available on- or off-site that might shed light on potential environmental concerns. Similarly, a call to the regulatory agencies, supplemented by an FOIA letter, is common practice. The agencies, however, seldom provide information over the phone; also information given by phone is difficult to confirm, may be incomplete, and often reflects at least inadvertently the bias of the regulatory official. Furthermore, the FOIA response will seldom be received early enough in the process to be of much value to the site assessment.

Topographical maps, Sanborn maps, and aerial photographs present another opportunity for differentiation. The ASTM standard acknowledges the adequacy of relying on these three sources of historical information, but there are often readily available opportunities to augment these documents. For example, while topographical maps will provide surface information, they provide no subsurface data. These data can often be found in Soil Conservation Service reports, geological data from adjacent or nearby sites, and any soil-boring logs or other geophysical data associated with construction on or near the site. Most of these sources are readily accessible with a little extra effort.

Finally, most site assessments rely on the topographical maps, Sanborn maps, and aerial photographs that are provided along with the data base search by the supplier. In well-developed, densely populated areas, these materials can often be supplemented by visiting the cartography section of the local library, a local historical society, or nonenvironmental municipal agencies, such as the municipal planning commission or zoning board. These sources will likely provide added information and insight and thereby augment the quality of the assessment.

By now it is becoming apparent that there are many steps beyond the ones required by the ASTM standard or any protocol. It is also becoming apparent that many of these additional activities will increase the time and cost of an environmental site assessment without necessarily providing a commensurate increase in its substance. The conventional wisdom suggests that the more you want to know about a site, the more it will cost and the longer it will take—and still you can never assume 100 percent confidence in the results. This may be a practical rule of thumb but it is somewhat inconsistent with the goals and principles of TQM.

Site Reconnaissance

The actual on-site inspection provides another illustration of how a quality assessment can be differentiated from a commodity assessment. In many cases, the site reconnaissance is conducted by rote, and the ASTM standard may inadvertently foster this approach. When the engagement is authorized, the next available auditor is assigned to the project. He or she then contacts the facility, schedules a visit, and proceeds to conduct the site reconnaissance. Seldom is much research done prior to the visit, and most site inspections are performed before the data base and other environmental documentation have become available.

The primary output of the site reconnaissance is the factual evidence. Is there an underground storage tank? Is there asbestos? Are there transformers? The quality component of the site reconnaissance goes beyond the basic factual assessment to the interpretation and implications of the facts. Even an assessor with little experience in tank remediation or asbestos abatement may be able to ascertain the facts more or less accurately; but he or she may be hard pressed to judge their implications accurately.

Finally, the TQM site reconnaissance will have quality assurance built in. If there are two assessors at the site, they should have complementary skills and experience. Prior to the site visit, the assessors should be well briefed by their supervisor and by anyone with specific knowledge of the site or a similar type of property. The same group should reconvene once the reconnaissance is complete to analyze the findings. This process should minimize the potential for missing material implications of what was observed.

Interviews

The ASTM standard recommends that interviews be conducted with owners, operators, a key site manager, a reasonable number of occupants of the site, and selected local officials. It also admonishes the interviewer to seek specific and comprehensive answers and to assess the quality of those answers. Again, the difference between a commodity and a quality interview depends on the person conducting the interview, the quality of the questions, and the preparation underlying those questions.

Interviewing is more than just reading questions and jotting down the answers. Because the assessor will rarely be able to select whom to interview, the quality of the interview itself becomes critical. The key ingredient to a successful interview is preparation. Ideally, the interviewer should be able to make the interviewee comfortable and facilitate an interactive atmosphere. While some interviewers are naturally more adept, the basic interviewing techniques can be mastered in a TQM manner. Familiarity with the material, prior knowledge of the property and the people being interviewed, and preparation inevitably improve the quality of the interview. The aphorism "you only get one chance to make a first impression" is particularly relevant to the site assessment interview. If you have not done your homework and you make the interviewee defensive, it will be that much harder to reap quality data from the interviewing process.

Exhibit 1: Phase I Environmental Site Assessment Report

Recommended Table of Contents and Report Format

X2.1.   **Summary**

X2.1.   **Introduction**
    X2.1.1.   Purpose
    X2.1.2.   Special Terms and Conditions
    X2.1.3.   Limitations and Exceptions of Assessment
    X2.1.4.   Limiting Conditions and Methodology Used

X2.2.   **Site Description**
    X2.2.1.   Location and Legal Description
    X2.2.2.   Site and Vicinity Characteristics
    X2.2.3.   Descriptions of Structures, Roads, Other Improvements on the Site (including heating/cooling system, sewage disposal, source of potable water)
    X2.2.4.   Information (if any) Reported by User Regarding Environmental Liens or Specialized Knowledge or Experience (pursuant to Section 5)
    X2.2.5.   Current Uses of the Property
    X2.2.6.   Past Uses of the Property, to the Extent Identified
    X2.2.7.   Current and Past Uses of Adjoining Properties, to the Extent Identified

X2.3.   **Records Review**
    X2.3.1.   Standard Environmental Record Sources, Federal and State
    X2.3.2.   Additional Environmental Record Sources, State or Local (if any)
    X2.3.3.   Physical Setting Source(s)
    X2.3.4.   Historical Use Information
    X2.3.5.   Additional Record Sources (if any)
    X2.3.6.   Helpful Document (if any)

Report

In consultant's terms, the ultimate deliverable of the site assessment process is the report. The records review, site reconnaissance, and interviews may have been thorough, comprehensive, and definitive, but if the assessment report fails to reflect that, it is of limited utility. The ASTM standard provides a model table of contents for a site assessment report. This model (**Exhibit 1**) has already begun to surface in many contemporary environmental site assessment reports and is likely to be adopted as the basic format for most site assessments.

Nevertheless, standardization of the report format does not guarantee a quality report. And the report, in many respects, is the ultimate indicator of an effective TQM approach. Boilerplate construction is efficient and cost-effective, but if a report is not tailored to the specific site, its boilerplate character becomes apparent. There is nothing wrong with using a standard report format, and it is not inconsistent with a TQM approach, as long as that format is constantly being reassessed and improved on. The fact that each site is unique and each client's needs are specific should be ever present in the minds of the author and the reviewer.

Finally, the internal review of the report is the consummate example of the continuous improvement process. It may sound trite to say that no report should be shipped before it is perfect, until one considers how few really are. Reasonable professionals may differ on the implications of a site assessment, but the facts of the assessment and the written product must be unassailable. As Peters and Austin quote Donald Burr, chairman of the former People Express Airlines, "[C]offee stains on the flip-down trays in the airplane means to our passengers that we do our engine maintenance wrong."[9]

Conclusion

Environmental site assessments provide a unique challenge to proponents of TQM. They provide ample opportunity for continuous improvement of the process and product, require a quality driven relationship with key suppliers and subcontractors, and present ongoing opportunities for evaluating and meeting customer needs. On the other hand, they are also fraught with obstacles to TQM: construction, geological, and hydrological characteristics are unique at each site; regulatory requirements differ by jurisdiction; access to historical information is inconsistent; auditors have varying backgrounds; and client needs and expectations differ.

The trend toward standardization of the terminology and substance of environmental site assessments, particularly the introduction and seemingly widespread acceptance of the ASTM standard as a benchmark, can be advantageous for the implementation of TQM. Establishing a common language and structure for the basic components of an environmental site assessment—records review, site reconnaissance, interviews, and reports—may lead some to think of environmental site assessments as a commodity. To advocates of TQM, though, standardization presents an ideal opportunity to differentiate between a commodity and a quality product.

Notes

1. For a basic overview of the concepts of TQM, see Mary Walton, *The Deming Management Method* (New York: Perigee Books, 1986), and Steven Cohen and Ronald Brand, *Total Quality Management in Government* (San Francisco: Jossey-Bass Publishers, 1993), especially after chapter 2.

2. ASTM Standard E.50.02.2, *Standard Practice for Environmental Site Assessments: Phase I Environmental Site Assessment Process*, December 1, 1992.

3. The ASTM standard explicitly distinguishes between an environmental site assessment and an environmental audit, id., p. 9.

4. See, for example, United States Environmental Protection Agency, Office of Enforcement and Compliance Monitoring, National Enforcement Investigations Center, *Multi-Media Compliance Inspection Manual*, 4th ed., July 1989.

5. See, for example, Lawrence B. Cahill and Raymond W. Kane, *Environmental Audits*, 6th ed. (Rockville, MD: Government Institutes, 1989); Mark Blumenfeld, *Conducting an Environmental Audit*, 2d ed. (New York: Executive Enterprises, 1989); and Valcar A. Bowman, *Preacquisition Assessment of Commercial and Industrial Property* (Northbrook, IL: Pudvan Publishing, 1989).

6. Tom Peters and Nancy Austin, *A Passion for Excellence: The Leadership Difference* (New York: Warner Books, 1985), p. 45.

7. ASTM Standard (cited in note 2), pp. 32-33.

8. Id. at pp. 3-12.

9. *A Passion for Excellence* (cited in note 6), p. 89.

Howard N. Apsan is the director of environmental management services, Northeastern Operations for Clayton Environmental Consultants in Edison, New Jersey. He has worked for regulatory agencies, consulted to EPA, and provides consulting support to a number of major commercial and industrial clients. He is also a faculty member of Columbia University's Graduate School of International and Public Affairs.

Conducting Quality Management Audits

Continuous Improvement through Environmental Auditing at AlliedSignal

20

Ann C. Smith

Environmental auditing evolved as a means of providing assurance to top management that its health, safety, and environmental responsibilities were being adequately discharged and that no significant noncompliances existed. The author takes an in-depth look at the HSE audit program developed at AlliedSignal to permit continuous improvement of environmental management systems.

AlliedSignal Inc. developed its environmental auditing program in the 1970s to provide top management and the Board of Directors with independent information on the status of health, safety, and environmental (HSE) programs at its operations. Over 500 audits have been conducted since then at AlliedSignal's more than 240 facilities worldwide.

The program has a dedicated staff of three full-time professionals, one of whom leads each audit team. In addition to the team leader, teams include an independent third-party auditor and many also include from one to three HSE professionals from other operations. Each audit lasts three to five days and features a standard approach controlled by a written protocol, interviews with key personnel, documentation review, visual observation of plant features, and a final audit report distributed to appropriate parties.

Defining the Environmental Audit

There are a number of activities conducted under the term "environmental auditing":

- Remediation investigation/feasibility studies (RI/FS) conducted in support of RCRA corrective actions or CERCLA (Superfund) cleanups
- Assessments of environmental liability associated with real property transfers
- Quality or product safety audits
- Environmental impact studies
- Hydrogeological studies
- Meteorological studies

- Audits designed to assess an operation's status of compliance relative to specific environmental statutes and other criteria

It is the last of these that this chapter addresses, as the objective of AlliedSignal's audit program is verification of compliance with the law and with corporate policies and procedures, and assurance that systems are in place to ensure continued compliance.

HSE Audit Program Overview

AlliedSignal Inc. is organized into three sectors: Automotive, Aerospace, and Engineered Materials, each of which operates with considerable autonomy.

The Vice President, Corporate Health, Safety and Environmental Sciences Department, reports to the Chief Operating Officer of the corporation. The department has sixteen full-time staff in Pollution Control, Product Safety, Occupational Health, Loss Prevention, and Environmental Auditing.

Each function is headed by a director, who is responsible for overall coordination of and guidance to the sectors and operating companies, program monitoring, and regulatory affairs interaction.

The three sectors also have environmental, health, and safety staff structured similarly to that of the corporate staff (but without an audit function), with day-to-day responsibility for compliance. The sector director reports at a high level and has staff commensurate with the risks inherent in the sector industries. A functional reporting relationship exists with corporate counterparts. Personnel assigned to specific facilities are likewise tied in functionally to sector HSE staff.

Corporate Policy

AlliedSignal's health, safety, and environmental policy commits the corporation to establish regulatory compliance programs and to adopt its own standards where laws and regulations may not be adequately protective or do not exist. The policy is supported by written corporate guidelines. To supplement the corporate guidelines, sectors, companies, and individual facilities also have written operating procedures that address environmental concerns specific to the individual businesses.

Organization and Staffing

A number of criteria were established when AlliedSignal Inc. considered an approach to organizing and staffing the audit program, including:

- Independence of the audit teams from those responsible for managing corporate and sector environmental programs, but with organizational proximity to facilitate communication and resolution of problems and conflicts

- Minimizing the full-time staffing commitment to the audit program, yet having a readily available supply of competent, objective team members, continuity in the conduct of reviews, and long-term accountability for the program

With those objectives, several options were considered, such as using external auditors; establishing an independent internal group housed within the corporate audit department or the corporate health, safety, and environmental sciences department; or using task forces made up of persons drawn from throughout the corporation. Each option was viewed as having advantages and disadvantages. For example:

- An external auditor would not require the addition of any full-time employees and would have a high degree of independence; however, there could be substantial barriers to coordination and communication. Also, this approach would involve relatively higher total costs.
- An independent group within the corporate audit department would have a high degree of independence from health, safety, and environmental program management, but would not have the needed understanding of subject matter.
- A separate, independent group of full-time auditors within the HSE department would afford a good opportunity for communication with health, safety, and environmental management, but its independence might be questioned.
- A task force would have broad participation, high flexibility, and relatively low cost, but carry the potential for loss of continuity and disruption of regular functions.

In order to achieve as many of these objectives as possible, the audit program was established within the corporate HSE department and is staffed by three full-time professionals. To ensure continuity and accountability, the team leader for each audit is one of those three professionals. The remainder of the audit team (which varies from two to five people depending on the review scope and size of facility) is comprised of corporate, sector, or division HSE professionals familiar with the review subject, but not directly involved in the programs being reviewed, and an outside consultant who provides the advantages of an external auditor.

Audit Scope and Focus

All of AlliedSignal's facilities worldwide fall within the scope of the audit program, with operations assessed as having lower health, safety, and environmental risk receiving less attention than those assessed as high-risk operations. The functional scope of the program includes:

- Air pollution control
- Water pollution control and spill prevention
- Solid and hazardous waste disposal
- Occupational health and medical programs
- Safety and loss prevention
- Product safety and integrity
- Special focus audits

The compliance scope includes all legal requirements, corporate policies and procedures, and good health, safety, and environmental practices.

With some 240 locations and seven functional areas, a comprehensive review of all subjects at all locations would be a formidable task. Therefore, most audits are limited to only one of the functional areas listed above (for example, air pollution control only) in order to maximize the amount of in-depth review in the time available. Thus, although the program covers a variety of topics, the scope of a specific audit is narrow.

Audit Selection Process

Approximately fifty audits are conducted annually. Thus, the program reviews only a relatively small sample of the corporation's facilities each year. The selection process uses a fairly sophisticated approach to choose locations that represent a cross-section of AlliedSignal's business interests and health, safety, and environmental concerns where potential risks are high. Audits are apportioned evenly among the various functional areas.

At the beginning of each year, the audit schedule for the year is sent to corporate and sector health, safety, and environmental staff. Two months prior to the review, the team leader sends a letter to the facility manager, with copies to the appropriate sector and corporate environmental staff, identifying the type of audit to be conducted, which is not revealed until this time.

Audit Methodology

The HSE audit program employs a number of tools and techniques such as formal internal control questionnaires, formal audit protocols (or guides), informal interviews with facility personnel, physical observations, documentation review, testing, and verification.

A written audit protocol covering each functional area of the review reflects the objectives of the audit, facility characteristics, and time constraints. The protocol methodically guides the auditor to an understanding of requirements affecting the facility and the facility's management system, the conduct of tests to confirm that the system is working, and the determination of specific deficiencies. Auditors carefully document the accomplishment and results of each audit protocol step in their audit working papers.

The audit process can be analyzed in four phases:

Phase I: Preparation

Among the pre-audit activities conducted by the audit team leader are the confirmation of review dates and organization of the audit team based on the functional scope of the review. Corporate files are screened to obtain and review information on the facility and its processes (for example, process flow diagrams, plant layout diagrams, policies and procedures, operating manuals, permits, required reports to the corporate office). Regulations applicable to the facility are also studied.

Phase II: On-Site Review

The on-site review commences with a meeting of the audit team, the facility manager, and appropriate facility personnel. During this meeting, the team leader discusses the objectives of the audit program and the review scope. Facility personnel present an overview of the facility's operations—products, processes, facility organization, and so on. The team is then given a tour by facility staff to gain a general understanding of plant characteristics.

Following the tour, the review team and appropriate facility environmental staff meet to complete an internal controls questionnaire. This questionnaire, administered by the audit team leader, aids the auditors in developing an initial understanding of facility operations, processes, personnel responsibilities, and environmental management controls.

Working from the audit protocol, with major sections apportioned among team members, each auditor gathers system information and performs relevant tests. In the course of the review, the auditor must use sampling techniques and exercise professional judgment in selecting the type and size of samples to be used to verify that the key controls in the system under review are in place and working. Testing is not done until the system is well understood and a carefully reasoned plan of testing is worked out. This understanding may come from interviews with facility staff, review of facility operating procedures and systems, observation of physical features of control systems, and so forth.

Testing of the systems can take a variety of forms. For example, verification testing for water pollution control can include:

- Visual observation downstream from an outfall;
- Comparison of analytical results with contaminant reports required to be filed with regulatory authorities;
- Review of programs to assure the reliability of treatment or monitoring equipment; and
- Determination that composite samplers, effluent flow measuring devices, and in-place monitoring devices are properly maintained and calibrated.

Each auditor carefully documents all testing plans and test results, sharing observations and information on deficiencies found throughout the audit with team members and facility staff. Also, time is set aside at the end of each day to exchange information and share any concerns that have developed during the day's work. The audit team continuously feeds back impressions about the system's compliance with established criteria to plant personnel. This continuous feedback is intended to:

- Eliminate misconceptions and false trails for the team member who may have misunderstood the initial description;
- Encourage team members to organize their thoughts;
- Give facility personnel an opportunity to participate in the audit process; and
- Maintain the audit as an open process among team members and between the team and facility staff.

Significant findings are compiled by the team leader on a summary sheet, which is used as the basis for discussion with plant management at a close-out meeting.

Phase III: Reporting and Record Preservation

The purpose of the written report is to provide information to top management (sector presidents) on the more significant findings of the audit. The written report states the auditor's opinion as to whether or not the facility is in substantive compliance and lists any observed exceptions. The report is based on findings listed on the audit findings summary form.

A standardized four-part format for the written report has evolved:

- Section I provides details on the place, date, scope, and personnel involved in the audit.
- Section II addresses compliance with legal requirements (federal, state/ provincial, regional, and local).

- Section III covers compliance with AlliedSignal's policies and procedures (corporate, sector, or facility).
- Section IV indicates deficiencies in the facility control systems that would make continued compliance with the law or company policy questionable (such as record retention, documentation, clear assignment of environmental responsibilities, and so on).

The length of the report depends on the number of findings; typically it is four to five pages.

Report Distribution

The written audit report is issued in draft form by the team leader to the involved line and staff personnel at both the operating company and corporate levels, the facility manager, and the audit team. Comments on this draft report are requested within two weeks of its issuance. When comments necessitate significant revision of the first draft, a second draft of the report may be prepared and circulated for review.

The final written report is issued to the sector president six to eight weeks after the review, with copies to appropriate facility, business, legal, and environmental management. The final report is accompanied by a request that the operating company provide a written corrective action plan.

Records Retention

A formal records retention policy for all audit documents exists to help keep the records volume at a manageable level and to ensure that all audit records are retained for a period of time consistent with their utility in the program and with applicable federal regulations. Thus, audit working papers are retained for three years. Audit reports and action plans are retained for ten years or longer where subject to specific records' retention requirements.

Other Reporting

In addition to the formal written report for individual reviews to the sector president, the Board Corporate Responsibility Committee receives regular reports on audit program activities at least twice a year. These reports, both oral and written, are given by the audit program director to the Board Committee. A representative of the program's consulting firm is also present to respond to board requests for independent information on the status of compliance programs and of the audit program. The purpose of reporting to the board is to confirm that the audit program is functioning and to provide assurance that concerns material to the corporation have been identified.

Phase IV: Company Action

The job of the audit team ends with the submission and management's understanding of the final report. The review *process*, however, continues until responsible management prepares and executes an action plan for correcting the identified deficiencies.

Once the action plan is developed by facility personnel and received by the audit director, the audit team leader reviews it to confirm that the final report has been understood and that the plan is responsive to the findings of the report.

Action plans are typically received within two to three months of the issuance of the final written report. The plan reports on corrective actions already taken as well as those that are planned. Operating management then assumes responsibility for follow-up and monitoring of the corrective actions. The audit group performs follow-up reviews to confirm the completion of approximately 20 percent of these action plans.

The corporation's environmental assurance system also includes other formal procedures for follow-up and corrective action on all environmental, health, and safety deficiencies.

Program Benefits

AlliedSignal has noted a number of benefits throughout the corporation resulting from the audit program. Among them are:

- For top management and the Board of Directors, the program provides independent verification that operations are in compliance with applicable requirements of environmental law and the corporation's environmental policy.
- For environmental management, the program serves as another source of information on the status of operations and the individual deficiencies and.patterns of deficiencies that may occur.
- For line management, there is added incentive for much closer self-evaluation to confirm that operations are in compliance. The program has stimulated line management to become more familiar with the detailed implications of environmental requirements. The program has also identified problems in their operations that require corrective action, or, more frequently, it has confirmed that environmental requirements were being met.
- For business management, improved understanding of health, safety, and environmental liabilities can improve planning and budgeting.

Continuous Improvement in Environmental Management

Environmental auditing developed as a means of providing assurance to top management that its health, safety, and environmental responsibilities were being adequately discharged and that no significant noncompliances existed. The concept and application were taken virtually wholesale from the financial audit field, where

> audits evolved as a means of verifying compliance with bookkeeping practices. They were created basically to uncover cheating—which, of course, is still a prime audit application. The intent of compliance auditing is to identify operations where standards aren't being adhered to and to then force changes in practices—or people—to make sure that standards are met. A standard might be a specification, law, policy, procedure, contractual agreement, or the auditee's own documents.[1]

Auditing will have no value, however, if the deficiencies it uncovers are not corrected. It is therefore a fundamental tenet that management be committed to fixing what is found.

The environmental management process can be viewed as diagrammed in **Exhibit 1**.

In this scheme, each goal is planned for, acted on, checked, and modified. The modification is actually a new plan, so the process is circular, as diagrammed, and continuous. Note that the "check" step is actually auditing. So the process of auditing supplies the feedback loop to permit continuous improvement of environmental management systems. In most cases, audit is not the only source of such information: regulatory agency inspections, insurance carrier audits, customer audits, and many other activities can also supply valuable inputs to improve management schemes.

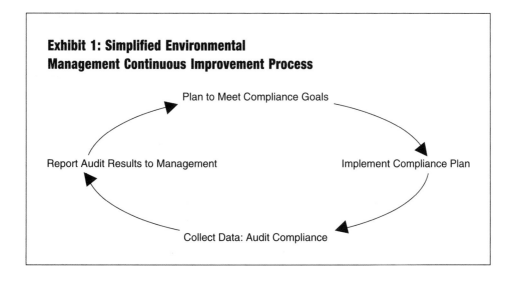

Exhibit 1: Simplified Environmental Management Continuous Improvement Process

Plan to Meet Compliance Goals

Implement Compliance Plan

Collect Data: Audit Compliance

Report Audit Results to Management

Because environmental auditing is itself a component of the environmental management system, it too should be subject to continual evaluation and feedback to enhance its functioning.

At AlliedSignal, we solicit feedback from all organizational levels of HSE management and from other parties affected by the audit program as a means of improving the program. Recent improvements have involved modifications to the audit selection process, reporting frequencies and methods, and audit field work.

There are a number of other quality assurance steps taken in AlliedSignal's audit program. For example, a member of the audit staff leads each audit to assure program consistency. The team leader's role includes supervision of team members to assure completion of all assigned tasks. In addition, the team leader takes pains to encourage open and full communication among the team and plant personnel.

Allied's audit protocols provide a structured framework to guide the auditors through a series of steps designed to create an understanding of the system under review, conduct appropriate tests to confirm that the system is working, and determine specific deficiencies.

Another quality measure relates to the audit working papers. The credibility of the audit depends on the thoroughness of the review and its documentation. Each team member must prepare working papers that document the information gathered, tests performed, and conclusions reached. At the end of each audit, the team leader reviews the working papers, which serve as support for the audit report and a way of evaluating the performance of each team member.

The program is guided by written procedures describing such things as site selection, documentation, record retention, training, audit conduct, and so on. Standard forms are likewise used to the extent possible in order to assure consistency of approach.

Finally, AlliedSignal's outside consultant provides an additional quality control check. A representative of the consulting firm participates in each review. All audit reports are reviewed by the consultant to ensure accurate and consistent audit reporting. The consultant periodically reviews working paper files at corporate headquarters to assure their quality.

Achieving Total Quality

The argument is frequently made that total quality is not achievable. Whereas *perfection* might be unattainable, aggressively and assiduously pursuing a continuous improvement process can be synonymous with achieving total quality. The argument will no doubt continue. While it does, let me assert that achieving total quality demands that certain fundamentals be in place:

- Adequate training of personnel to assure that they know how to meet requirements;
- Personal and organizational commitment, or wanting to do the job right every time;
- Doing the job;
- Having the humility to know that mistakes will be made; and
- Correcting and redoing the process in response to the mistakes and their implicit lessons.

An environmental audit can serve as a catalyst for gearing up programs in a continuous improvement mode, rather than simply as an analysis for deficiency. It develops information on the current compliance status. Properly used, this information permits process and program changes that improve HSE management. Re-audits then evaluate the effectiveness of corrective actions, permitting even more refined modifications. Over the years, AlliedSignal's environmental auditing program has proven its value as an effective tool for continuous improvement of the management of the corporation's health, safety, and environmental responsibilities.

Note

1. Aquino, "Improvement vs. Compliance: A New Look at Auditing," *Quality Progress*, October 1990.

Ann C. Smith heads AlliedSignal Environmental Services Inc.'s worldwide consulting practice. She currently chairs the Environmental Auditing Roundtable, the international professional society of environmental auditing.

Auditing for Environmental Excellence at Union Carbide

21

Paul D. Coulter

Union Carbide formed its current Health, Safety, and Environmental Audit Program in 1985 following the Bhopal, India, tragedy in December 1984. Although our pre-Bhopal record confirmed our belief that we had an excellent program, with the help of a consulting firm we went back to the drawing board and questioned everything. We raised the bar and set as one of our goals the development and implementation of an audit program that is "second to none." This chapter details the specific tools being used by Union Carbide auditors to ensure environmental excellence at our numerous plant sites.

Although each of Union Carbide's major businesses has staff professionals who are responsible for a full range of traditional health, safety, and environmental (HS&E) functions, the Health, Safety and Environmental Audit Program reports directly to the chief executive officer and the Health, Safety, and Environmental Affairs committee of the board of directors. As an independent unit of Union Carbide, we are responsible for auditing our worldwide companies and affiliate operations and some suppliers. In addition to auditing against applicable regulations, we audit a location's compliance with Union Carbide's own HS&E standards that in many cases exceed legal requirements.

The objective of the compliance audit program is to provide independent assessment of line management and location performance against the following criteria: compliance with applicable internal standards and governmental requirements, and the existence of management systems that assure continued compliance.

The program is composed of the following elements:

- Standard Operating Procedures (SOPs)
- Audit protocols
- Facility profile data base
- Hazard ranking model data base
- Audit Timeliness Index (ATI)—site selection
- Location audits
- Performance classification

- Written reports
- Action plan reviews and response
- Action plan follow-up
- Root cause/findings analyses

Preparing for the Audit

We have developed a comprehensive set of standard operating procedures for compliance audits. These procedures give detailed instructions to the auditors regarding the planning, execution, and completion of the auditing process. There are general SOPs that cover the overall procedures for the department, and the purpose, scope, and key elements of the audit program. The fundamental SOPs address such items as (1) pre-audit planning, (2) audit preparation, and (3) on-site compliance audit activities such as the opening meeting, the understanding of management systems, assessing management systems, gathering audit evidence, sampling strategies (e.g., random number tables) and techniques, evaluating the audit evidence, management feedback meetings, preparing and issuing the audit reports. Also described in the SOPs are interviewing techniques, working papers requirements, and the post-audit dispute resolution process. Other SOPs cover recordkeeping retention requirements, good travel practices, emergency procedures, and security. The SOPs are regularly reviewed and updated as appropriate.

Audit Protocols

We have developed thirteen audit protocols to cover three issue areas. The three issue areas are: health and safety, which includes occupational health and medicine, plant and employee safety, and operational safety events; environmental, which covers air emissions, waste management, groundwater and surface water protection, and environmental emergency preparedness; and product responsibility, including product risk assessment, product safety communications, product quality, the Toxic Substances Control Act (TSCA), and product distribution. In addition, a general protocol is used to direct the auditor review of management systems and miscellaneous issues. The protocols are regularly reviewed and updated as appropriate. Each protocol is maintained on a computer network disk. Before each audit, based on the functional areas they are to cover, the auditors print out the most recent version of the applicable protocol to take along with them.

To maximize the benefits and intent of the auditing process, sites must be selected and audited in a timely manner. Only then can management derive the maximum benefit from the program consistent with the resources employed. The principal components of Union Carbide's scheduling criteria are hazard potential, compliance potential, facility size, and past audit performance, to which we add a special site-specific component. In addition, we select a representative group of

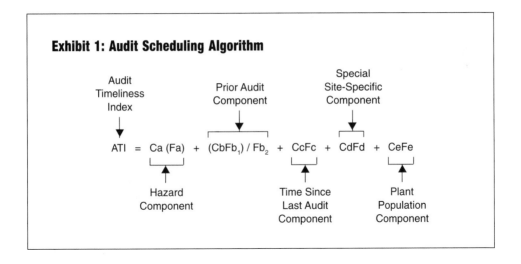

Exhibit 1: Audit Scheduling Algorithm

$$\text{ATI} = C_a(F_a) + (C_bF_{b_1})/F_{b_2} + C_cF_c + C_dF_d + C_eF_e$$

Audit Timeliness Index → $C_a(F_a)$

Hazard Component → $C_a(F_a)$

Prior Audit Component → $(C_bF_{b_1})/F_{b_2}$

Time Since Last Audit Component → C_cF_c

Special Site-Specific Component → C_dF_d

Plant Population Component → C_eF_e

locations from all businesses and geographical areas. Because of the large number of sites covered by our program, we developed a mathematical model for prioritizing audit sites for scheduling purposes. The site data used for the model and to calculate the site's hazard ranking are contained in a facility profile data base, which is updated regularly by the locations and reviewed for accuracy by our auditors during an audit.

Audit Timeliness Index

The audit scheduling algorithm is shown in **Exhibit 1**. We refer to it as the Audit Timeliness Index (ATI). Each of the five components is related to one of our scheduling criteria. The hazard component is based on the location score from the hazard ranking data. The prior-audit component is based on performance classifications from the last two audits. The time-since-last-audit component is based on the number of years since the last audit. The plant-population component is proportional to the number of employees and on-site contractors at the location. The special site-specific component allows us to tune the model for site-specific factors, such as laboratories with special considerations, new businesses, or other situations that are not adequately covered by the other four components.

The scaling constants are chosen so that sites that should be audited during the current year receive an ATI numerical score of 10 or higher. The effect of prior audit performance and hazard ranking is illustrated in **Exhibit 2**. In general, the better the prior audit performance, the longer the time interval between audits.

Information about the site, prior audits, and ATI index are consolidated on a computer printout, a page of which is shown in **Exhibit 3**. Each site has a description, a business group code, an internal audit unit number code, the total number of sites contained within that audit unit, the date of the most recent audit of the

---

Exhibit 2: Effect of Prior Audit Performance and Hazard Ranking

Location A	(GM, GM)[a]	= 11
	(SM, M)	= 9
	(M, M)	= 7
Location B	(GM, GM)	= 13
	(M, M)	= 9
Location C	(X, RSI)	> 10

[a] For an explanation of these abbreviations, see Exhibit 4.

---

location, and the year and performance classification of the two most recent audits.

The log of the Hazard Ranking score is in the numerical section of the printout plus flags, such as "+," "-," or "%," that indicate whether any data are missing from either the facility profile or chemical thesaurus (used in the calculation of risk). Next come the components calculated from the hazard ranking score—classifications received in prior audits, last audit (factor proportional to the numbers of years since the last audit), any site-specific data, and the population factor—and finally, the ATI score itself. An asterisk after the ATI score indicates that an audit has been scheduled for the current year.

The use of the ATI score as a tool by an experienced audit team has allowed Union Carbide to reach its goal of making site selection less subjective and more objective.

The Audit Process

After the audit schedule has been established, the team leader assigned to the audit issues a notification letter and requests materials for auditor review before the audit team visits the site. For non-U.S. sites and for non-owned Union Carbide facilities, notification is given thirty to forty-five days before the scheduled audit. All other locations receive a ten-day notice.

The audit team leader assigns specific functional areas to each of the team members and arranges the logistics. The team leader is also responsible for arranging a pre-audit meeting with audit management and other Union Carbide health, safety, and environmental personnel as appropriate.

Once on site, the audit is conducted in a manner that is consistent with the five-step process described in the book *Environmental Auditing: Fundamentals and Techniques* by Maryanne DiBerto, J. Ladd Greeno, and Gilbert S. Hedstrom (Cambridge, Massachusetts: Arthur D. Little, 1987), and in accordance with Union Carbide's SOPs. In approximately 25 percent of our audits, a consultant auditor participates in the audit to provide an independent assessment of our performance.

During the performance classification, we assess the current level of the location's health, safety, and environmental protection performance. Performance classification allows Union Carbide to set benchmarks for health, safety, and envi-

Exhibit 3: Union Carbide Audit Timeliness Report 92

Description	Location					
	A	B	C	D	E	F
Group	CP	CP	CP	CP	CPD	MEL
Aud Unit	183	043	255	092	162	005
Lin Count	2	13	3	2	1	29
Most Rec Visit	MAR 89	JUN 89	MAY 91		OCT 91	JUN 91
Most Rec Year	89	89	91		91	91
Most Rec Perf	GMX	N/A	GMX		SMX	SMX
Prev Yr	87	87	88		89	90
Prev Perf	N/A	RSI	GMX		GMX	GMX
Log SRS	4.1-	4.6+	4.6	3.5	4.9	4.6%
Component Hazard	6.7	7.3	7.6	5.7	7.8	7.3
Prior Audit	.0	.0	.0	.0	.0	.0
Last Audit	1.5	1.5	.5	3.5	.5	.5
Site Spec	.0	.0	.0	.0	.0	.0
Pop Num	2.4	1.8	2.5	1.3	2.3	2.8
ATI	10.7*	10.6	10.6	10.6	10.6	10.6

* An audit has been scheduled for the current year.

ronmental protection objectives and to measure improvement in performance from year to year.

Several steps are taken to establish a performance classification. We develop a list of exceptions, which is used to integrate and summarize exceptions within a functional area. Performance classifications for each functional area are evaluated and the overall location performance classification determined.

For each exception, we determine whether it is of imminent concern (demands immediate management attention); priority concern (has the potential for serious adverse health, safety, environmental, or corporate impact); or other (all other situations). For each functional area, we determine whether the degree of compliance is high, substantial, general, or limited. Using the severity and compliance factors and the table shown in **Exhibit 4**, we determine the performance classification for each functional area.

For an audit rating of "Meets," at least 75 percent of the functional areas must be "Meets," no functional area is "Generally Meets" or "Requires Substantial Improvement," and there is no other relevant information that suggests that the overall rating should be different from a "Meets." Similarly, we determine "Substantially Meets" and "Generally Meets." The location receives a "Requires Substantial Improvement" (RSI) classification if more than 25 percent of the functional areas are

Exhibit 4: Functional Area Performance Classification

Compliance Factor	Severity Factor	
	Priority Concern	Other Concern
Full	GM	M
Substantial	GM	SM
General	RSI	GM

M = Meets governmental and internal compliance requirements
SM = Substantially meets these requirements
GM = Generally meets these requirements
RSI = Requires substantial improvement to meet requirements

classified as RSI.

By assigning a value to the various classifications, we can develop an index for groups of audits. Visual representation of progress can be made by plotting the index versus time, as shown in **Exhibit 5**. Generally, such plots indicate an increasing improvement in a location performance classification. However, if an analysis is made based on the classification of a location on its first audit, following the second and third audits, and after four or more audits, a slightly different story emerges, as is shown in **Exhibit 6**.

Over a period of time, the results of first audits are nearly constant, whereas the results of second and third audits and four or more audits show a higher degree of improvement. Because of the progressively greater number of locations having four or more audits, the overall audit performance classification index climbs steadily. This illustrates the importance of visiting sites periodically to help them identify weaknesses. As most of the improvement occurs in the early audits and tends to plateau after repeated audits, sites that have been audited repeatedly and are showing a high degree of compliance should have less frequent audits.

Each of our auditors has a laptop computer, which is used to write individual findings and, ultimately, the au-

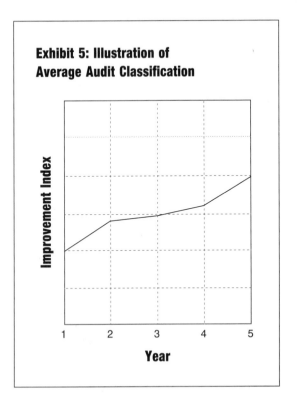

Exhibit 5: Illustration of Average Audit Classification

dit report. Each audit team carries with it a portable printer. On the evening before the closeout meeting, the team meets, merges all their findings, prioritizes them within each functional area, and prioritizes the functional areas. The audit summary is written and is combined with the findings and the standard boilerplate to generate a draft report. Unless the performance classification is RSI, or the audited location requests time to respond to some of the findings, the draft report, with any minor editorial changes as necessary, becomes the final report and is left with the site.

In those unusual and special situations in which an RSI is proposed as the performance classification, the report is reviewed by audit management and issue specialists in the Corporate Health, Safety, and Environment Department. When the RSI performance classification is confirmed, the location is notified and the final report is issued to business group management.

In all cases, the final report is entered into our computer data base and sent to the responsible Union Carbide managers.

Audit Follow-Up

Within sixty days of the issuance of the final report, each audited location is required to develop a detailed action plan to correct the deficiencies noted during the audit. This action plan must reference each finding, the action being taken to correct the deficiency, the projected completion date, and the responsible person. The action plan is reviewed by health, safety, and environmental professionals in the business unit and forwarded to the accountable vice president for his or her endorsement and submittal to the audit group. All action plans are reviewed by the audit team leader. If the team leader has questions about some of the proposed actions, the action steps in question are reviewed with the appropriate issue manager within the corporate HS&E department. If it is deemed that some proposed

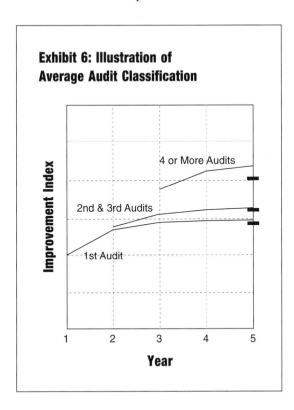

Exhibit 6: Illustration of Average Audit Classification

actions are not adequate or, less commonly, overstated, the action plan is sent back to the location requesting revision.

Approximately 10 percent of the submitted action plans are subjected to an in-depth review, which includes both the team leader review and a review of each item by appropriate issue managers and audit program management.

Each location is required to submit a semiannual update on its action plan until all items are completed. On repeat audits, the auditors verify that physical or system revisions noted in the action plan are complete and correct the problem.

Recently, we have improved our root cause analysis. During the preparation of the final report, each auditor makes an analysis of the root cause(s) of each exception and codes them in the audit report. We have developed a comprehensive list of factors so that we can analyze recurring weaknesses within our overall health, safety, and environmental program. We are able to analyze by business, type of plant, process, or geographical area. We believe this will allow us to continue progressing toward excellence in our health, safety, and environmental programs.

Paul D. Coulter is director of the compliance audit program at Union Carbide Corporation in Danbury, Connecticut. Since 1960, he has been particularly interested in the application of computers to solving problems. Currently, he is involved in using computers in compliance audit scheduling, classifying, deficiency analysis, report preparation, action plan tracking, and related items in the audit program. He is a member of the American Chemical Society, the American Academy for the Advancement of Science, and the Environmental Auditing Roundtable.

Environmental Auditing and
Continuous Improvement at Lockheed

22

Mark C. Posson and Craig A. Barney

Continuous Improvement can be applied to every business function, including environmental auditing. The benefits of customer focus and performance measurement are realized in a more efficient business system and a higher level of environmental compliance. Lockheed has successfully used Continuous Improvement principles in the development and implementation of its environmental auditing program, which are described in this chapter.

Lockheed Missiles and Space Company, Inc. (LMSC) recognizes that internal audits are essential to a comprehensive environmental quality and protection program. Environmental audits at LMSC provide an internal review of the practices and procedures of manufacturing, research, and support operations located at facilities throughout the United States.

Customers of the audit program are divided into three broad groups: company management, audited unit manager and employees, and Environmental Protection Programs (EPP). The primary purposes of the audit program are to facilitate compliance with environmental laws, regulations, and company policies, and to effectively reduce the potential for environmental impairment, penalties, or adverse publicity. The program scope includes evaluation of broad environmental management practices with a focus on hazardous waste management, air and water quality protection, and hazardous material storage and handling requirements.

LMSC's program includes total quality management principles (Continuous Improvement (CI) is the LMSC vernacular) in program development, implementation, and evaluation. The use of CI principles accelerates program development and implementation, provides a measure of customer satisfaction, and sets improvement targets.

Developing the Program

The development of our program includes evaluation of broad environmental management practices with a focus on five major activities:

1. Identify and prioritize risks of noncompliance.

2. Establish the framework for the program.
3. Write the audit protocols.
4. Prioritize operations by risk and develop the schedule.
5. Practice Continuous Improvement activities.

In the early developmental stages, we recognized the need for focusing our program on activities that posed the greatest compliance risks. The primary focus of the audit is determined by considering LMSC's compliance history, previous internal reviews, and regulatory agency priorities as reflected by recent California enforcement trends.

After identifying the risks, we developed three parallel activities:

1. Establish the framework for the program;
2. Write the audit protocols; and
3. Prioritize operations by risk and develop the schedule.

The first parallel activity established the program framework, which included a description of the exception categories, the format and use of checklists, the timing and format of reports, the nature and timing of required response, the procedures for agreeing on corrective action, and the systems for tracking closure.

Our benchmarking activities at this stage were crucial and involved a dual approach: Lockheed internal audits and world-class companies in environmental auditing. After reviewing the well-established and successful program of Lockheed Corporation for internal audits, we developed a list of questions regarding the specifics of environmental auditing. This step provided us with valuable insight into which audit methods to apply and helped us avoid many of the problems experienced in new audit programs. We then met with technical and management personnel from world-class companies in environmental auditing. We offered our ideas about applying internal audit protocols to environmental auditing and received valuable insights concerning the methods used by these companies. Finally, the framework was presented to our customers, the LMSC environmental professionals and representatives from manufacturing units, as a "straw man" for their comments and recommendations. As a result of the benchmarking and early customer involvement, the framework has contributed to exceptional program performance.

The second parallel activity was developing the audit checklists. A critical part of any audit program is consistency of review and reporting. The checklists serve as the basis of the audit and contain the key elements of the compliance programs. In developing the checklists, we built on what was available from sources, such as the California Environmental Protection Agency and other companies such as automobile, semiconductor, and computer manufacturing. Suggestions for the format and use of checklists were obtained from auditor training classes, standard text-books, and benchmarked companies. In addition, we added a unique element of expertise to the process by teaming with Lockheed's internal audit professionals, who are instrumental in helping us to understand the standards, practices, and ethics of a good audit program. The product of this activity is a company document describing the procedures and responsibilities for the auditor and audited organization.

In selecting operating units to be audited, our objective is to select those units which present the greatest exposure for noncompliance. We prioritize the operating units to be audited by calculating the percent contributed by each organization to the total amount of waste generated and to the number of permitted sources of air emissions. The potential risk of noncompliance is closely related to these factors. We critically review the operations in areas that pose special risks such as solvent cleaning, photo processing, and coatings operations.

Satisfying Customer Expectations

Quality is defined as the perceived value by our customers of our support and services. The success of the audit program is critically dependent on "buy-in" by our three customer groups: upper management, the audited unit, and Environmental Protection Programs. We believe company management and the audited unit are the primary customers of the program, and the needs of these customers are fundamentally different. Company management wants a periodic compliance "snapshot" and a description of trends that need to be addressed at a higher level. This summary-level information allows upper management to identify the companywide actions they can reinforce to assure compliance. The manager of the audited unit wants to have specific exceptions brought to his or her attention so that prompt corrective action can be implemented to prevent future recurrence. This requires detail-oriented findings focused on the unit's compliance programs.

For the audited managers, we provide immediate feedback to their employees as soon as an exception is noted during the audit. In most cases, the item is immediately correctable. The responsible supervisor receives a handwritten "exception report" on the same day the deficiency is discovered. In addition, we offer a daily debriefing to the manager, which provides feedback concerning daily activities, opportunity to request additional clarification, and discussion of noted exceptions.

At the conclusion of the audit work, a closing conference is held with the unit manager to present a draft report containing a compliance summary, details of all exceptions, and an explanation of the required written response. Each item is discussed at the closing conference to correct any factual errors and to agree on corrective action. If requested, the auditors provide recommendations on corrective actions based on what has worked in other operations. This service satisfies the audited manager's needs by providing compliance help, and meets upper management and EPP needs by establishing the responsibility of the audited manager for corrective action.

To meet upper management's needs, the audit data are periodically summarized using broad categories representing the major areas reviewed during the audits. The presentation concludes with a discussion of the major issues and recommendations for improvement.

Developing Audit Metrics

Audit results are difficult to quantify and measure due to the variability of risk areas and the severity of exceptions. Audit data do not lend themselves to routine measurement as in manufacturing. Manufacturing measures how many products are produced per unit effort, whereas audits measure how many potential compliance deficiencies are noted and corrected. The customer does not receive a tangible product such as an electronic part, but rather gains assistance and information. In addition, not all audit findings are comparable. Noted exceptions may engender vastly different potential liabilities, depending on the type and prevalence of exceptions, and the nature of the audited unit. Audit results, however, must be quantified and measured if companies hope to improve business systems.

We divide audit data into two distinct types: (1) elements that can be analyzed using "hard divisors" and (2) elements that must be analyzed using "soft divisors." Employee training and container labeling fall into the first category, compliance with permit conditions and performing self-inspections into the second. For example, one can calculate the deficiency rate for findings with a hard divisor, thus:

56 training records examined, 1 person had not completed training.
$1/56 = 1.8\%$ deficient, or

85 hazardous waste drums inspected, 3 incomplete labels.
$3/85 = 3.5\%$ deficient

For items with no hard divisor, like self-inspections, we calculate:

83 audits performed, 3 operations evidenced some type of deficiency.
$3/83 = 3.6\%$ deficient

The use of soft divisors accounts for the fact that not all deficiencies, with respect to compliance systems like self-inspections, are alike, and that the sizes of audited organizations greatly vary.

In order to make a more precise comparison, we have devised and are evaluating a scoring system. We determined that the self-inspection program is essential to LMSC's compliance; subsequently, a way to score the completeness of programs implemented in different organizations has been devised. As in Olympic gymnastics, each organization starts with ten points and loses points for specific deficiencies. As an example, deficiencies with respect to hazardous waste requirements are weighted fivefold with respect to hazardous materials requirements to reflect the difference in potential liabilities. We are evaluating such a scoring system to compare the degree of compliance with all the requirements of a comprehensive self inspection program, and to determine which elements are the greatest cause of exceptions.

The Customer Survey

A critical element of our CI program is the direct measurement of customer satisfaction. For our audit program, we use a customer survey to measure our performance in six critical areas: (1) advance audit information, (2) anticipated usefulness, (3) opening conference, (4) closing conference, (5) improvements made by the audited organization, and (6) auditor effectiveness.

The managers are asked to rate the program on a scale of 1 to 7 and to provide comments. Our response rate for completed surveys is about 70 percent. The responses are analyzed by calculating the average, median, and mode for each question. To determine the potential improvement targets with the greatest effect on the program, we used two analytical tools taken from our CI toolbox: the gap analysis and the interrelationship diagram. These tools provided valuable insight regarding the meaning of the numerical data. The average responses for each question are charted on a radar chart against the perfect score (gap analysis). The chart demonstrates that our system needed improvement in the areas of the initial contact and the opening conference.

We then can draw the interrelationship diagram (ID), which is used to determine the steps in the process that have the greatest effect on others and, by inference, on the overall audit program. By using the ID, we have discovered that the "initial contact" affects the greatest number of other systems in the program. When the ID was compared to the results of the gap analysis, we determined that we could best improve our program by enhancing the initial contact: both the phone call and the announcement letter sent to the manager prior to the audit.

The data also show that, by the end of the process, most responders are more satisfied with the results than they had anticipated. The surveys provide a direct measure of customer satisfaction and the results have shown improvement.

Mark C. Posson is the manager of environmental protection programs at Lockheed Missiles and Space Company, Inc., and teaches Principles of Hazardous Materials Management at the University of California, Davis, and the University of California, Berkeley. **Craig A. Barney** is an environmental and safety specialist for Lockheed Missiles and Space Company. His responsibilities include developing and implementing the internal environmental audit program for all LMSC locations.

Preparing Quality Audit Reports: Ten Steps (and Some Leaps) to Improve Auditing

23

Lawrence B. Cahill

Good writing is never easy, but it is critical to the effectiveness of environmental audit reports. This chapter discusses ten issues to consider while producing audit reports that will enhance a company's quality effort.

"Writing is easy. All you do is stare at a blank sheet of paper until drops of blood form on your forehead." Sadly, this quote from Gene Fowler accurately describes the frequent desperation involved in writing an environmental (health and safety) audit report. It is the most difficult part of the entire audit process. Yet, the report is the cornerstone of any audit program.

There has been much written on developing effective environmental audit reports. And this is usually done with some trepidation. Authoring an article on how to write effective audit reports is a bit like giving a speech on how to be an effective speaker. Anything but perfection will not be tolerated.

Notwithstanding this heart-felt reservation, this article examines ten issues that need to be considered when developing an audit report that will enhance a company's overall quality effort. These are issues that never quite go away, no matter how many reports are written or how often the frustrated audit team leader refers an auditor to Strunk and White's classic writer's guidebook, *The Elements of Style.*

1. Keep the Customer in Mind.

One of the key tenets of Total Quality Management, "keeping the customer in mind," is often forgotten in the heat of the battle. Audit reports should be written principally for the site management, those responsible for correcting the deficiencies.

Yes, there are other customers. Senior management should have a sense of whether they have a problem site on their hands after reading the executive summary. And there should indeed be an executive summary, for quite often that is all some reviewers will read.

But the body of the report, the findings, must be written so that the reader both understands the nature of the problem and can readily envision a corrective action. Thus, when the team leader reviews the report, he or she should ask, for every finding, do I understand the problem well enough to know how to fix it? If the answer is yes, then the auditor has done the job of serving the customer.

2. Organize for Monitoring.

Many reports are rambling narratives in which it is difficult to sort background information from the findings. This does little to help the site or to allow for later tracking of corrective actions.

The audit report should be organized so that the findings are broken out, listed, and codified. It is usually best to list only findings that are deficiencies. It makes little sense to codify a finding that requires no corrective action. If positive findings are listed, there will be a numbering gap in the sequencing of corrective actions that can confuse those responsible for managing the closeout process. Save the positive findings and commendable items for the executive summary.

One company, Hoechst Celanese, assigns each finding of each report a two-field numerical code, which includes the year of the audit and the number of the finding. When coupled with a code for the plant that was audited, this allows for computerized tracking of the closure of all findings. This "closure" step is critical to the success of a program. In my independent reviews of audit programs, problems with the management of the findings' follow-up and closure system are one of the most commonly observed deficiencies.

3. Pay Attention to Repeat Findings.

The handling of findings that remain uncorrected from the previous audit is quite a challenge for most programs. Many lawyers will argue, rightfully, that labeling them as repeat findings in the audit report creates added liabilities for the organization. Yet, for senior managers, it is important to know if documented problems are being corrected. Some would say that not knowing whether problems are being fixed is an even greater liability than documenting repeat findings, and I would tend to agree.

DuPont has a specific and proactive policy regarding repeat findings. The policy calls for auditors to pay particular attention to uncorrected problems identified in the previous audit. In classifying these findings, auditors are asked to consider assigning them a higher risk priority than otherwise would be the case.

4. Be Clear and Precise.

The importance of writing clear and precise audit reports and findings has been discussed at length in the classical audit texts. Here, the intent is to reinforce the importance of the topic and to suggest an approach to writing findings that can help achieve a quality product. Most audit findings can be broken up into three components: the situation, the requirement, and the reference. A sample finding written in this format is presented below:

The Situation: At the ninety-day hazardous waste accumulation point in Building 27, there was one drum with an open-top funnel containing waste solvents.

The Requirement: RCRA requires that containers holding hazardous waste be closed except when adding or removing waste.

Reference: 40 CFR 265.173(a)

Each finding does not have to be organized with the three headings listed as shown. But the intent of the organization is to precisely describe the situation so that the reader could readily go to the location in question (Building 27) and locate the deficiency (the drum with the funnel). This helps the customer solve the immediate problem.

Paraphrasing the requirement helps the site staff understand what is needed and listing the reference allows them to conduct additional research if necessary. With a little more effort, even management systems findings can be handled in this way.

5. Be Careful of "Good Practices."

Most audit programs classify findings into one of three types: regulatory, company policy, or good management practice (GMP), sometimes also called good engineering practice or observations. In my experience, difficulty often arises in crafting effective GMP findings.

I have observed hour-long discussions (or, more precisely, arguments) between the audit team and site management over the validity of a single GMP finding. The discussion usually centers on the justification for the finding. When the auditor says "that's the way we do it at our site" or "we will accept nothing less than best-practice procedures," this usually raises the hair on the back of the site manager's neck.

There is a place for GMPs in an audit report. Regulations or company policies do not always address all practices that might pose a risk to the organization. However, there needs to be solid justification for each GMP finding.

One way to develop that justification is to frame GMP findings in the same way as suggested in point 4 above. What is the situation? And what is the requirement (e.g., protection of groundwater)? Too often, GMP findings begin with phrases such as: "The site should..." or "The site needs to..." These are *not* findings; they are really "soft" recommendations. This is the trap that many auditors fall into, crafting GMP findings as recommendations with no supporting justification.

6. Set Priorities.

Not all findings are created equal. Some are more important than others. Thus, it is usually helpful to categorize findings by significance. Some companies do this by bringing forward the most important findings into the executive summary. In other cases, individual findings are classified by level of significance. This can, of course, create headaches for the legal profession, but it can be a valuable tool for management.

Some organizations (e.g., the U.S. Air Force) use a classification system suggested by the U.S. EPA in its Federal Facilities Compliance Strategy. This results in a three-tiered classification, as follows:

Significant. A problem categorized as significant requires immediate action. It poses, or has a high likelihood to pose, a direct and immediate threat to human health, safety, the environment, or the installation mission. Some administrative issues can be categorized as significant. For example, failure to ensure that hazardous waste is destined for a permitted facility, failure to report when required, and failure to meet a compliance schedule are all significant deficiencies.

Major. A problem categorized as major requires action, but not necessarily immediately. This category of deficiencies usually results in a notice of violation from regulatory agencies. Major deficiencies may pose a future threat to human health, safety, or the environment. Immediate threats must be categorized as significant.

Minor. Minor deficiencies are mostly administrative in nature. They may involve temporary or occasional instances of noncompliance.

The above classification scheme can be helpful because the definitions are based on U.S. EPA's sense of significance, and it allows the auditor to highlight truly significant findings.

DuPont has taken this scheme and modified it to serve the purposes of its own environmental audit program. DuPont classifies its audit findings as follows:

Level I: Immediate Action Required. Situations that could result in substantial risk to the environment, the public, employees, stockholders, customers, the company or its reputation, or in criminal or civil liability for knowing violations.

Level II: Priority Action Required. Does not meet the criteria for Level I but is more than an isolated or occasional situation. Should not continue beyond the short term.

Level III: Action Required. Findings may be administrative in nature or involve an isolated or occasional situation.

This classification has been helpful in setting facility action priorities within DuPont. No matter what approach is used, however, there should be some way to establish priorities among findings and to truly highlight those items that are in need of immediate attention.

7. De-emphasize Numbers.

Total Quality Management principles suggest that "numerical quotas should be eliminated." In the context of an audit report, this suggests that one has to be very careful how the *number* of findings are handled within the organization. It seems that no matter what is said or done, line managers, and others, have a tendency to add up the findings and compare. This is neither a meaningful nor constructive exercise and should be discouraged by senior management.

It is near impossible to make effective performance evaluations by solely keeping track of the number of findings. First, individual site situations, even within the same class of facility, differ greatly due to such factors as the surrounding area (e.g., wetlands, non-attainment areas) and the regulatory stringency of the state in which the facility is located.

Second, audit teams differ in composition and makeup. Based on many of my own training experiences, one can send two different audit teams to the same location and have them audit something as straightforward as an accumulation point and wind up with a wide variance in the number of findings.

And third, as audit programs have evolved over the past few years, there has been a movement toward evaluating management systems. This has resulted in the "rolling up" of individual compliance findings into an overall system finding. This makes comparisons over time even more difficult.

In sum, using the number of audit findings as a measure of performance is fraught with problems. As an alternative, some companies have asked audit teams to classify the site overall. A sample ranking system, based in part on a scheme sometimes used by financial auditors, might be to classify the site as follows:

- Good
- Qualified
- Needs improvement
- Unacceptable

This approach is more compelling, although each of the classifications would have to be defined.

8. Accept No Mistakes.

Not much needs to be said here. Audit reports should be mistake-free. Even the smallest typographical error should not be allowed, not even in a draft report. In fact, in the audit business, much like the consulting business, there is really no such thing as a draft report. If it is to be sent to the client or customer it should be considered final, no matter if words like draft or preliminary are used.

Every report should have a third-party review by someone not on the audit team. Also, do not rely solely on word processor software "spell checks" to eliminate all typos; they will not. A human must conduct the final check.

And based on experience, it is better to take the heat for a report being a day or two late than to take it for it being sloppy. It is quite interesting that people will remember that report with all the typos for ten years and will forget the perfect report within a month.

9. Remove Barriers to Efficiency.

Auditors must be given the tools to be able to develop a quality report. This would include a sample audit report to be used as a guide. Many companies, such as Kodak, have also developed a separate audit report-writing guide, which typically includes a discussion of the writing process and pitfalls to avoid and a report with sample findings. Kodak has gone one step further and has developed a database of over one thousand written findings from past reports codified by category, which assist auditors in the field. Also, in-field use of laptop computers has done much to improve the efficiency of the process. Draft reports can now be developed on the fly.

10. Train the Auditors.

Train, train, and retrain! All auditors should receive formal training before they embark on their first audit. And a good part of this training should be on report writing or, at minimum, on the writing of individual findings. Providing a new auditor with on-the-job training in writing findings at 11:00 p.m. the night before the report is due is no fun. Unfortunately, this happens all too frequently. Preparing a quality audit report is a most difficult task. It takes time and effort to make it lucid. The effort, however, is well worth it. The report is *the* decision-making document for the environmental audit program.

Lawrence B. Cahill is a senior program director with ERM, Inc., and the author of *Environmental Audits*, now in its sixth edition, published by Government Institutes, Inc. Mr. Cahill has over fifteen years of experience in all aspects of environmental auditing and he has trained people worldwide in auditing skills. **Note:** Any discussion in this article of a company's individual environmental audit program is based on information provided to the public at large through technical papers, presentations, and the like.

Evaluating Your Environmental Audit—Moving beyond Band-Aids in Developing Corrective Actions

24

Gilbert S. Hedstrom and Roger W. Voeller

Although audit programs have helped companies make big improvements in performance, more progress is still necessary and available. In this chapter the authors show how still bigger improvements are possible by expanding the corrective action process and utilizing total quality principles in developing corrective actions and evaluating company performance. With sufficient knowledge about the nature of its problems, not just the degree of its problems, a company should be able to rethink its basic management approaches and achieve dramatic improvements in performance.

Environmental auditing has experienced significant growth and evolution over the last decade as senior managers and corporate environmental managers have recognized the audit as a key component of a company's environmental management system. Today, hundreds of companies in North America and, increasingly, in Europe and Asia, have formal environmental, health, and safety audit programs in place. Typically, these programs are designed to provide a company assurance that its operations are being managed in accordance with government standards and corporate policies. As a result, audit programs have helped companies:

- Pinpoint areas for immediate correction
- Determine how successfully a facility is managing its environmental responsibilities
- Compare facilities
- Make a "snapshot" of the operation and effectiveness of environmental management systems
- Decide whether or not environmental performance is improving year to year

Environmental auditing has enabled many companies to assess their environmental performance, correct deficiencies, and reduce their overall risk—especially the risk of noncompliance with key governmental regulations.

Despite enormous progress developing and implementing audit programs, many corporate and plant environmental management personnel are not yet comfortable with their answers to questions such as these:

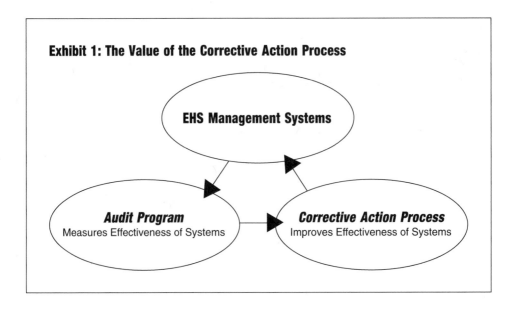

Exhibit 1: The Value of the Corrective Action Process

EHS Management Systems

Audit Program
Measures Effectiveness of Systems

Corrective Action Process
Improves Effectiveness of Systems

- Do reaudits find the same, or similar, problems?
- Do similar problems show up again at the same facility? Do different facilities share common problems?
- Are a plant's corrective actions fixing only the symptoms, or are they also getting at the root causes behind recurring problems?
- Is senior management satisfied with its overall environmental record?

In our work assessing company audit programs and evaluating overall environmental performance, we are beginning to sense some discomfort regarding these questions. We have begun seeing a disconnection between the environmental audit program and continuing improvements in environmental management systems. Companies that find their audit programs most valuable understand the key relationship between environmental audits and a successful corrective action process in improving environmental performance (**Exhibit 1**). In other words, an environmental audit program is only as good as the company's success in identifying the root cause of each audit finding and then taking the "right" corrective action.

As corporate environmental audit programs and overall environmental management systems mature, the focus of the audit program tends to shift. When a company first establishes its environmental auditing program, the focus is on identifying problems to be corrected (**Exhibit 2**). As the audit program evolves, the emphasis moves from identifying problems to determining compliance status, and then on to assessing the effectiveness of the environmental management control systems. Thus, as a company's environmental performance improves, the empha-

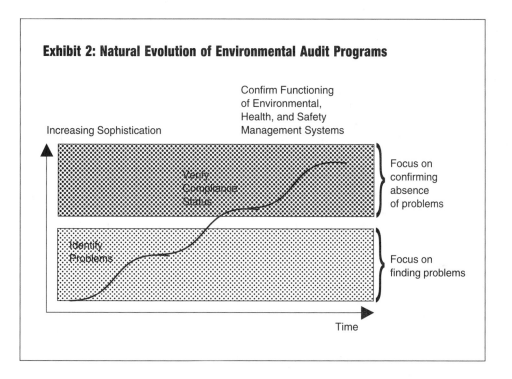

Exhibit 2: Natural Evolution of Environmental Audit Programs

Increasing Sophistication

Confirm Functioning
of Environmental,
Health, and Safety
Management Systems

Verify Compliance Status

Focus on confirming absence of problems

Identify Problems

Focus on finding problems

Time

sis should shift from identifying problems to confirming the absence of problems—a much more difficult task. The most significant benefits from a well-established audit program are successful environmental performance and a feeling of increased comfort and security that environmental risks are being managed.

A similar evolution should occur in how companies act on the results of their audits. In the early stages of audit programs, immediate attention is given to fixing the problems identified. In some cases, companies develop sophisticated tracking tools to ensure that such corrective actions do, in fact, occur. A more comprehensive approach, not yet taken by many companies, is to analyze the problems identified during the audit for cause and effect and develop and implement appropriate corrective actions for those underlying causes. Those companies that simply stick to fixing the problem may not achieve the performance desired and may even begin to consider their audit programs to be ineffective.

When performance improvements are not quickly forthcoming after implementation of an audit program, some companies blame the program itself for being ineffective. It may well be, however, that the focus of such blame should be placed on the corrective action process. Unfortunately, many companies have little experience in analyzing the corrective action process or the effectiveness of the corrective actions implemented, despite their relative sophistication in gauging the audit program's ability to find the problems.

Expanding Corrective Action Planning

In order to successfully correct problems, keep the problems corrected. And head off finding the same problems in other facilities by expanding the corrective action process (**Exhibit 3**). In this expanded model for corrective action, audit findings are evaluated for underlying causes, and corrective actions are focused on developing management solutions to such root causes. Frequently, when findings are grouped for commonality, it is possible to identify common root causes. When the focus of corrective actions is on correcting common root causes, the effectiveness of the audit is increased tremendously.

The expanded corrective action process can be applied at any level—plant, division, or overall corporation. We rarely find that the root cause for serious facility problems stops at the plant gate; it usually extends upward into the division or corporate parent.

There are many different ways to enhance the corrective action planning process. One method we have used successfully is to group findings in categories built on the following phases in a simple model for corporate risk management:

- Identify hazards and evaluate risks
- Develop control programs
- Implement control programs
- Maintain and oversee programs

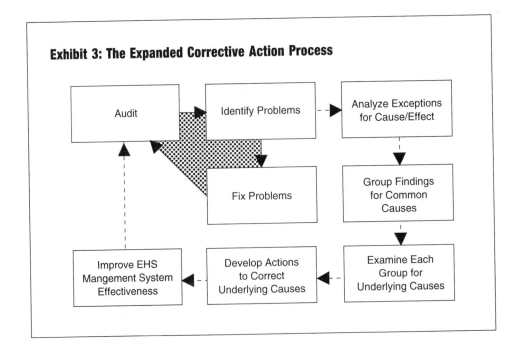

Exhibit 3: The Expanded Corrective Action Process

By placing problems identified during an audit or audit program into such risk categories, it may be possible to see patterns in the findings, which can then help to focus corrective actions. The results of such groupings can help to answer the following questions:

- Are facility or corporate personnel aware of requirements?
- Are control programs missing important elements? If so, why?
- What prevents full implementation of control programs, even when the program itself seems sound?
- Do plants have internal measurement processes to continually gauge the effectiveness of their programs?

In fact, grouping findings into categories like the four phases described above can provide one of the simplest methods for evaluating overall company performance, for making comparisons between facilities, and for measuring facility improvement. Audit program managers are always looking for ways to use audit results more broadly. It is not uncommon for senior management to fall into the trap of making year-to-year and facility-to-facility comparisons by counting the number of findings in an audit. Counting findings does not do it, however, because no two findings typically carry the same risk. On the other hand, if most findings at a facility are weighted toward Phase I (identify and evaluate), it may say a lot about the facility's overall environmental risk management systems (no programs!).

Applying Total Quality Management Tools

This expansion of the corrective action planning process lends itself well to Total Quality Management approaches. We have found that some of the traditional TQM tools can be useful in helping companies get at the root of the problems they identify through their audits. Nominal group and brainstorming techniques are helpful in setting priorities for the identified problems and for delving into issues of cause and effect. A fishbone diagram can help to array all possible causes of a problem, and other TQM tools such as the Pareto chart, run chart, histogram, and scatter diagram can help in the "investigative" process.

For example, the fishbone diagram can be introduced to begin brainstorming about possible breakdowns in the environmental management system—whether, for example, the causes of breakdowns relate to programs and procedures, people, equipment, or materials. In our example on hazardous waste violations (**Exhibit 4**), we can see that "materials" is not likely to be the largest problem area, while "people" or some combination of "people," "programs/procedures," and "equipment" may be.

Once arrayed, each of these problem areas can be considered against the four

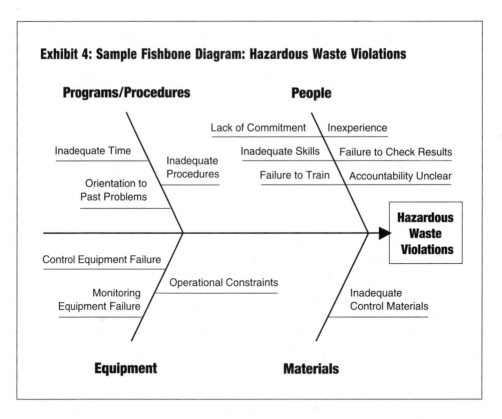

Exhibit 4: Sample Fishbone Diagram: Hazardous Waste Violations

Programs/Procedures   **People**

Lack of Commitment   Inexperience

Inadequate Time   Inadequate Skills   Failure to Check Results

Inadequate Procedures   Failure to Train   Accountability Unclear

Orientation to Past Problems

Hazardous Waste Violations

Control Equipment Failure

Operational Constraints

Monitoring Equipment Failure   Inadequate Control Materials

Equipment   **Materials**

phases of the risk management process and patterns begin to emerge. Our invented example (**Exhibit 5**) shows that this company has some serious problems in its failure to identify hazards and to develop controls. A company whose findings tend to fall into the first two categories is facing serious environmental risks and has probably not devoted sufficient resources companywide to managing its environmental responsibilities. In such cases, plant-level corrective actions must have a base of support at a high level in the company. On the other hand, when findings tend to fall into the two latter categories, problems are more likely to be facility specific, and corrective actions are more likely to focus on the individual facility.

Application of the Four-Phase Approach

This four-phase approach has been used quite successfully in a number of real world situations. One of our clients is a company which is managed horizontally, rather than vertically. This horizontal organization means that each facility is treated as a substantially independent entity with very little corporate oversight, other than in the financial arena. The company also strongly adheres to the principles of employee empowerment. Each site is managed by only a skeleton staff of salaried management personnel with several hourly employees taking on a great deal of management responsibilities.

Several environmental requirements apply to the company's plants.

As a result of a regulatory enforcement problem at one plant, this company chose to audit each of its plants. This company had been proud of its previous environmental record and was embarrassed by the enforcement action; it wanted to ensure that no similar problems existed elsewhere.

After completing audits at each facility, the audit teams brainstormed possible causes of the findings and placed each finding in one of the risk management categories mentioned earlier. **Exhibit 6** illustrates the pattern of findings for each environmental topic for one plant. **Exhibit 7** illustrates the pattern of findings for all plants within the topic of spill prevention and emergency response.

From the figures it is clear that this company's plants have problems identifying applicable requirements or risks and in developing effective control programs. When we discussed the problem with the company, it became apparent that much may be directly related to the company's horizontal management structure, where each plant was left to itself to identify complex regulatory requirements. In addition, the company had a general reluctance to get formal in its program development because of its strong culture of employee empowerment.

As a result of the audits, and perhaps more as a result of the evaluation, the company has taken steps

Exhibit 5: Sample Four-Phase Analysis: Hazardous Waste Violations

	Failure to Identify Hazards	Failure to Develop Controls	Failure to Implement Controls	Failure to Maintain/Oversee Program
1. Hazardous Waste Storage Tank				
2. Hazardous Waste Labeling	✓			
3. Waste Oil Management	✓	✓		
4. Hazardous Waste Manifests		✓		
5. Emergency Contact List	✓			✓
6. Emergency Response Plan	✓			
7. Hazardous Waste Transportation	✓	✓		

Exhibit 6: Evaluation of Environmental Audit Findings

Plant One	Failure to Identify and Evaluate Risk	Failure to Develop Complete Program	Failure to Implement Program	Failure to Maintain and Oversee Program
A. Air Pollution Control				
1. Recordkeeping and Monitoring		X	X	
2. Ambient Air Quality Monitoring	X			
3. NO Emissions from Coal Fired Boilers				X
4. Particulate Emissions			X	
5. Sulfur Content of Fuels	X			
B. Water Pollution Control				
1. Discharge Monitoring Reports	X			
2. Discharge Limit Compliance		X		
3. Recordkeeping for Underground Injection Wells		X		
C. Spill Control and Emergency Planning				
1. SPCC Plan	X			
2. Tank Truck Unloading Control	X			
3. Discharge of Accumulated Rainwater	X			
4. Recordkeeping of Past Spill Events				X
5. SARA III Reports			X	
D. Solid and Hazardous Waste Management				
1. Missing Manifest Reports	X			
2. Waste Minimization Program	X			
3. Ash Management				X
Percentage of Findings in Category	50	19	19	19

to correct its weakness at the root—not by abandoning its culture, but by developing corporatewide environmental programs that mesh with its culture.

Roles in Corrective Action Planning

Who should be involved in this expanded corrective action planning process? We believe that the expanded corrective action process can be most successful by soliciting input broadly. For example, the traditional role of the typical audit program has not included involvement by audit team members or program managers in the corrective action planning process. The audit program has been limited, frequently, to monitoring the status of corrections for the deficiencies noted dur-

Exhibit 6: Evaluation of Environmental Audit Findings

Companywide Spill Control and Emergency Planning	Failure to Identify and Evaluate Risk	Failure to Develop Complete Program	Failure to Implement Program	Failure to Maintain and Oversee Program
A. Plant One				
1. SPCC Plan				X
2. Tank Inspections		X		
3. Spill Control Training		X		
4. Secondary Containment	X			
5. Spill Control Equipment			X	
6. Emergency Planning Notifications	X			
7. Tier Two forms	X			
B. Plant Two				
1. SPCC Plan	X			
2. Fuel Unloading Control			X	
3. Tank Integrity Testing			X	
4. Spill Reporting	X			
5. Stormwater Management	X			
6. Storage of Incompatible Materials	X			
7. Emergency Coordinator Responsibility				
C. Plant Three				
1. SPCC Plan	X			
2. Tank Truck Unloading Control	X			
3. Discharge of Accumulated Rainwater	X			
4. Record keeping of Past Spill Events				X
5. SARA III Reports			X	
D. Plant Four				
1. SPCC Plan	X			
2. Secondary Containment				X
Percentage of Findings in Category	57	10	19	14

ing the audit. It has been established wisdom that those involved in managing the facility program know far better than an audit team how a problem should be corrected in their facility. This conventional wisdom, however, may no longer be valid.

As audit programs become well established, those involved accumulate a wealth of knowledge and experience in managing environmental issues, which can and should be shared in developing corrective actions. In addition, a thorough audit process includes development of a detailed understanding of facility management systems. This independent understanding may be very valuable to a facility in identifying and evaluating root causes for problems. In developing the audit report, the audit team itself could analyze findings for root causes, based on the understanding of management systems developed by the team during the audit. The team's understanding of possible root causes can be provided in closing meetings or in the audit report or both.

In some companies, facility management already applies Total Quality Management principles in developing their corrective actions to specific audit findings. Such approaches can lead to dramatic improvements in the overall effectiveness of corrective actions if the various environmental customer/supplier relationships in a plant are brought together in developing corrective actions. In bringing everyone into the process, it is more likely that workable, creative solutions will be found. For example, in some manufacturing facilities environmental problems can be mitigated through aggressive waste minimization or pollution prevention programs. In order to be successful, such programs require the full support of the manufacturing supervisors and the work force, and representatives from such groups should be involved in the process. Depending on the specific problems to be corrected, representatives to the expanded corrective action process may include staff from transportation functions, financial functions, production planning, and others.

Likewise, audit results from many different plants can be evaluated at the company level to help determine companywide root causes and develop appropriate

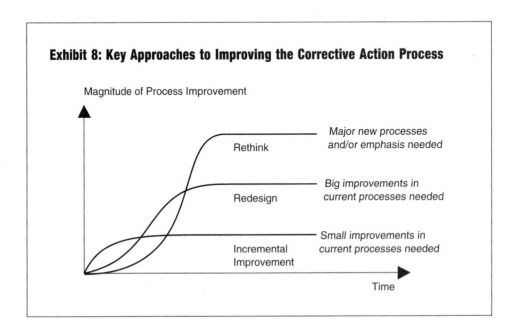

Exhibit 8: Key Approaches to Improving the Corrective Action Process

companywide solutions. Weighting factors can be placed on the phases in the risk management model to help develop an improved company perspective of its overall performance. And much of this can be done without a great deal of sophisticated effort or modeling. Identifying problems can help determine whether the gains a company is seeking in its environmental performance should come from incremental improvements or from rethinking its management systems.

Rethinking Environmental Management

The degree of improvement in environmental performance can be seen as resulting from three alternative approaches inherent in a company's approach to developing and implementing corrective actions (**Exhibit 8**). *Incremental improvements* result from small changes to current management systems or control methods. This approach may be helpful at first for fixing problems, but over time it will reach a level of diminishing returns. Larger performance improvements result from *redesign* of the management system—likely resulting in relatively high returns with low risk. The greatest returns, however, come from *rethink* approaches—that is, significant new processes designed at higher initial cost and risk, but highly rewarding when successful. The expanded corrective action planning model is more likely to lead companies to develop corrective actions for audit findings that are *redesign/rethink* oriented than has been typical in the past.

Gilbert S. Hedstrom is a vice president of Arthur D. Little and managing director of the firm's Environmental, Health, and Safety Consulting Practice. He has responsibility for the company's work in environmental, health, and safety auditing; environmental and risk management; and environmental business strategy. He is a past member of the first board of directors of the Environmental Auditing Roundtable and is currently serving a third term on the board. He is a principal author of *Environmental Auditing; Fundamentals* and *Techniques* and *The Environmental, Health, and Safety Auditor's Handbook*. **Roger W. Voeller** is a senior consultant in Arthur D. Little's Environmental, Health, and Safety Auditing Practice and has participated in over fifty environmental audits, many as team leader. In addition to field work, Mr. Voeller has developed audit programs for corporate and government clients, provided training in auditing skills and techniques, and reviewed existing programs.

25

RCRA Inspections and Enforcement

Gabriel G. Crognale

EPA continues to issue ever-increasing fines to violators of the Resource Conservation and Recovery Act (RCRA), the Clean Water Act (CWA), the Clean Air Act (CAA), the Toxic Substances Control Act (TSCA), the Occupational Safety and Health Act (OSHA), and others, in a concerted effort to keep handlers in compliance with the respective federal regulations. This chapter focuses on how RCRA inspections are prioritized, planned, and conducted, and how such inspections may lead to enforcement actions to return RCRA handlers to compliance. To provide some insight into the inspector's agenda, the "FY94 RCRA Implementation Plan" (RIP) will be discussed in some detail.

With the advent of the next generation of enforcement initiatives converging on the affected industries—i.e., the regulated communities subject to the various environmental and health and safety regulations—companies and facilities need to keep abreast of these initiatives as one of the new costs of doing business in today's dynamic business environment.

In RCRA civil and criminal matters, both the revised RCRA Civil Penalty Policy (RCPP) and the revised U.S. Sentencing Guidelines for environmental criminals have combined for consistently higher penalties being issued to RCRA handlers. On August 24, 1993, the *Wall Street Journal* reported that EPA's Region I fined United Technologies $5.3 million for a series of abuses in handling and discharging hazardous wastes in recent years. And in a similar situation, reported in the September 11, 1992, *Hazardous Materials Intelligence Report*, Dexter Corporation entered into a $13 million settlement for various RCRA and CWA violations.

These two examples help to reinforce the idea that EPA is determined to convey to the regulated community that enforcement action penalties can no longer be perceived as "the cost of doing business."

While the agency, and to some degree, state agencies, continue to issue more stringent enforcement actions to companies for noncompliance with the regulations, EPA is also striving to make pollution prevention more commonplace within the regulated community. Such an example is EPA's Interim Final Waste Minimization Guidelines (Fed. Reg. May 28, 1993). These guidelines spell out a six-point program to commit generators of hazardous wastes into certifying they have a waste minimization program in place under RCRA in an effort to reduce the volume and toxicity of hazardous wastes to an extent that is economically practical. Projecting forward, this could very well become an enforceable "bean" in a subsequent fiscal year (FY) RCRA Implementation Plan (RIP), as the guidelines allow for a program implementation and evaluation that can be readily tracked by enforcement databases.

EPA has at its disposal an array of databases to facilitate this tracking. For any given RCRA handler, the results of an inspection (or a complaint) will ultimately be logged as data for any one or all of the following: RCRIS (Resource Conservation and Recovery Information System) (replaces HWDMS), CM&E (Compliance Monitoring and Enforcement) Informed Form (replaces CMEL), GIS (Geographic Information System) if the handler is undergoing groundwater monitoring, and the IDEA (Integrated Data for Enforcement Initiatives) System.

It is very likely that EPA, with these tracking tools, can keep good tabs on a RCRA handler once an inspector (actually a data specialist) has input the inspection's findings into the system. Of course, the likelihood that such findings may prompt an enforcement response will depend on the severity of the regulatory findings, the handler's compliance history, and other factors. These will be discussed in greater detail below.

The RIP—Outline for the Inspector

EPA's Office of Enforcement developed the FY94 RIP to define national policy and strategic goals and to delineate priority activities. The underlying themes of each of these EPA efforts directed toward the regulated community are the promotion of waste minimization initiatives, the sustaining of environmentally sound waste management practices, and reducing risks of releases of hazardous wastes and/or materials.

In an effort to attain these goals and guide further implementation, EPA and the states initiated a strategic management framework (SMF) in FY92. At that time, EPA and the states began a systematic environmental priority ranking of treatment/storage and disposal facilities (TSDFs), evaluated the appropriate prevention and cleanup measures at the high-priority (HP) facilities, and set about to account for visible results in meeting the goals of the SMF.

Among the noteworthy objectives of the FY94 RIP are priority setting, compliance monitoring, and enforcement. Priority setting evaluates both environmental significance and environmental benefits for each handler in question. Specifically, the environmental significance must be determined for land disposal facilities (LDFs), incinerators, TSDFs, and other solid waste management units (SWMUs). Each HP facility identified as part of the SMF must also be reflected in STARS (Strategic Targeted Activities Results System) and other tracking measures. This is a crucial point because the core of RCRA's focus, as EPA sees it, is to address HP facilities first.

Continuing further, compliance monitoring and enforcement of each identified handler helps to target future multimedia inspections, and provides handlers an opportunity to implement and practice pollution prevention/waste minimization activities within their normal business practices.

Looking at the RCRA core program as a whole, it is the intent of both EPA's regions and the states to

- Maintain a visible enforcement and compliance presence
- Determine the environmental significance of facilities
- Maintain both statutory and other RCRA program commitments
- Conduct compliance monitoring
- Ensure enforcement
- Return facilities to compliance

Planning the Inspection

In a typical RCRA inspection, the inspector usually has at his or her disposal a series of enforcement tools with which to plan the inspection. These include the FY94 RIP, EPA's enforcement response policy, agency operating guidance, and policy memoranda. These tools serve to clarify enforcement issues within EPA and provide overall enforcement guidance and contribute to developing the RIP each fiscal year.

In planning the inspections, the inspector may refer to one or all of a series of in-house databases to help prioritize which environmentally significant handlers should be inspected first. During this process, the EPA inspector may consider state referrals and/or complaints. In this fashion, an otherwise low-priority handler could be subject to an inspection, depending on the circumstances. Any of this information also may prompt the initiation of a multimedia inspection.

As an example, an accident occurred at a RCRA handler several years ago in which two workers were killed when the drum they were using to mix solvents exploded, possibly as a result of improper grounding of the drum. That handler was soon afterwards investigated by EPA's Office of Criminal Investigations, with the help of several EPA inspectors from various media programs. The inspectors' findings at this handler did not point to criminal activity. This case was subsequently referred to OSHA for further investigation of employee safety and health issues in the workplace.

Conducting the Inspection—What the Inspector Looks For

That case aside, which was an exception, (known) environmentally significant handlers are still EPA's highest priority. As previously mentioned, these include LDFs, incinerators, TSDFs and other SWMUs.

At each of these handlers, the inspector's objective is to view and evaluate sufficient on-site information. The inspections can be announced or unannounced,

EPA- or state-led or joint, single- or multi-media, and, most importantly, either civil or criminal.

The inspector uses a combination of two methodologies, the walk-through and the records review, to achieve the stated objective.

During the walk-through, the inspector may wish to see

- Hazardous waste storage area(s)
- "Satellite" accumulation points
- Process area(s), noting waste stream(s) generated
- The entire site
- On-site waste treatment or pretreatment area(s)
- Hazardous materials storage area(s) and any other pertinent area(s)

During the records review, the inspector may concentrate on

- Contingency/personnel training plans
- Job descriptions and documentation of employee training
- In-house inspection logs or other regulatory tracking systems
- Hazardous waste manifests, LDR forms, and other shipping papers
- Waste minimization and biennial reports
- General TSD requirements
- Targeting specific employees for subsequent interviews

The interview process may provide insight to both the facility representative and the inspector as it may provide clarification or help explain situations noted by the inspector. For example, the inspector may note a full, unlabeled drum in an area where chemicals are used, and may reasonably suspect this to contain hazardous wastes, and note it as a possible RCRA violation.

During an employee's interview, that issue may be raised by the inspector. Thus, having the information on hand to explain the contents of that drum can make the difference as to whether it becomes a violation or not. In any other situation, a good facility environmental representative should have any questionable regulatory issues resolved *before* they become violations, and if disagreements with the inspector occur, they should be resolved in a professional manner. If they can't, the facts should be documented and forwarded via certified mail to the inspector's section chief for resolution.

Tips for a Company to Protect Itself

Presuming the inspector has found one's particular facility in good compliance order, this is the time to improve on the RCRA compliance program, not after a scathing EPA administrative order. The program's environmental manager, in concert with plant management, should take the time to evaluate the program, assess the program's strengths and weaknesses, and strive to improve those weak program areas.

These areas may include

- In-house inspection records, manifest files, incident report files
- Environmental audit report files
- EPA/state correspondence files
- Any contractors' or consultants' work files

In each of these instances, one should strive to maintain up-to-date information, and when problems are spotted, they should be noted, and timely and appropriate corrective action should be taken. Of course, this presumes that there are sufficient corporate funds available, coupled with a sincere corporate commitment to execute the corrections.

If one is at a loss as to where to turn for assistance, EPA's hotlines can be a good source of general regulatory information, provided one then follows up with additional research. It is also a good practice to attend EPA-sponsored workshops and seminars, whenever possible, if available to the public. Networking groups are also a good source of information. In addition, the environmental manager (EM) should strive to develop and maintain effective environmental audit programs and, if appropriate, to seek help from qualified outside consultants.

Items that the EM should not lose sight of during this self-check are current regulations and other changes coming down the road, such as the revised Sentencing Guidelines, that will be discussed in detail below.

With respect to the regulations, a few tips are worth noting:

- Keep all applicable media waste management regulations current.
- Build a library of trade publications and compliance handbooks to supplement the regulations.
- Attend relevant seminars and conferences.
- Become active in industrial trade association meetings.

With respect to the Sentencing Guidelines, the U.S. Sentencing Commission created an advisory working group to advise it on how to deal with environmental crimes committed by organizations. That group proposed a discussion draft of stringent organizational environmental guidelines that were circulated for public comment on March 5, 1993. The discussion draft is not a final proposal of the working group, and is referred to as the draft environmental guidelines. As drafted, these follow the same general approach as the organizational guidelines, with several important differences, such as a base fine that accounts for the economic gain; an upward or downward adjustment depending on aggravating or mitigating factors; the impact of repetitive acts; and the extent or absence of compliance programs. (See Hale and Dorr's *Criminal Enforcement Bulletin*, April 1993.)

Compliance programs play a substantial role in mitigating the fine, if issued, and it clearly is in the handler's best interest to maintain an exemplary program. Under the draft guidelines, seven minimum criteria are listed for a compliance program:

- Established compliance standards and procedures
- Specific management-assigned responsibility for compliance
- Due care exercised *not* to delegate responsibility to individuals who may engage in criminal conduct
- Effective steps taken to communicate standards to employees
- Reasonable steps taken to achieve compliance through appropriate monitoring, reporting, or other systems
- Standards consistently enforced through measures
- After offense is noted, appropriate action taken and future violations prevented

Clearly then, under the draft environmental guidelines, internal compliance programs have become even more important—their presence decreases the fine and their absence increases it.

Conclusion

The management of a comprehensive RCRA compliance program requires responsible, knowledgeable professionals to ensure its success. The responsible EM should set the tone for determining the requirements for any program's successful implementation, develop procedures and practices, develop efforts to reduce the number of unreasonable regulations, ensure that employees are well-trained, re-evaluate staff needs, secure corporate resources to accomplish these tasks, and, above all, be sharp and alert.

Gabriel G. Crognale is an environmental consultant specializing in the development and enhancement of environmental management systems and audit programs for industrial clients. Previously, Mr. Crognale was with SAIC, where he developed an environmental audits training program for a foreign petrochemical company, and he was a consultant for Arthur D. Little, Inc, where he provided hazardous waste management expertise.

Environmental Auditing Roundtable Establishes Formal Standards for Environmental, Health, and Safety Audits

26

William A. Yodis and Gilbert S. Hedstrom

The Environmental Auditing Roundtable's Standards for the Performance of Environmental, Health, and Safety Audits are featured in this chapter. With many global initiatives converging in the development of environmental auditing and management standards, this document represents a vital building block, unique from many others in that it was built by a broad-based consensus effort of actual practitioners. Over 95 percent of the Roundtable members who voted on the standard endorsed it.

The Environmental Auditing Roundtable (EAR) is the original professional organization of environmental, health, and safety (EHS) auditors. Founded in January 1982 (back when only a handful of companies had formal EHS audit programs) the Environmental Auditing Roundtable has grown to a membership of over 400 practitioners. During this period of growth, there have been several important milestones, including adoption of a code of ethics and formal bylaws in 1987, and incorporation as a not-for-profit organization in 1991. Today the EAR is the organization of choice for leaders in EHS auditing, and for those who strive to be leaders, with members from the Americas and Europe.

Why Did the EAR Develop These Standards?

Prior to 1990, a number of organizations in North America and Europe had been engaged in codifying current environmental auditing practices and developing environmental auditing principles. At the same time, the term "auditing" was increasingly being used to represent a very broad set of activities, and many EHS auditing practitioners were, quite frankly, very frustrated that some of the emerging "standards" were being written by people who had relatively little auditing experience.

In recognition of this, and desiring to have a voice in the emerging standards, the EAR formed a Standards Committee in September 1990. The committee was charged with developing a set of standards defining the minimum criteria for the performance of EHS audits, whether done internally or externally to the entity audited.

How Were the Standards Created?

The standards were created in three phases, each designed to achieve broad consensus. First, twelve subcommittees spent six months studying other audit standards (including the Institute of Internal Auditors' Standards for the Professional Practice of Internal Auditing and those from the General Accounting Office and the American Society of Quality Control) as well as environmental principles (from the U.S. Environmental Protection Agency and the International Chamber of Commerce, among others). This was all part of an effort to define the basic principles and practices that represent the core of the EHS audit. During Phase 2, the output of these twelve subcommittees was integrated into a working draft. The final phase consisted of numerous revisions to the draft until the subcommittees, the EAR board of directors, and, ultimately, the EAR membership endorsed the document.

The New Standards

These standards are intended to provide core, minimum criteria for conducting EHS audits.

- They define "audit" relatively narrowly, much as the U.S. Environmental Protection Agency and the International Chamber of Commerce do. Thus they focus on audits against established criteria. They are not intended to represent standards for the acquisition/divestiture (due diligence) audits, risk assessments, management systems assessments, pollution prevention audits, or the like.
- They focus on the actual audit itself—from preparation through report writing. They do not include standards for the design of an audit program (the subject of a current Environmental Auditing Roundtable initiative).
- They are an effort to describe sound auditing methodology, but are not intended to be legally binding. Those individuals endorsing these standards were not saying that each of their company's audits completely fulfilled the standards.

To obtain a pamphlet-sized copy of the standards or to receive further information about the activities of the Environmental Auditing Roundtable, contact the Environmental Auditing Roundtable, Inc. c/o SBI, 12 Indian Head Road, Morristown, NJ 07960.

Standards for Performance of Environmental, Health, and Safety Audits

© 1993 Environmental Auditing Roundtable Inc.

Introduction

These standards have been prepared by the Environmental Auditing Roundtable (EAR), a professional organization, to provide minimum criteria for the conduct of environmental, health, and safety (EHS) audits. These are the generally accepted auditing standards that EAR members believe are necessary for the professional conduct of EHS audits.

Some important points about these standards are:

1. An *EHS audit* is defined as an activity directed at verifying a site or organization's environmental, health, or safety status with respect to specific, predetermined criteria. An audit is distinct from other evaluation methods that may involve conclusions based on professional opinion or limited evaluation, or unique instances not associated with specific criteria.

2. These standards apply to activities that take place within the scope of an audit engagement. Standards of audit program design and implementation are not addressed. Principles or standards for audit program design and implementation are a natural extension of these standards; however, to emphasize only core issues, these standards focus solely on the audit engagement.

3. These standards are deliberately concise. They intend to define *what* is required to conduct a competent audit, not *how* to implement each aspect of the standard.

4. In these standards, the word "must" denotes a mandatory practice, while "should" denotes a desired "best practice" recommendation.

5. Throughout this document, "audit" and "auditor" mean "environmental, health, and safety" audit or auditor.

The scope of EHS auditing is broad, and the term *EHS audit* is used in a variety of ways. Activities that could be covered by these standards range from internally motivated audits (such as those for property transfer or regulatory compliance) to audits conducted with the intent of disclosing findings to the public (such as reporting on the goals and performance of the environmental program of an organization). A "client" authorizes the performance of an audit, and must assure the consent and cooperation of the "auditee" (the organizational unit or facility) to be audited. The scope of an audit must be defined in advance, and the verification criteria selected and agreed on prior to beginning the audit. Agreement on required audit resources is part of the scope. The organization being audited must provide the auditors with access to documentation, information, location, and other resources needed to make judgments and form opinions required to achieve the objectives of the audit. Audit "findings" are the conclusions reached by auditors regarding elements of the audit scope and verification criteria. Audits must be conducted in an ethical manner. The EAR Code of Ethics governs the activities of its members in performing audits. The Code is attached to these standards.

Standards are developed in the complex legal and regulatory environment of auditing. Standards must be sufficiently flexible to be adaptable to the unique needs and circumstances of any individual audit. Although these standards define good commercial and customary practices for performing audits, there are specific circumstances that might mandate a departure from the standards established here. This document reflects a consensus of environmental professionals on key components of the performance of audits. It is not intended to serve as a legal analysis of liability issues or as legal advice. This document will be updated periodically, as judged appropriate to changing audit practices and legal requirements. The EAR Standards Committee will review this standard at least annually for possible revision.

I. General Standards

A. Auditor Proficiency

Auditors must have adequate qualifications, technical knowledge, training, and proficiency in the discipline of auditing to perform their assigned audit tasks. Proficiency is the responsibility of the organization managing auditing activities and of each individual auditor. Qualifications of the audit team assigned must be commensurate with the objectives, scope, and complexities of the audit assignment.

1. Auditors must be qualified to perform audits. Organizations and individuals responsible for planning the audit engagement must establish suitable educational and professional experience criteria for auditors. Auditor proficiency and professional experience in the following areas must be adequate to achieve audit objectives.
   a. Auditing processes, procedures, and techniques.
   b. Characteristics and analysis of management systems.
   c. Regulatory requirements and environmental policies.
   d. Environmental, health, and safety protection systems and technologies.
   e. Facility operations.
   f. Potential environmental, health, and safety impacts and hazards/risks associated with the types of facilities and operations to be audited.

2. Auditors should have training and demonstrated abilities in areas needed to perform audits, including, but not limited to:
   a. Interpersonal and communication skills.
   b. Work scheduling and planning.
   c. Analytical abilities to evaluate potential deficiencies noted during the audit.
3. Auditors should understand the operations of the facility/organization to be audited as they relate to the audit scope.

B. Due Professional Care

Due professional care is the application of diligence and skill in performing audits. Exercising due professional care means assuring accuracy, consistency, and objectivity in the performance of audits; using good judgment in choosing tests and procedures; developing conclusions and, if necessary, recommendations; and preparing reports.

1. Auditors must conscientiously complete audits in compliance with these auditing standards.
2. Auditors must apply the diligence and skills expected of a competent, reasonably prudent and knowledgeable auditor in the same or similar circumstances.
3. Auditors must apply established auditing standards consistently, and should seek authoritative interpretations when such standards are conflicting or vague.
4. Auditors must conclude that sufficient and reasonable evidence exists to allow formation of opinions.

C. Independence

Auditors must be objective and independent of the audit site and/or activity to be audited, free of conflict of interest in any specific situation, and not subject to internal or external pressure to influence their findings.

1. Factors that can impair independence include personal or organizational bias, and external or internal influence on the auditor's judgment or authority, whether implied or direct.
2. Where a conflict of interest exists, it must be communicated to the client. In some cases, the client may waive the conflict of interest. A statement of this waiver should be provided in the audit report.
3. An objective auditor must base findings on observed, measurable, and verifiable evidence, and not allow personal opinions or beliefs to influence the conduct of audits or conclusions that might be reached.

II. Conduct of Audits

A. Clear and Explicit Objectives

The objectives of an audit must be clearly established and fully communicated beforehand to the client and to the auditee. The objectives of specific audits should be consistent with the needs of intended recipients of audit results and the provisions of these standards.

B. Systematic Plans and Procedures for Conducting Audits

Audits must be based on use of systematic plans and procedures that provide uniform guidance in audit preparation, field work, and reporting. Explicit written plans and procedures promote consistency and uniformity of approach.

1. The audit planning process and procedures must include the use of protocols, checklists, and/or guidelines consistent with the audit scope to provide a clear methodology for conducting the audit.
2. Audit documentation must be consistent with the defined scope of the audit.

C. Planned and Supervised Fieldwork

Fieldwork must be properly planned, implemented, and supervised, to foster efficiency and consistency and to achieve audit objectives. Effective supervision and leadership are necessary parts of environmental auditing.

1. A team leader must supervise fieldwork performed by members of the audit team.
2. Audit fieldwork should be conducted in accordance with a prepared protocol and an established audit plan.
3. While on site, auditors must gather information necessary to fulfill the audit objectives. The information collected must be relevant, accurate, and sufficient to support findings, conclusions, and recommendations. Appropriate sampling schemes should be utilized in selecting samples.

D. Audit Quality Control and Assurance

Audits must undergo quality checks to assure accuracy and encourage continuous improvement of audit management systems, procedures, and implementation. Quality control measures the extent to which an audit is conducted according to the objectives and scope of the audit, and to these standards.

1. Quality checks should be conducted to ensure that audit findings are consistent with evidence recorded by the auditors.

2. Quality checks should be conducted to ensure that audit findings are reliably communicated in reports.

E. Audit Documentation

The auditor prepares documentation of ongoing activities during an audit in "working papers."

1. Each subject reviewed in an audit should be documented sufficiently so that another auditor of similar skill could confirm the conclusions of the auditor without consulting further resources.
2. Disposition of working papers should be consistent with established policies of the auditing organization or as agreed upon when defining the scope of the audit with the client.

III. Audit Reporting

A. Clear and Appropriate Reporting

A formal report must be prepared for each audit to communicate information, consistent with the audit scope and objectives. Reports should clearly communicate information and findings in a timely manner to the intended recipients, and in sufficient detail and clarity to facilitate corrective action.

1. The audit report should describe the audit scope and conduct, and report the audit results and conclusions, consistent with audit objectives.
2. Audit findings must be documented and based on relevant, accurate, and sufficient evidence. Audit reports may contain recommendations to correct the deficiencies identified in the audit report. An auditor's opinion as to the overall status of the facility may also be included, if the opinion is consistent with the defined scope and objectives.

Environmental Auditing Roundtable Code of Ethics

Introduction

The reliance of the public and business community on the information reported by environmental, health, and safety auditors imposes an obligation that auditors maintain high standards of technical competence and integrity.

Professional Conduct

Article I.   Members as professionals shall exercise honesty, objectivity, and diligence in the performance of their professional duties and responsibilities.

Article II.   Members shall not engage in any act or omission of a dishonest, deceitful, or fraudulent nature.

Article III.   Members shall continually seek to maintain and improve their professional knowledge, skills, and competence.

Article IV.   Members shall not knowingly misrepresent facts and when expressing an audit opinion shall use reasonable care to obtain sufficient facts to support statements. In their reporting, members shall reveal facts which if not revealed could distort the report.

Article V.   Members shall avoid any activity which would prejudice their ability to carry out their professional duties and responsibilities objectively.

Article VI.   Members shall not use confidential information gained in the course of an audit for personal gain. Members shall not disclose confidential information acquired in the course of an audit unless disclosure of such information is required by law.

Conduct of Members

Article I.   Members shall abide by this Code of Ethics and support the objectives of the Environmental Auditing Roundtable.

Article II.   Members shall not represent their acts or statements in such a way as to lead others to believe that they officially represent the Environmental Auditing Roundtable unless they are duly authorized to do so.

Article III.   Members shall not directly market their professional services at Roundtable meetings.

Article IV.   Applicants for membership and candidates for elective office in the Roundtable shall not misrepresent any credentials submitted in support of their application or candidacy.

Article V.   Members in good standing may communicate their membership and their acceptance of this Code of Ethics. However, they may not in any way imply that they are endorsed by the Roundtable or its Board of Directors.

William A. Yodis is the president of the Environmental Auditing Roundtable and the manager of corporate health, safety, and environmental audit at AlliedSignal Inc. **Gilbert S. Hedstrom** is the secretary of the EAR and a vice president of Arthur D. Little, Inc.

The Power of Information Technology

The Power of *IT*:
How Can Information Technology Support TQEM?

27

Lynn Johannson

This chapter presents a discussion among experts on how information technology can enhance the effectiveness of TQEM efforts.

Business is undergoing unprecedented changes. With the globalization of markets, the opening of international trade borders, growing customer demands for "environmentally friendly" products, and spiraling government controls, competition is taking on a whole new meaning. Organizations must make evolutionary changes at revolutionary rates to play in this market. It is fast becoming a truly international market—even from the comfort of your own home office.

To be able to compete in this aggressive climate, one must, as Campbell's Soup (and others) affirm, "do the right things right." This approach is not based on good luck. It is the result of planning, doing, checking, and acting on information, focused on improving your product, process, and service to meet customer needs. As any quality manager knows, customer needs have a habit of changing. The speed of these changes can be frightening to those who are not trained or who lack the appropriate tools. It is less a barrier to those who are familiar and comfortable with constant change. For those with the right tools and knowledge base, change is not only accepted, but also sought with the same enthusiasm as skiing on fresh powder, teeing off on a new course, or riding the curl of a wave.

In this chapter we are going to explore how the power of information technology (IT) can reinforce your effectiveness in applying quality management to ecological (environmental) issues. Information technology is one of the fastest growing industries, and has, in fact, been described by Nuala Beck, a well-known Canadian business consultant, as one of the engines that is driving the new economic era. Businesses are realizing that environmental management is among the highest corporate priorities. In fact, IT provided us with the evidence of mankind's impact on the environment when space exploration gave us our first truly global perspective.

Supporters of this global perspective include such groups as the International Chamber of Commerce (ICC), Canada's National Round Table on the Environment and the Economy (NTREE), and the U.S.-based Global Environmental Management Initiative (GEMI). However, many organizations remain in a quandary as

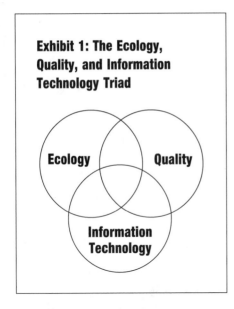

Exhibit 1: The Ecology, Quality, and Information Technology Triad

Ecology

Quality

Information Technology

to how to effectively use this knowledge and rise to meet the challenges of this new global economy.

As shown in **Exhibit 1**, *Ecology*, the science of structure and function of nature, and *Quality*, the management science of human values in qualitative and quantitative forms, share common elements with *Information Technology*. IT provides a skill base and a systems perspective that enhance the two sciences, forming an important triad.

To best understand how *Ecology, Quality* and *Information Technology* interrelate, a brief explanation is in order. *Ecology* refers to the structure and function of nature of whatever system you are a part of.

Quality, in its broadest sense, is anything that can be improved. In the TQEM context, quality is not only associated with products and services; but it also includes the way people work, the way machines are operated, the way systems and procedures are dealt with, *and the ecological systems involved in the creation of the product, process, and service*. It includes all aspects of human behavior. Frequently the term *kaizen* (meaning improvement) is used. *Kaizen* assumes that our way of life—be it working, in a social context, our home life—deserves to be constantly and forever improved.

Information technology is not just data. It encompasses computer and telecommunication products and services, which allow access to data, with the means of access and options to use these components that are astounding.

At the risk of beating a dead horse, remember that once the philosophical acceptance of quality is achieved, the act of improvement requires an ongoing assessment of customer needs. Why? *The basis for making decisions founded on quality, environmental quality, is improved information.* Hence information technology, the use of computer and telecommunication products and services, forms a crucial link in meeting the goals of this new economic era. IT will be instrumental in the development of sustainable products, processes, and services that will allow your organization to thrive in the new economy. (See **Appendix** for an outline of general benefits.)

To assist your understanding of how IT can make your total quality environmental management process more effective, I contacted a number of experts whose services, products, or experience demonstrate the power of IT.

Richard Underwood, NASA

Our first respondent is Richard Underwood, now retired, who served as the technical assistant to the director of photography and television technology for National Aeronautic and Space Agency (NASA). He lectures around the world using an incredible collection of slides to show the rate and extent of environmental changes that have occurred over the last three decades. I have started the responses with Richard Underwood's, as it provides us with an understanding of how IT and space exploration initiated the environmental movement by giving us a truly global perspective and reinforces the need to make TQEM a global process.

"For more than thirty years space photographs have captured on film the Third Planet," Underwood says. "One may well ask, 'What was the value of those NASA trips to the moon more than twenty years ago?' I believe that the greatest value, by far, was the fact that they went translunar 'blunt end forward.' That is, they never saw the moon until they were in orbit about it. The window always looked back to planet Earth getting smaller and smaller each passing minute. It gave them their psychological connection to the home planet.

"Christmas in 1968, Frank Borman said it best as he was about to make the first lunar orbit. *'Planet Earth, I can hold out my thumb and block it out.'* It is truly a minor planet going around a minor star near the edge of a minor galaxy. Not very important in the great celestial scheme, but it is the only planet we have and we must take better care of it, or we may very well lose it.

"Being in the space photo business since it began, I feel that those photos of a small disk (Earth) against the pitch blackness of space have changed the world. I had the great fortune to be the first person to see them and they changed the world. Photos like AS-17-148.22727, a fully-lit earth disk, brought about the birth of the environmental movement on a worldwide basis. People saw a finite Earth for the first time. More people have seen it than any other photo in human history, and it was taken en route to the moon.

"The space photos of Earth cover large areas for a synoptic view. One can cross North America in nine minutes; thus they show the exact environmental status of vast areas with no respect for political, geographical, geomorphic, or any other type of boundary.

"For instance, over thirty years of space photos have shown the rapid growth of African deserts due to imprudent land use procedures of primitive people. It has determined why it happened, recorded by the destruction of vast areas, and clearly shows what will happen: the destruction of many tens of millions of people in the next two decades. What we predicted twenty (and more) years ago is now headlines from the Somali situation. The power of customs and religion will destroy everything. Somalia, unfortunately, is but the tip of the iceberg. It may well develop into the human equivalent of a "feedlot" mentality. The predictable cause and effect have been clearly seen in space photographs for a quarter century, but, alas, nobody would listen. And, of course, today we clearly see the destruction of worldwide rain forests (and other forests); the polluting of oceans, rivers, lakes, etc; industrial environmental problems, the destruction of arable lands, acid rains, etc., all clearly seen worldwide in the space photography. The space photos of the former Soviet Union showed unbelievable environmental disaster and were dismissed as merely anti-Soviet propaganda from the U.S. Then the great wall was knocked down in Berlin and the light of reason crossed Eastern Europe and beyond the Urals toward the Pacific. The horrors seen from space are in no way propaganda.

"The potential use of the Space Station for understanding the worldwide environmental situation and then having the knowledge to take proactive action is unlimited. But, alas, nobody listens."

David Olson, Geomatics International

Our second respondent is Dave Olson, U.S. Operations Manager for Geomatics International, who shares information on a specific information tool and its applications. Geomatics International is an environmental consulting firm specializing in the use of Geographical Information System (GIS) and remote sensing technologies for mapping, analysis, and management of environmental and natural resources.

"For those readers who have not had exposure to GIS technology previously, it should be thought of as an information integration and analysis tool. GIS is a computer data base that stores information in a form that relates data attributes or conditions to spatial locations—i.e., a line that represents a road being identified by type, traffic volume, bearing capacity, construction material, or other criteria. Any information that can be tied to a geographic location can be sorted, displayed, analyzed, and reported. Almost any function that can be done in more familiar types of data bases can be done with GIS, in addition to many types of spatial and temporal analysis that standard data bases cannot do.

"GIS has evolved over the last thirty years, beginning primarily as a mapping tool and more recently as a practical, powerful, and flexible analysis tool. Many societies, such as the American Society of Cartographers and Surveyors, American Society of Photogrammetric Engineering and Remote Sensing; periodicals, such as GIS World and Geo Info Systems; as well as many symposiums and conferences coordinate, report, and track developments in GIS technology for many different application areas, including environmental management. GIS is a rapidly maturing technology that has just recently made the transition from dedicated mainframe computers and complex software with large learning curves to a flexible, easily upgradable and intuitive graphical user interface analytical tool accessible to PCs and nondedicated users. This reduction in complexity and cost, coupled with greater analytical capability, has opened many new areas of economically attractive applications for this technology.

"Some examples of applications which directly relate to environmental management include:

Network Analysis—Use road information to select the shortest path for hazardous material transportation routes that represent logistical or operating constraints, such as maximum load bearing capacity, avoidance of schools or high population density areas and sensitive resources, scheduling to avoid heavy traffic volumes, or other criteria that would result in reduced risk and optimized efficiency.

Emergency Response—Use selected routes and transfer schedules to track transport of materials so that in the event of an incident or problem the shipment can be quickly located and all of the appropriate agencies and authorities notified, as well as potential environmental impact pre-evaluated. This application can also be used to analyze the placement of rapid response equipment and materials to be able to respond with the appropriate resources within designated performance objectives.

Visual Impact Assessment—Generate perspective views of planned projects to determine visual impacts of facilities before they are built for the permit of public review process. This application can also identify locations that an object can be seen from—e.g., from what locations would you be able to see an exhaust stack that is one hundred feet tall in this location and how will it look from those perspectives.

Point Source Dispersion Models—Almost any mathematical model that has been developed, from atmospheric to wind tunnel, can be applied to GIS. Many models significantly improve from incorporating spatial and temporal (time) elements that can be integrated in GIS modelling—e.g., running a model of dispersion of exhaust from a smoke stack using wind speed, direction, temperature, and humidity information for an entire year from a data recorder on the stack to estimate the average deliveries to the surrounding areas. These data can be used for reporting or controlling emissions during certain weather conditions to reduce impacts on high population areas or sensitive resources.

Non-Point Source Pollution Modeling—This type of application is even more dependent on GIS technology because much of this type of analysis becomes complex with multivariate factors to the extent that the relationships are not 'humanly graspable' in their entirety. An example that we are currently working on is to calculate the amount of phosphorus that can be transported into Lake Ontario. This analysis takes into account the type of crop grown, the fertilizer treatment, the soil type, the drainage, the tillage practices, proximity to the lake, and interactions of the fertilizer with sediment and aquatic plants. Imagine all of these variables over a hundred square miles and you have a task that is not humanly grasp-able, but is relatively easy for GIS once the scientific relationships of the variables have been defined and the data base of the conditions has been mapped.

"In addition to improvements in the quality and timeliness of analyses, the analysis of processes too complex and variable to be accomplished otherwise, GIS also improves communication through geographical representation of informa-tion. Some government agencies, like the Washington State Department of Natural Resources, are already requiring that regulation compliance reporting to their agency is in GIS-compatible formats. It should be expected that as this tool continues to grow in usage, the trend for agencies to require reporting in their specifications for compliance and monitoring will grow as well.

"As with any tool, if GIS is diligently applied to the appropriate types of tasks, it can make significant qualitative improvements to and impacts on operations and provide a good return on your investment. The best advice is while looking for ways to continuously improve products, services and efficiency, make a serious evaluation of this tool, learn where it can work for you, and begin to take advan-tage of a technology that has an incredible amount to offer for total quality efforts in environmental or natural resource management."

Doug Archibald, SESI

Our last respondent is Doug Archibald, president of SESI, a firm that markets software technology developed to assist organizations in the management of haz-ardous materials.

"In this age of high technology the emphasis has been on *technology* and how technology can be utilized to improve quality of life, corporate results, health care, etc.

"At SESI our emphasis is on *information* and how technology can be used to provide more timely, accurate, and current information. Information is the life-blood of industry and commerce and must be available instantly to all levels of management to facilitate the decision-making process.

"As we march toward the next century, all sectors of the global economy are coming under intense pressure from the citizenry (through all levels of govern-ment) to become more and more environmentally and ecologically conscious of their effects on our globe.

"These same sectors are also under intense economic pressure from sharehold-ers to continually provide maximum return on investment. These demands are, to a certain extent, mutually exclusive; however, this will not be the first time that business and industry have addressed and overcome this conundrum. The key to decreasing or negating these pressures is the prudent and strategic use of informa-tion in a timely manner.

"The original principles of data processing have not changed dramatically in the past forty years—the technology that allows us to enter, store, update, manipulate, access, display, transmit, and secure data has changed dramatically over the past forty years—indeed, over the past ten years.

"There is absolutely no excuse for corporations of all sizes not to have access to information that is necessary to ensure successful and profitable operations. The software currently available and under development at SESI is designed to ensure that data, once entered, can be used, reused, processed, and reprocessed to provide the information necessary to support the complete function of management, which demands timely decision-making based on accurate and current information.

"The starting point for all information systems is the establishment of accurate and comprehensive data bases. Data entry technology is becoming available which is lessening this onerous task—e.g., scanners.

"These data bases, once established, must be kept current by the daily transactions of the business—e.g., wastes produced (by type and quantity), at which processes, exactly where the wastes are stored and exactly how much is stored there, wastes shipped (again by type and quantity), sites to where the wastes are shipped, which company transported which wastes, etc.

"It is apparent that the information available in the data base can be used to produce (virtually at the push of a button) regulatory documentation—e.g., manifests, NPRI reports, environmental ministries reports and summaries, TRI reports, storage facility information, and transportation information. These data are also available for the provision of information to management at all levels to make decisions relative to operations, storage, treatment, transportation, and disposition of toxic wastes and hazardous materials produced and used during the production process.

"Timely use of the available information also ensures that the corporate executives, officers, and directors are informed as to the corporation's adherence to EPA/CEPA regulations."

Summary

The power of IT therefore can be summarized as follows:

Technology provides the tool, information provides knowledge, and knowledge is power.

The age-old expression "a picture is worth a thousand words" comes to mind when sitting through one of Dick Underwood's presentations. It would be hard to imagine how someone could not grasp the need to change, when exposed to pictorial proof of our impacts on this planet.

The benefits of David Olson's explanation of GIS and its applications and Doug Archibald's description of the power that good software provides its users are intended to expand your TQEM toolbox and assist you in the implementation of your TQEM goals. As change is a constant, these tools will allow managers to be more effective with stewardship and efficient in the use of resources, leading to greater competencies in the TQEM process. We all share the responsibility for the rate of change that the globe is experiencing. We are fast being held accountable for the results of these changes. A focus on compliance is not the answer. Define who your customers are in the context of TQEM and determine what their needs are. The faster we can input and synthesize data leading to better decision making, the sooner we will be able to achieve sustainable development using these new tools as part of our TQEM toolbox.

Appendix

The benefits of IT are described by the Information Technology Association of Canada (ITAC) in a five-level process referred to as the "Enabling Effect" (see "Things Change," ITAC, September 1992).

Level 1—Cost Reduction
Dramatic reductions in costs—direct and indirect—for such things as energy, materials, labor, and transportation; typically soon after implementation.

Level 2—Quality Enhancement
Minimize breakdowns, shorten delivery delays, eliminate product defects and close client-product expectation gaps; typically early in the implementation.

Level 3—New Products and Services
Launch an organization into new, IT-dependent product areas.

Level 4—Enhanced Strategic Management
More productive use of management time and better information to see where to focus, deploy resources, set standards, uncover deficiencies, forecast, plan, and analyze.

Level 5—New Concepts and Models
Some applications are new concepts themselves; some are so influential that the workplace of five years ago is unrecognizable.

Lynn Johannson is the director of E2 Management Corporation in Georgetown, Ontario.

Supporting Auditing Programs with Automated Tools

28

Barbara Jo Ruble

With more and more companies initiating and expanding their environmental, health, and safety (EHS) auditing programs, there is an increasing need to facilitate the management of protocols, working papers, audit reports, and other documents. In addition, auditors need to stay abreast of rapidly changing regulatory requirements and managers need to track audit findings and corrective action projects.

Not surprisingly, many organizations are developing automated information management tools that will support their auditing programs. This chapter examines some of the ways in which information management technology can most effectively support auditing programs. It looks at how to identify information management needs and discusses implementing an information tool and the benefits such a tool can actually provide.

Automated tools that support environmental, health, and safety (EHS) auditing programs generally perform one or more of the following functions:

- Query and find regulations
- Provide and manage checklists and protocols
- Prepare audit reports
- Track corrective actions and follow-up
- Analyze trends

There are many good products available commercially. Each one has a slightly different focus or approach so it is likely that among the offerings you can find a tool or set of tools that will meet your needs. It may be helpful to understand some common features when making your selection.

Regulatory Information Tools

The largest number and variety of commercially available software tools that support EHS auditing are regulatory information systems. These are tools that allow you to query and find information on EHS regulatory requirements.

Regulatory information tools come in three basic types determined by how and where the information is stored:

- PC hard disk
- CD-ROM
- Dial-up

Although the largest differences are in the software and the content of the regulatory database, there are some differences that are inherent to the media. PC hard disks are very fast, but in order to store all the regulatory information you want, you will probably need a very large disk or multiple disks. This may mean a hidden hardware cost for implementation.

CD-ROM tools store information on compact discs that look just like music CDs. You will need to have one or more special CD-reader devices hooked up to your computer or network in order to use such tools; this may mean additional hardware costs. CD-ROMs are not quite as fast as hard disks, but they are reasonably speedy and the CD-readers are usually less expensive than a large external hard disk.

Dial-up systems store information on a remote computer, usually a large mainframe that can provide high-speed disk storage for very large volumes of regulatory information. They are accessed through a modem and some type of communications software that runs on your PC. Although the mainframe disk access time is very fast, the response time you see at your computer will be much slower after all the communications time is added. Again, there may be hardware costs for modems; however, a top-of-the-line modem is usually about half the cost of a medium-quality hard disk or CD reader.

These systems can generally be used by either an individual PC or a network; however, individual system software may have limitations so you should inquire carefully about implementation in your specific computing environment.

Almost all the commercial regulatory information services offer the text of U.S. federal regulations from Titles 40 (EPA), 29 (OSHA), and those parts of Title 49 (DOT) that address the transportation of hazardous materials. Some products offer other titles having to do with nuclear energy, fossil energy, pipelines, shipping, coast guard, or environmental taxes. Coverage of laws or statutes is much less certain than coverage of regulations, so if laws are important to you, be sure to check carefully on what laws are covered and how the information is handled and updated.

The biggest differences among products are in the coverage of state, local, and foreign laws and regulations. When you are evaluating tools, check carefully to see whether the states or other jurisdictions of concern to your business are included in the database. In addition, it may be prudent to determine specifically what sources are used for the information. Does the information come from code books, registers, compliance bulletins, and/or guidance documents? Are the paper sources you currently use included in the database?

Another critical feature is timeliness of the information. How often is the information updated? How often are updates provided? Is all the information updated at the same frequency? How are updates presented? Some products integrate updates into the text of the regulation every time updates are provided. Some display newly updated material differently, e.g., in bold or with bars down the right-hand margin, in order to highlight it. Other products leave updates as separate documents for a period of time, such as a year, before integrating the updates with the text of the original regulation. Each of these approaches has advantages and disadvantages, and which tool is best depends on the way you intend to research and use the information.

The commands you use to search for regulations and the way you see the information displayed will depend on the software that the vendor has created for the tool; this is known as the user interface. No two tools are exactly alike, though most use some sort of word or phrase searching as the basic element and most allow some amount of Boolean logic to link search terms. Generally you can search for a specific regulatory reference or for the presence or absence of one or more words.

Some tools categorize the database by major regulatory topic such as waste, water, or air. They may also limit a single search to regulations within a topic, which could be an advantage if your job focuses on a specific issue, or conversely, it could be a disadvantage if you have very broad compliance responsibilities.

Some tools have very simple searching commands with a template already laid out on your screen; this may be ideal for folks who do not use computers very often. Other tools have a less-structured search screen, and some are completely free-form offering only a single prompt where you may type in any kind of search specifications. Although these might be intimidating to the unfamiliar, they may allow more powerful or precise searching. A very nice feature, offered by several products, is on-screen, context-sensitive help.

Different users will undoubtedly have different preferences for the use interface, and it may be difficult to find the common ground among your colleagues. This does not mean, however, that the simplest tool or the least common denominator is the best choice. Depending on the number and location of users and the nature of their needs, more than one tool could be justified.

Costs for hard-disk and CD-based systems are usually presented as annual subscriptions where you receive regular updates in the mail or through an electronic bulletin board. Subscription prices may vary depending on which topics or jurisdictions you subscribe to. Dial-up services are usually priced by the amount of time you use and may or may not have some base fee for signing up. This difference in the pricing structure will make your cost evaluation more difficult if you have no idea how much time you will spend using the tool. Think carefully about how you and your colleagues will use the tool and how much of your time you currently spend on regulatory research. Although these tools will help you do your research faster, you will probably not spend less time researching, you will just get more and better quality information for the time spent.

Audit Checklist and Protocol Tools

Though less prolific than regulatory information tools, there are several good products on the market that will provide audit protocols or checklists, record findings from audits, and prepare reports. These tools generally operate on a PC with the data stored on the hard disk. With modern hardware technology, you can put the protocol software on a notebook computer that weighs less than five pounds.

Very few auditors, however, carry a PC notebook around the facility while they audit. It is inconvenient to try to type answers as you go. Most auditors who use these tools print out paper protocols and then type in their answers later, either in a conference room or office at the facility, back at their hotel in the evening, or when they return to their home office. New products are being developed that will operate on PCs with special pens that activate the software when touched to the screen. These pen devices work much like any computer mouse with the added feature that you can write limited amounts of information and the software will recognize your writing (if it is neat). These types of PCs may make it easier for some auditors to actually use the computer while they walk around, but they won't necessarily eliminate the need for a clipboard and working papers. Auditors have a lot to do while they are in the facility, and most are too busy looking around and talking to employees to want the added task of entering data into the computer. If you are considering an audit protocol tool, you may want to evaluate how easy it is to print out the protocol questions, what volume of paper is involved, and whether the paper format leaves space to write answers and notes.

The key things to consider when evaluating audit protocol tools are the nature of the protocol questions and the features of the user interface. Different products may address slightly different sets of regulatory issues. The level of detail and style of questions may be different. In addition, the way that the software allows you to move from question or issue to issue will probably be very different.

Most of the products have menus that allow the user to choose what function to perform or what section of the protocol to display. Once the user is in the middle of a function or protocol, however, the ease of movement among functions and return to the original place may vary dramatically. Windows users who are used to bouncing from one window to another may want to check this feature carefully.

Most of the protocols have some introductory or preaudit questions that determine which detailed protocol questions will be presented to the auditor. Audit questions are usually detailed and referenced to a specific regulatory citation. Most of the products allow the auditor to answer yes, no, or not applicable. They generally also allow the auditor to enter brief comments. This style of question may or may not fit well with your auditing program. EHS compliance issues are rarely black and white. More and more, auditors are looking to see if the management systems, procedures, awareness of requirements, and quality assurance measures are structured to reasonably provide compliance. As audit programs and auditors become more sophisticated, audit findings may become more subtle.

Most of the products provide protocols that address federal requirements. Some have protocols to address a few state's requirements, but the selection is limited. A nice feature, offered by a few products, allows you to enter your own requirements and protocol questions. This would be a handy way to include company policies in the scope of your audit.

Reporting Tools

Most of the audit checklist or protocol tools also provide reporting features. Each tool usually offers several different format options such as complete reports of all answers and notes; exception reports, where only those findings that would indicate noncompliance are reported; or summary reports that tally the number of compliant and noncompliant answers by topic. Some packages allow users to design their own reports, although the options may be limited.

One major advantage of these self-reporting protocol tools is that it is much easier for auditors to produce an audit report before leaving the facility. Even a preliminary report may facilitate the close-out meeting with facility personnel and help the auditor set expectations for the final report and follow-up activities.

Tools That Track Corrective Actions

Software tools can also support the auditing process by helping to identify findings that require corrective actions and/or track the corrective action project to its completion. Some audit checklist or protocol tools provide this feature. In addition, there are stand-alone products that focus on the tracking and management of corrective action projects.

The tasks involved in tracking corrective action projects depend on your own level of involvement. Some auditors or audit managers are not involved beyond the point of identifying the need for corrective action or recommending a specific approach. Others may need to track that the corrective action has been accomplished, perhaps by a specific date. Still others will be involved in defining project tasks, budgets, schedules, responsibilities, and verifying the completion of tasks.

Depending on your needs, features to look for may include the following:

- Ability to enter textual descriptions of projects and tasks
- Ability to define responsibilities for projects and tasks
- Ability to define budgets for each task or subtask and compare budgets against actual costs
- Ability to define project and task schedule, display and print Gantt or Pert charts, and modify them to reflect actual progress
- Ability to copy task descriptions, budgets, or schedules from project to project to save time and effort when you are managing several similar projects

If you are looking for a tool to help track and manage corrective actions, don't forget to look beyond the tools that are developed specifically to support environmental or auditing programs. There are many good PC-based and easy-to-use general project management tools. One of these may be the best choice, especially if you will be involved in all aspects of managing corrective actions.

Trend Analysis

One of the reasons that computers were developed was to facilitate the analysis of large volumes of data and identify trends and patterns; at the time, the major emphasis was on finding and breaking codes. An emerging use of computer technology is to identify trends in audit findings. Although not widely available yet, a small number of software tools have been developed to help you correlate audit findings with items like time, type of business or operation, or with broad compliance management issues such as training, housekeeping, or records management. The benefit of these types of tools is that they can help you identify places or conditions that need extra attention.

For example, if an analysis of findings from 100 audits shows that 40 percent of all noncompliance issues occurred in relation to soldering operations, you might decide to implement new procedures for those operations, or you might decide to audit them more frequently. If an analysis of audit findings showed that 40 percent of all findings had something to do with employees not understanding the requirements, you might decide to enhance training programs.

If you cannot find an environmental auditing tool with the features you want, you might look at some of the more general statistical packages or even spreadsheets. These kinds of trend analyses do not require sophisticated statistical calculations.

Identifying Your Information Management Needs

Before you can select an information management tool that truly will be worthwhile and likely to make your job easier, you need a clear understanding of how you and your colleagues use information. Ask yourself these questions:

- What information do I use?
- When and where do I use it?
- What do I use the information for?

Identify all the people, projects, and activities that need and benefit from the information you use and produce. Identify possible ways in which those benefits might increase if you had an automated tool. Lastly, determine the time, effort, and costs currently associated with producing and using the information, as well as the costs to purchase and implement any information management tool.

As an illustrative example, let's say you are an auditor and you are considering purchasing a regulatory information tool.

You audit manufacturing facilities in New Jersey, New York, and Pennsylvania. You need to know the current EHS requirements for the federal government and those three states. Currently, you have copies of the applicable EHS laws, the federal and state code books, and a few applicable standards, like NFPA. You have subscriptions to the federal and state registers as well as some bulletins and newsletters that discuss regulatory compliance and enforcement issues. You would like the regulatory information database to include all these documents but you might be willing to settle for a tool that would provide just the registers because you are familiar with the existing requirements and are most concerned with new requirements.

You audit one facility each month, and you update your protocol with new requirements the week before each trip. You want information updates at least once a month, and you want the release time of the updates to fit with your auditing schedule.

You mostly use the code books and registers in your home office, but you sometimes take copies with you on the audit for a quick reference, just in case. It would be nice to be able to access the database from the field, if that would actually reduce the amount of stuff you had to carry.

At least three other auditors in your company have approximately the same needs for regulatory information. At least seven other EHS staff use similar information in other ways for other purposes.

Identify the Beneficiaries

The primary benefit of having access to the regulatory information you use is the ability to do your job competently. In the interest of simplicity, we will assume that because you are paid to do this job, management of your company has decided that the success and/or profitability of your company is in some way enhanced by your performance.

After looking at several potential tools, you have estimated that any of the systems would allow you to perform your regular research in less time, perhaps 30 to 40 percent less time. Currently you spend sixteen hours each month reviewing regulations. Over the course of a year, you might save a week and a half. In that time, you might spend one more day on each audit and be able to expand the scope or increase the level of detail, or you might be able to attend a training class or three professional meetings.

If the three other auditors could save as much time as you, your company could save six weeks of effort. That's enough to perform another audit, completely overhaul your audit protocols, develop and produce a new regulatory guidebook, or start a new training program.

Identify the Costs

As we mentioned, you currently spend sixteen hours each month reviewing regulations. Let's say that with salary, benefits, and overhead, that represents $8,000 each year. If the tool would save you 35 percent of that time, that would be a savings of $2,800. If the tool costs $5,000 a year, then at least one more auditor would have to see the same time savings in order to equal the tool's cost.

A real-life needs analysis is rarely this simple. For example, unless the two auditors, whose time savings justify the purchase of the tool, plan to take the extra time as unpaid leave, they will have to do something with the time saved that is at least as valuable to the company as their regulatory research. In addition, if it will take them any extra time over the first several months to learn to use the new tool, that effort will have to be deducted from the savings. There will be other deductions if new hardware is needed or if a computer technician has to install the software or update the database on a regular basis.

Setting Reasonable Expectations

One of the biggest problems with automated information tools is that users and others who expect to benefit from the tool frequently have unrealistic expectations of the benefits they will see and how quickly they will see them. Automated tools are not magic bullets and they don't solve all problems, but in the same way that it is easier to turn a screw with an electric screwdriver, it will be easier to manage information with the appropriate software tool. There are two key tasks that will help you set reasonable expectations for your automated information management tool. First, you should identify and understand the limitations of the tool; second, you should reconcile the costs of the tool and its implementation with the benefits you will receive.

One of the best ways to develop reasonable expectations about the benefits and limitations of an automated tool is to talk with other people who have been using the tool. You should get at least two opinions. Ask the vendor for names of customers who use the tool, especially customers who have used it for more than a year. You might also ask your peers in other companies or friends who participate in the same professional organizations if they have used the tool. Ask the tough questions:

- How long did it take to become proficient with the tool?
- What unexpected costs did they encounter?
- How many times has the vendor made improvements to the product since it was bought?
- What are the best and worst features?
- What would they do differently the next time to avoid mistakes, problems, and unexpected costs?

You may wish to set up a trial of the tool. Don't expect to learn everything from a trial. By their very nature, software trials set up unrealistic working conditions. People find extra time to use the tool or they try especially difficult problems. The vendor's support team is primed and ready for your calls and is pulling out all the stops to win your business. This isn't to say that trials are not valuable. On the contrary, there is nothing like working with the software at your own desk. However, you cannot expect to learn in a week what it will actually be like to work with a tool over the long haul.

When it comes to reconciling costs and benefits, don't stop at the cost of the tool and the benefits to the primary users; include all the implementation costs and all the downstream beneficiaries. Try to find quantitative measures for each cost or benefit. Is there a measurable benefit if the facility receives an audit report sooner? If so, count it. If a technical assistant will have to receive and load database updates every week, or care for and maintain another hard disk, be sure to count the cost. If you are very cost sensitive, you may want to double your estimates of the implementation costs and halve the expected downstream benefits before you decide if the tool is cost-effective.

One frequent pitfall of reconciling costs and benefits occurs when the costs of a tool are absorbed by people or groups that do not benefit from its use. Depending on your company's cost accounting structure, the information systems group might be expected to pay for a new automated tool, or it might be charged to the environmental group. Trouble might occur, however, if facilities or production groups are charged for a tool that supports auditing, especially if the facilities do not have a direct need for the tool or if they are not given access to it for their own work.

Sometimes, the added burden of implementing a new tool is just too daunting for already overworked employees. You may need to create incentives to implement a new automated tool; for example, auditors may be more willing to make the extra effort to learn to use a new tool if they can choose how to spend the time they save.

Conclusion

There are many ways in which automated information management tools are helping companies do a better and more efficient job of environmental, health, and safety auditing. The selection of commercially available tools offers such a wide variety of features and user interface options that you will probably be able to find one that is right for you. It is, however, a good idea to do your homework. Look carefully at how you work, talk to others in similar positions, and learn from their experiences.

Once you have selected a tool, don't get carried away; advertise the benefits and the limitations of the new tool. Give everyone a clear picture of the cost and effort that will be required to make the tool a useful part of your routine, and let them know why it will be worthwhile.

The extra time invested in planning the automation project will help ensure that the results meet your needs and expectations, and that in itself is a reasonably good definition of quality.

Barbara Jo Ruble is senior project manager in the Management Systems and Programs practice at ENSR Consulting and Engineering in Boston, Massachusetts. She has been a member of the Environmental Auditing Roundtable for five years and currently serves as co-chair of the Computer Applications Work Group.

29

Case Study:
Browning-Ferris Industries' Computerized System for Managing Audit and Environmental Performance

Curtis J. Johnson

While some companies have established scoring systems within their audit programs, few utilize the full potential for measurement of the information gathered and subsequently produced from audits. In this chapter, the use of a computerized tracking system developed and used by Browning-Ferris Industries is discussed, along with a data report that details the completion of audit items and helps assure that action plans resulting from environmental audits are completed. This and other summary reports from the computer tracking system have provided meaningful measures of individual facilities' and overall company performance.

Browning-Ferris Industries (BFI) has over four hundred operating locations in North and South America, Europe, and the Pacific Rim consisting primarily of solid and medical waste collection companies, recycling centers, transfer stations, composting operations, medical waste treatment facilities, and landfills. Management is decentralized, with individual facility managers having full authority and responsibility for each location. Oversight, coordination, and assistance are provided through regional offices and the corporate headquarters. The company's audit program, which is run out of corporate headquarters, has a staff of six who will complete about one hundred compliance audits in 1994. About two hundred audits were conducted between 1991 and 1993.

A common argument against conducting audits is that an identified problem may not be rectified in a timely manner, thereby increasing the potential for criminal enforcement. When BFI's audit program was established, the need to track audit findings and their associated corrective actions to completion was considered paramount. BFI made the decision early on to develop its own computerized environmental audit management system, because the commercially available audit software packages reviewed at the time were primarily designed to produce findings from established protocols. The systems reviewed had no tracking components to assure completion of audit items.

Findings as Data

BFI's computer program not only records a text description of the finding, action and follow-up activity in the database, but also records certain data and descriptors that we have found can also be used as measurements of performance.

Each finding is characterized with a specific citation, a reference category, and a ranking. It is important to provide a citation so that the audited operation can be certain of the auditor's concern and design the appropriate action. If the auditor cannot identify the specific regulation or company policy he or she believes is not being followed, it is probably not an exception to requirements. It may, however, be a legitimate observation for improvement that still should be presented.

The reference categories identify the broad regulatory titles (e.g., Clean Water Act) and operational categories of our business (e.g., landfill gas management, medical waste transportation). Subcategories were established to identify specific subject areas within the reference category. For instance, the category of Clean Water Act has sub-categories established for discharge permits, spill prevention plans, and wetlands issues.

Reviewing the collective category data from numerous audits and expressing them as a frequency (i.e., total number of findings in a particular category divided by the number of audits) has been useful in root cause analysis. These data have helped identify potential areas for systematic improvement. Management has been able to assess these data and identify issues potentially in need of more or different explanation in training materials to enhance employee understanding, or the need to establish alternative procedures to improve or streamline the process.

Rankings

A ranking is assigned to each finding—identifying each finding as a regulatory issue, a company policy issue, or a management observation. The category for management observation is used for suggested areas of improvement or efficiency that are not an exception to regulation or company policy.

Regulatory issues are assigned one of three grades. A grade of "G1" is reserved for the most critical issues, such as lack of a required permit or plan. A "G2" ranking is for exceptions relating to implementation of a permit or adequacy of a required plan. The ranking of "G3" represents that the plan or permit implementation appeared adequate, but that some of the supporting documentation was missing or inadequate.

Review of the ranking frequency from numerous audits and comparing them with similar data from a later time frame can show a shift in type or severity of findings. For instance, a reduction in "G" findings and increase in "C" findings would indicate that compliance with the regulations is improving, but that internal requirements are probably getting tougher.

Action Plan Development

An absolute requirement of BFI's audit program is that any and every exception uncovered must have an action plan established, and that the action plan must be completed. BFI's tracking system has been an important part of this process, but before any tracking system is worthwhile, procedures must be in place to establish a comprehensive and specific action plan. While there are numerous papers and texts available on proper audit technique[1] and the Environmental Auditing Roundtable (a professional association of EHS auditing professionals) has recently approved a set of standards for conducting audits,[2] little help is available on effective development of actions plans. A handful of components are critical, however, to ensure that an effective action plan is developed; these are discussed below.

The action plan must be written, and must address every finding, including action on those items that were completed quickly (i.e., before the report of findings is completed). In these cases, actions must be fully described so as to document what actions were actually taken, and to allow for review of the acceptability and appropriateness of the actions. Not every issue can be quickly resolved, however, and for those items, a written plan should be developed in the form of a proposal by the audited facility manager. The manager should be responsible for drawing upon whatever internal and or external resources are necessary and appropriate to the circumstances of issue complexity and their own capability. The proposed plan should then be subject to a draft review by persons with the following responsibilities:

- Audit Team Leader—to help assure that the Action Plan addresses the actual issues of concern stemming from the findings,
- Facility Manager's Supervisor—to help assure that conflicting objectives are limited or non-existent, and assist in coordination of outside resources,
- Senior Environmental, Health and Safety Representative—to help assure that all required steps are included and that, where appropriate, solutions uniform to the company's other locations are implemented (i.e., that wheels are not re-invented), and
- Legal Counsel—to also help assure that all required steps are included (particularly, reporting requirements) and to help assure that language in the proposed plan can withstand potential enforcement scrutiny.

There should be a written dispute resolution process in place, involving supervisors of the original reviewers of the draft plan, to deal with the potential differences of opinion relating to selection of the best option and timetables for implementation. If necessary, the individuals' supervisors (and so on) are brought in until the conflicts are resolved. More often than not, merely suggesting that the dispute resolution process should be utilized is enough to break any deadlock and find the acceptable solution.

The process to develop and endorse an action plan should not impede the implementation of the actions themselves. However, production of the action plan itself cannot be allowed to be unduly delayed. Audits are snapshots of operations at a particular time, and as such, findings and actions have a "shelf life" beyond which they may no longer make sense under changing circumstances. If too much time has elapsed between the audit and design of the action plan, too much time will be wasted on regaining a handle on current conditions and cleaning up the record. It may make more sense to redo the audit in entirety and start the process over. To prevent this waste of resources, a timetable should be in place during which it is expected that the action plan will be initially proposed, reviewed and finalized. Someone other than the facility manager should be responsible for tracking this for reporting purposes. In this manner, a "neutral" outsider can prompt plan development when necessary, and incentives and/or penalties for responsiveness can be fairly and uniformly dispensed. This issue is discussed further, below.

Establishing clear, specific descriptions of what is intended to be done, so that one is able to determine when it has actually been completed, is one of the most difficult aspects of writing action plans. Clearly, a target date for completion must be included with every item, but setting a date does not assure that the action can be determined to have been completed. The following example shows the need for definability of completion:

"Facility Management will do a better job of inspecting the fuel tank."

In this example it is difficult, if not impossible, to determine whether management has, in fact, done a better job of inspecting the tank. Assigning a target date to this item merely confuses the issue:

"In 14 days, facility management will do a better job of inspecting the fuel tank."

The first question that comes to mind is, why not sooner? Opposing counsel might ask whether facility management purposely intended to do a substandard inspection for the two-week period. In order to correct this example, specification of exactly what will be done needs to be added to ensure an accurate understanding of the action and to be able to determine whether it was done:

"The SPCC Plan will be revised within 14 days to include daily inspections of the fuel tank."

One finding may necessitate multiple steps to rectify the original problem and prevent a recurrence. For instance, the fuel tank finding probably requires several additional steps, including removal and management of contaminated soil, getting the engineer's certification of the revised plan, and training facility personnel in the elements of the revised plan. There may also be a requirement to report a discharge to the governing agency. No matter how many steps are needed, each step should be identified and have its own target date assigned.

Actions as Data

In BFI's tracking system, all actions must have not only a text field used to describe the intended action, but also a target date for completion. The need to identify the action in specific, definable steps becomes quite apparent at this point, when a target date has to be identified. As discussed above, the action has to be defined in such a manner as to be able to show when it has been completed. In the earlier example of doing a "better job inspecting the fuel tank," there is no closure date that can define when this has been completed. On the other hand, a revision of an SPCC Plan is something that has a tangible date associated with its completion.

When an item has been completed, the actual completion date can be recorded along with the text description of the action taken. In this manner, each action is defined as being open or closed based on whether the completion date is recorded in the computer system.

Follow-Up Tracking

An important component of BFI's system to assure completion of action plans is a report of any open actions that is produced from the computer system and sent to the facility manager for obtaining status information. This report, called an Action Plan Status Report (APSR) is sent to the facility manager who is to identify actions completed (along with the actual date of completion) and the status of all other pending actions.

The APSR, with the facility manager's entries, is forwarded to that person's regional supervisor, who must also sign the report before returning it to the corporate office. In this manner, the facility manager's supervisor, who is in the best position to influence the objectives of the facility manager, is informed of the status of actions. The regional supervisor's signature is also meant to attest to the accuracy of the report and acknowledge that sufficient evidence exists to prove that the item was completed. The regional supervisor, therefore, becomes accountable for verification that the actions were implemented. Note that this process is subject to review by the environmental auditing department through repeat or verification audits as a quality assurance measure.

Following review of the signed APSR at the corporate office, data in the computer system is updated. If items remain to be completed, an additional APSR is sent out, and the process continues until all items have been completed.

Per Cent Completion Report

Most of the elements of BFI's audit program are fairly standard—when an audit is conducted, an action plan is produced, draft reports are reviewed prior to finalization, and status reports are produced that describe progress on the Action Plan. One area, however, in which audit programs are subject to failure (failure being defined as not completing all action items in a timely fashion) is where there is difficulty in communicating whether the items were completed. Anyone who has had to regularly review progress reports knows that they are often quite lengthy, usually quite technical, and almost always dry. Presenting the completion data in numerical form helps overcome the difficulties associated with the text descriptions.

To present this information, a one-page report titled the Per Cent Completion Report was developed that presents the following data for each individual audit:

- Total number of findings within each rank
- Total number of actions associated with those findings
- Percentage of total actions completed
- Percentage of actions that were completed within the target date set for their completion
- Total number of unfinished actions that have their target dates set within the next month and quarter

If any unfinished item is overdue (i.e., the target date has passed), it is specifically identified by its unique tracking number, ranking, target dates, and number of days overdue, along with a short text description of the intended action.

The Per Cent Completion Report can be produced for a single facility or for any pre-set grouping of facilities, such as by geographical region, business type (i.e., landfill, medical waste) or fiscal year. By grouping data, improvements in overall company performance can be quantified. When grouped reports are produced, senior management can receive a single-page report detailing the completion performance for each individual audit in that group. While the specificity of ranking is lost (i.e., only the total number of findings is presented), detailed knowledge of the plethora of regulations and requirements is not necessary in order to determine whether action was taken in a timely manner. Senior management receives a report in a language with which they are intimately familiar.

Response to this report has been remarkable due to its simplicity and numerous benefits. Management is able to quickly identify managers who need assistance or prodding to complete their action plans. Simply by presenting the items numerically as completed on time or not, managers who were and were not able to accurately define the time required to complete actions can be easily identified.

Managers always want to know how their audit compares to ones of other facilities. The Per Cent Completion Report gives a meaningful comparison of their abilities to design and implement the plan. Managers who perform well by completing their Action Plans on time can be recognized and rewarded. By lessening the importance of comparing the number of findings, a more open relationship can be cultivated between the auditor and the audited. Measuring managers on their ability to complete actions better supports the theme of continuous improvement, in that one should not be satisfied with having fewer than a threshold number of findings.

Compensation Tie-In

To amplify the importance of timely completion of all Action Plan items within BFI, regional management compensation has been tied to the on-time completion performance for the facilities in their region. Full compensation cannot be achieved without completing every action on or before its target date.[3] To prevent delays in the production of the Action Plan itself, the requirement for facility management to produce the draft Action Plan within thirty days is put into every Action Plan automatically by the Corporate Office. In this manner, anyone who delays submission of the plan itself cannot attain the desired 100 percent on-time completion performance, and full compensation cannot be achieved.

An additional report that has been developed uses the same data concerning action item target dates and their actual dates of completion, but expresses it as follows:

- total elapsed time to complete action items since the audit, and
- average number of days to finish the action items.

While this report has not yet enjoyed the same level of interest as the Per Cent Completion Report, it has been useful in demonstrating an overall shortening of the time taken for the company to complete its action plans. It has also provided management with data supporting how much time it should take to complete a particular set of actions. With this information, facility managers can be prevented from establishing action item target dates too far in the future.

Program Enhancements

Several aspects of BFI's tracking system have been identified for improvement. First, the updating system of action plans is somewhat cumbersome. It is paper-intensive, and as the updating report itself collects signatures as it is routed from the corporate office, to the facility, to the regional office, and back to the corporate office, several weeks can pass. Clearly, there is an opportunity for significant delay between the time an action is completed and the time its completion is reflected in the computer system. While steps have been taken to shorten the time taken to complete the loop, the optimum solution would enable data entry at the facility or regional level. Nevertheless, even when a facility manager gets management "attention" for the apparent failure to complete an action plan based on outdated data in the Per Cent Completion Report, three important goals are still achieved:

- The facility manager knows that someone is paying attention.
- During the resulting dialogue between the facility manager and superiors, the fact that the items were completed is communicated.
- The facility manager usually takes steps to ensure rapid completion of subsequent reports so as to avoid continued management "attention."

Feedback from managers involved in overseeing completion of action items has prompted the development of additional reports and data fields associated with the action items. In addition to tracking the projected and actual date of completion, the program is also able to track the estimated and actual work effort (in work-days) associated with an action item. With these data, it will be possible to compare managers not only on their ability to complete action items within a projected time frame, but also on their ability to successfully predict the cost and effort associated with action items. To date, insufficient data has been gathered to justify inclusion of cost and effort prediction success in the compensation system.

Lastly, in some specific circumstances, completion of an action item may indeed be outside the direct control of the facility manager. To enable communication of this circumstance, a data field was added that defines the action as internally controlled or as dependent on an external action (e.g., agency approval required before construction can commence).

Program Results

Since BFI began use of its computerized system for managing audit data, an improvement in overall company performance has been demonstrated. In landfill operations, audit results from 1991 to 1992 indicated the following:

- The average number of findings per facility has dropped from 17.3 to 9.4.
- There has been a shift away from the more serious regulatory findings.
- The incidence of on-time completion of action items has improved from 41 percent to 77 percent.

- The average number of days necessary to complete action plans has dropped from near two hundred to less than fifty.

Between 1992 and 1993, about a 6 percent improvement was demonstrated in on-time completion performance, and the reduced number of average days to complete action items in all business systems and the shift away from the more serious regulatory findings continued.

While many factors are certain to have contributed to this improvement in performance, the company's computerized tracking system and particularly the use of the Per Cent Completion Report are believed to have been important factors. Fundamentally, quantifying the improvements would not have been possible without use of the tracking system.

Notes

1. See: Environmental Auditing Roundtable Procedures Work Group 1990, "Guidelines for Written Environmental Audit Program Procedures;" Greeno, L., G. Hedstrom and M. DiBerto, Center for Environmental Assurance, Arthur D. Little, Inc. 1985. Environmental Auditing, Fundamentals and Techniques; Smith, A.C. 1991, "Continuous Improvement Through Environmental Auditing," in *Total Quality Environmental Management/Winter 1991/92,* page 121-129; Smith, A.C. and W.A. Yodis, Environmental Auditing Quality Management, Executive Enterprises Publications, 1989.

2. Environmental Auditing Roundtable, February 1993, Standards for Conducting Environmental, Health and Safety Audits. Contact the EAR at 12 Indian Head Road, Morristown, NJ 07960 for more information.

3. On Time Completion Performance is one aspect of the incentive compensation program. A discussion of this system can be found in "Evaluation of Facility Managers," B.A.Gantner, in *1992 Proceedings of Corporate Quality and Environmental Management, II,* Global Environmental Management Initiative, Washington, DC.

Curtis J. Johnson is divisional vice president of environmental, health, and safety auditing at Browning-Ferris Industries in Houston.

Appendix

federal register

Tuesday
June 21, 1994

Part IV

Environmental Protection Agency

Environmental Leadership Program;
Request for Pilot Project Proposals;
Notice

ENVIRONMENTAL PROTECTION AGENCY

[FRL-5001-5]

Environmental Leadership Program: Request for Pilot Project Proposals

AGENCY: Environmental Protection Agency (EPA).

ACTION: Request for Environmental Leadership Program pilot project proposals.

SUMMARY: This notice requests proposals for Environmental Leadership Program pilot projects, and outlines the criteria facilities must meet to be considered for participation. These pilot projects will explore ways that EPA and States might encourage facilities to develop innovative auditing and compliance programs and to reduce the risk of noncompliance through pollution prevention practices. In addition, the pilots will help EPA design a full-scale leadership program, and determine if implementing such a program can help improve environmental compliance. Any future full-scale leadership program based in the Office of Compliance will be consistent with the goals of the Administrator's Common Sense Initiative, which focuses on comprehensive environmental protection strategies for entire industry sectors.

These voluntary pilot projects will benefit the public by encouraging industry to take greater responsibility for self-monitoring, which will lead to improved compliance, pollution prevention, and environmental protection. The projects will benefit industry by providing an opportunity to receive recognition for outstanding environmental management practices and to address barriers to self-monitoring and compliance efforts. Finally, the projects will benefit government by strengthening Federal-State partnerships and allowing EPA to gather empirical data on environmental compliance methodology and measures.

EPA plans to select three to five (3-5) pilot projects. The pilots will be selected from the pool of proposals received based on how completely they address the seven criteria outlined in this notice, and their potential to demonstrate possible components of a full-scale leadership program. Depending on the level of interest in the projects, the quality of the proposals received, and available resources, the Agency may be willing to expand the pilot project phase to include additional projects.

DATES: Proposals for pilot projects will be accepted until August 22, 1994. Proposals will be reviewed on a rolling basis as they are received, with selection of the finalists in the fall of 1994.

ADDRESSES: Applicants should mail three (3) copies of their proposal and all required documentation to: U.S. Environmental Protection Agency (1102), Attn: Ira R. Feldman, ELP Pilot Project Director, 401 M Street SW, Washington, DC 20460. Facilities may submit their proposals directly to EPA after discussions with their State environmental agency, or to their State agency for forwarding to the EPA.

FOR FURTHER INFORMATION CONTACT: Ira R. Feldman, ELP Pilot Project Director, U.S. Environmental Protection Agency (1102), Office of Compliance, 401 M Street SW, Washington, DC 20460, phone (202) 260-7675, fax (202) 260-8511 or Mike Schiavo, U.S. Environmental Protection Agency (1102), 401 M Street SW, Washington, DC 20460, phone (202) 260-2824, fax (202) 260-8511.

I. Introduction

A. Original ELP Proposal

On January 15, 1993, EPA published a **Federal Register** notice (58 FR 4802) requesting comment on the possible creation of a national voluntary program to encourage and publicly recognize environmental leadership and to promote pollution prevention in the manufacturing sector. The Agency requested responses to 56 specific questions about the structure of such a program, possible goals and measures, the need for incentives, the role of compliance screening, and other related issues. Two basic components were proposed for the "Environmental Leadership Program" (ELP)—a "Corporate Statement of Environmental Principles" and a "Model Facility" Program.

The Agency received a wide variety of comments on the original proposal from industry, States, environmental groups, and other non-governmental organizations. In addition, the Agency held a public meeting on May 6, 1993 in Washington, DC and received additional comment from 30 groups. While no true consensus emerged on the best structure or goals for the program, the comments clearly indicated an interest in a voluntary program to recognize environmental excellence. (A summary of public comments is available from EPA upon request.) After extensive review and analysis of the comments by the Office of Enforcement, the Office of Pollution Prevention and Toxics, and the Administrator's Pollution Prevention Policy Staff, the Agency refined the goals and the immediate focus of the project.

B. Model Facility Pilot Projects

In the January 28, 1994 Federal Register (59 FR 4066), the Administrator announced EPA's intent to further develop the ELP concept, initially through a small number (3-5) of voluntary, facility-based pilot projects. The new Office of Compliance (OC), within the reorganized Office of Enforcement and Compliance Assurance (OECA), will coordinate the "model facility" pilot project effort with significant Regional and State partner involvement. At the same time, EPA opted not to further develop its own "corporate State-ment of Environmental Principles," but rather to work cooperatively with organizations that have developed their own corporate or industry-specific codes. (The Office of Pollution Prevention and Toxics will continue to lead any future Agency involvement in this area.)

This *pilot project* effort is distinguished from a possible future, *full-scale* Environmental Leadership Program. A major goal of the pilot projects is to further explore possible compo-nents of a full-scale program. Options were raised during public comment last year on various program elements, including the review and selection process, recognition mechanisms, and other possible incentives for facilities. The pilot projects will explore these options, and will have a definite life span of about 12-18 months. At the end of this time, EPA will determine if a full-scale program is feasible, and if implementing such a program can help improve environmental compliance.

The pilot projects, therefore, represent the experimental first step in the evolution of the ELP. The pilot phase is also an excellent opportunity to strengthen partnerships between government, industry groups, and regulated entities as a prelude to more extensive emphasis by the Agency on voluntary compliance initiatives. The pilot projects, and any future leadership program, will be a vehicle for facilities to continue building positive, proactive relationships with EPA and State and local agencies

C. Benefits to Pilot Project Participants

EPA foresees a number of potential benefits to facilities that are selected for pilot projects. The Agency will publicly recognize these facilities that demonstrate outstanding environmental management practices, and also provide them with an opportunity to help shape the possible future, full-scale leadership program. EPA will use the pilot projects to evaluate recognition mechanisms and other incentives that could be offered in a full-scale program. While mechanisms for recognition will be determined in discussions with each facility, they may include press releases, letters to community groups, local and State agencies, and/or site visits by EPA officials. It is important to note that any future program would offer recognition and other incentives on a continuing basis (similar to the OSHA Voluntary Protection Program), not as a one-time award.

The pilots represent an opportunity for facilities to inform and directly participate in EPA's effort to reassess its environmental auditing policy. In addition, it is anticipated that the projects selected will generate empirical data useful for evaluating EPA's compliance policies and spur the development of method-ologies for evaluating compliance behavior. Finally, EPA is interested in discussing possible policy modifications and other incentives that could help facilities overcome barriers to self-monitoring and compliance efforts. Facilities should address this issue in their proposals for pilot projects. Proposals should focus on incentives that can be offered by EPA's Office of Enforcement and Compli-ance Assurance under existing law using administrative authority or policies that lie clearly within OECA's jurisdiction. Proposals to change statutory deadlines, amend environ-mental standards, or that require actions by other agencies are not appropriate for this program.

The remainder of this notice will outline the

criteria facilities must address in their proposal to be considered for a pilot project, briefly outline the role of States and EPA Regions, and discuss the proposal review and selection process.

II. Criteria for Facility Pilot Projects

The following criteria for pilot projects were developed in response to extensive public comment on the original ELP proposal. In this phase of the ELP, facilities of all types, including small businesses, municipalities, and Federal facilities,[1] are encouraged to submit proposals for pilot projects that address these criteria. Each criterion must be addressed in some way in the proposal; however, facilities may choose to emphasize individual criteria that are appropriate to their unique situation in setting specific goals for a pilot project.

A. Compliance History

EPA believes that the greatest potential for the pilot projects is to demonstrate "state-of-the-art" environmental management systems that establish and maintain compliance with environmental statutes and regulations. These systems, when combined with an emphasis on pollution prevention, can lead to improved efficiencies that help facilities exceed minimum compliance standards. To be selected to participate in a pilot project, facilities must demonstrate a commitment to compliance. Therefore, facility proposals must describe their local, State, and Federal compliance

---

[1] The Federal Facilities Enforcement Office (FFEO) is developing a "Federal Government Environmental Challenge Program," as required under Section 4-405 of Executive Order 12856. This section of the Executive Order requires EPA to develop a Code of Environmental Management Principles for Federal agencies, a program to recognize individual Federal facilities as "Model Installations," and an award system for individual leadership in pollution prevention. For more information on the Model Installation Program, please contact Louis Paley at (703) 308-8723, or (202) 260-8790.

Since the Federal facility Model Installation program is still in its early stages, Federal facilities may submit proposals for ELP pilot projects. The Office of Compliance and FFEO will work together to use these proposals, and any subsequent Federal facility pilot projects, to help develop the Model Installation program and to ensure that it is consistent with any future, full-scale ELP.

history, explain how they have resolved compliance issues in the past, what they Are doing to address any outstanding compliance issues, and how they are trying to position themselves to go beyond compliance.

B. Environmental Management and Auditing Programs

Industry leaders have long recognized the value of self-auditing for environmental compliance and the need to have processes and personnel in place to achieve compliance goals. Facilties applying to the ELP must describe their existing or proposed environmental management and auditing programs, their systems to resolve issues raised by these programs in a timely manner, and their systems to evaluate and adjust these programs on a regular basis. One of the major goals of implementing these management systems and auditing programs should be to move the facility into compliance and position it to go beyond compliance.

Guidance on environmental auditing and state-of-the-art environmental management practices is available from many sources. As a starting point, EPA refers potential pilot participants to the following sources.

• The EPA Environmental Auditing Policy Statement (**Federal Register**, July 9, 1986) which includes a discussion of elements of an effective auditing program:

• The "Draft Corporate Sentencing Guidelines for Environmental Violations," (*BNA Environment Reporter*, 11/26/93), which includes a discussion of "Minimum Factors for Demonstrating a Commitment to Environmental Compliance" in Part D.

Voluntary standards on environmental management systems and environmental auditing may also provide guidance to facilities interested in preparing pilot project proposals. EPA is participating in work groups organized by the International Organization for Standards (ISO) and the National Sanitation Foundation (NSF International). The American Society for Testing and Materials (ASTM) is coordinating U.S. participation in ISO Technical Committee 207 (TC-207) on environmental management systems (EMS). Contacts for these organizations are listed at the end of this notice.

Similarly, EPA is aware that initiatives such as the Global Environmental Management

Initiative (GEMI), the Responsible Care Program, and the CERES Principles have been developed in the private sector and by non-governmental groups. These and other private sector efforts may be useful for facilities interested in submitting pilot proposals, and facilities are encouraged to develop proposals with industry and trade association involvement and support.

C. Disclosure of Audit Results

EPA is currently reevaluating its environmental auditing policy and will take an empirical approach so that any decision to either reinforce or change existing policy is informed by fact. The ELP pilot projects may generate useful data on auditing methodology and measures, and may serve as a vehicle for experimenting with policy-driven incentives.

EPA is particularly interested in examining how disclosure of audit results could improve the public's confidence in and acceptance of industry's self-monitoring efforts, and how disclosure could help facilitate the flow of information to the personnel responsible for implementing audit recommendations. Facilities applying to the ELP must demonstrate a willingness to disclose in some manner the results of their audits. EPA recognizes the controversial nature of this issue, and for that reason wants to explore the potential benefits and perceived risks of disclosure in the context of the pilot projects.

As part of their proposals, therefore, facilities should suggest the type and extent of information they would be willing to disclose, the mechanisms they would use to disclose the information, the parties to whom they would disclose that information, and finally, any conditions they would seek from regulators in order to make the disclosure. Proposed incentives should be limited to items that can be offered by EPA's Office of Enforcement and Compliance Assurance under existing law using administrative authority or policies that lie clearly within OECA's jurisdiction. Proposals to change statutory deadlines, amend environmental standards, or that require actions by other agencies are not appropriate for this program.

D. Pollution Prevention Activities

EPA's new Office of Compliance is

organized principally around economic sectors, in order to support integrated approaches to compliance that promote pollution prevention as a means of meeting environmental requirements and realizing environmental improvements. Facilities must describe their existing or proposed comprehensive, multimedia pollution prevention program that is integrated into their overall operations. In describing this program, facilities should include descriptions of their pollution prevention program that is integrated into their overall operations. In describing this program, facilities should include descriptions of their pollution prevention planning process, their State pollution prevention plan (if required, see "Other Required Documentation," below), their systems for implementing pollution prevention projects, how resources are allocated to pollution prevention, and how they measure pollution prevention progress. At a minimum, facilities should include the two-year projection of waste generation required by the Pollution Prevention Act and their RCRA waste minimization certification (see "Other Required Documentation" below).

E. Setting an Example

Facilities must show that they are currently using, or would be willing to use, their auditing, pollution prevention, and/or other environmental management programs as models or benchmarks for other facilities within their company or industry, or for their customers, suppliers, and contractors. EPA recognizes that there may be many mechanisms for doing this, and that confidentiality issues may limit the amount of information and technology facilities are able to share. Given these conditions, facilities must propose how they would help others learn from their experiences and the type and extent of information they would be willing to share

F. Performance Measures

Good environmental management systems set performance objectives, and measure and report on progress toward those goals. While EPA recognizes that there are many possible measures of environmental performance, at the pilot project stage the Office of Compliance is primarily interested in developing methodologies that can demonstrate and measure compliance success and pollution prevention results, as complements to the traditional enforcement measures of actions and penalties. Therefore, facilities must propose quantitative and/or qualitative measures that will track the compliance improvements and pollution prevention results that would accrue from their participation in a pilot project. Facilities must also include brief descriptions of additional performance objectives that they are striving to meet, and of the systems they use to track and monitor progress toward these goals. Any future, full-scale leadership program will attempt to incorporate overall measures of environmental management performance, in addition to measures of compliance and pollution prevention.

G. Employee and Community Involvement

Sensitivity and responsiveness to employee and community concerns is a key component of environmental leadership. In proposals for the ELP, facilities must demonstrate that their employees and their communities are involved in developing and implementing their environmental management programs, and should suggest mechanisms (for example, employee interviews, interviews with local Emergency Planning Commission (LEPCs), etc.) which can be used to verify this involvement.

III. Other Required Documentation

Facilities should include in their proposal the information they deem necessary to address the criteria outlined above, and the following required information:

• Contact person, mailing address, telephone number, and fax number.

• Company and/or facility environmental policy statement.

• State pollution prevention plan, if required under State law, in summary form.

• RCRA waste minimization certification, in summary form.

• Toxic Release Inventory (TRI) and Pollution Prevention Act (PPA) data, all available years, in summary form.

• A brief summary of participation in other EPA or State voluntary programs.

• While not required to do so, facilities may attach additional *summary* information related to the criteria outlined above that may help

EPA evaluate their proposal.

IV. Suggested Proposal Format

In order to expedite the proposal review and selection process, EPA suggests that facilities use the following format to organize their proposals:

Section 1—Table of Contents, 1 page.

Section 2—Executive Summary, 1-2 pages.

Section 3—Main Narrative, organized by the seven criteria and containing a clear statement of pilot project goals, 25-30 pages maximum.

Section 4—Exhibits and Attachments, 25-30 pages.

Section 5—Bibliography of Supporting Material, including a *list* of local, State, and Federal permits, and a *list* of applicable Federal technology-based standards, 3-5 pages.

V. Role of the States

States have been invited to work in partnership with EPA in the pilot project phase; the pilots will be more likely to succeed if EPA and States work in concert. EPA recognizes that States' level of involvement may vary according to available resources. The Agency strongly encourages candidate facilities to contact their State environmental agency as soon as possible to express their intention to prepare a pilot project proposal, and to begin discussions about the State's role, including opportunities to build on existing partnerships and programs. Strong proposals will include documentation showing that the proposal has been reviewed, sponsored, or endorsed by the appropriate State agency.

Recognizing the valuable role of States as laboratories for new approaches to environmental protection., EPA is eager to have significant State participation in the pilot effort. A number of States have already expressed interest in working with EPA to further develop the ELP concept. As of the date of this notice, the following States have approached EPA and offered to work as partners in the pilot project effort:

• Alaska
• Arizona
• Massachusetts
• New York
• North Carolina
• Washington

Contact people for these States are listed below.

EPA has invited *all* States to participate in the ELP, and is actively working to build additional partnerships. Facilities in States not listed here are encouraged to contact their State environmental agency as soon as possible to express their intention to prepare a pilot project proposal, and to begin discussions about the State's role, including opportunities to build on existing partnerships and programs. EPA recognizes that States may not be able to, or may choose not to, become involved in the pilot project phase. The Agency will keep all States informed of the status of the pilot projects on a regular basis, and, during the next phase of the projects, will convene a workshop to discuss the pilot experience, ideas for launching a possible full-scale leadership program, and other ideas for further expanding the leadership/excellence concept.

VI. Role of EPA Regions

EPA Regions have also been invited by the Office of Compliance to participate in the pilot project effort. In this phase of the ELP, Regional involvement may vary according to available resources. At a minimum, Regions will play a role in the screening and review of proposals. Through the pilot projects, EPA hopes to more accurately gauge the level of resources necessary for Regional participation in any future full-scale program.

Each Region's ELP contact is listed below. Interested facilities should contact their Region as soon as possible to express their intention to prepare a pilot project proposal, and to begin discussions about the Region's role, including opportunities to build on existing partnerships and programs. More general questions about the ELP pilot project phase should be directed to the Headquarters contacts listed at the beginning of this notice.

VII. Proposal Review and Selection Process

Facilities may submit their proposals directly to EPA after discussions with their State environmental agency, or to their State agency for forwarding to EPA. The ELP pilot project team will be using an expedited process—in partnership with EPA Regional Offices, State environmental agencies, and other OECA offices—to review proposals and to select the pilot participants. Pilot projects will be selected from the pool of proposals received based on how completely they address the seven criteria outlined above, and their potential to demonstrate possible components of a full-scale leadership program.

Proposals for the initial group of pilots will be accepted for 60 days from the publication of this notice, and reviewed on a rolling basis. Final selections will be announced in the Fall of 1994. The pilot projects will have a definite life-span, most likely 12-18 months. At the end of this time, EPA will evaluate their success and determine if a full-scale leadership program is feasible, and if such a program can help improve environmental compliance.

Dated: June 14, 1994.

Steven A. Herman
Assistant Administrator, Office of Enforcement and Compliance Assurance.

EPA Regional Contacts for ELP Pilot Project Proposals

Region 1
Joel Blumstein, Office of Regional Counsel, Phone (617) 565-3693.

Region 2
Gary Nurkin, Office of the Deputy Regional Counsel, Phone (212) 264-5341.

Region 3
Bill Reilly, Office of Program Integration, Phone (215) 597-9302.

Region 4
Sheila Hollimon, Enforcement Planning and Analysis Staff, Phone (404) 347-7109.

Region 5
To be determined.

Region 6
To be determined.

Region 7
To be determined.

Region 8

Mike Gaydosh, Office of the Regional Administrator, Phone (303) 294-7005.

Region 9

Fred Leif, Office of the Regional Administrator, Phone (415) 744-1017.

Region 10

Barbara Lither, Office of the Regional Administrator, Phone (206) 553-1191.

State Contacts for ELP Pilot Project Proposals

(As of the date of this notice.)

Alaska

David Wigglesworth, Pollution Prevention Office , Alaska Department of Environmental Conservation, 3601 C Street, Suite 1334, Anchorage, AK 99503, Phone (907) 273-4303; Fax (907) 562-4026.

Arizona

Beverly Westgaard, Arizona Department of Environmental Quality, 3033 N Central Ave., Phoenix, AZ 85012, Phone (602) 207-4249; Fax (602) 207-4346.

Massachusetts

Patricia Deese Stanton, Assistant Commissioner, Massachusetts Department of Environmental Protection, One Winter Street, Boston, MA 02108, Phone (617) 292-5765; Fax (617) 292-5500.

New York

Frank Bifera, Division of Environmental Enforcement, New York Department of Environmental Conservation, 50 Wolf Road, Albany, NY 12233, Phone (518) 457-2286; Fax (518) 485-8478.

North Carolina

Linda Bray Rimer, Assistant Secretary for Environmental Protection, North Carolina Department of Environment, Health, & Natural Resources, 3825 Barnett Drive, P.O. Box 27687, Raleigh, NC 27611-7687, Phone (919) 715-4140; Fax (919) 715-6902.

Washington

John Williams, Agency Enforcement Officer, Washington Department of Ecology, P.O. Box 47703, Olympia, WA 98504-7703, Phone (206) 407-6968; Fax (206) 407-6902.

Other Contacts

National and International Standard Setting Efforts

Mary McKiel, Director, EPA Voluntary Standards Network, Office of Pollution Prevention and Toxics (7401), U.S. EPA, 401 M Street, SW., Washington, DC 20460.

International Organization for Standards (ISO), U.S. SubTAG for ISO-TC-207: Environmental Auditing. Write to: Mr. Cornelius C. (Bud) Smith, Principal, ENVIRON Corporation, 210 Carnegie Center, Princeton, NJ 08540.

International Organization for Standards (ISO), U.S. SubTAG for ISO-TC-207: Environmental Management Systems. Write to: Mr. Joel Charm, Director: Health, Safety and Environmental, Allied Signal, Inc., P.O. Box 1013, Morristown, NJ 07692.

National Sanitation Foundation (NSF). Write to: Mr. Gordon Bellen, Vice President, NSF International, 3475 Plymouth Road, P.O. Box 130140, Ann Arbor, MI 48113-0140.

American Society for Testing and Materials (ASTM). Write to: Rose Tomasello, 1916 race Street, Philadelphia, PA 19103.

Federal Government Environmental Challenge Program: Model Installation Program

Louis Paley, Office of Federal Facilities Enforcement (2261), U.S. EPA, 401 M Street SW., Washington, DC 20460. Phone (703) 308-8723, or (202) 260-8790.

EPA Common Sense Initiative

Steve Harper, Office of Air and Radiation (6101), U.S. EPA, 401 M Street SW., Washington, DC 20460. Phone (202) 260-8953.

Vivian Daub, Office of water (4101), U.S. EPA, 401 M Street SW., Washington, DC 20460. Phone (202) 260-6790.

[FR Doc. 94-14949 Filed 6-20-94; 8:45 am]
BILLING CODE 6560-50-P

Appendix

Environmental Leadership Program: Update
Vol. 59, No. 019
59 FR 4066
Friday, January 28, 1994

AGENCY: ENVIRONMENTAL PROTECTION AGENCY (EPA)
DOC TYPE: Notices
NUMBER: FRL-4831-1

WORD COUNT: 611
TEXT:
EPA announces the next steps in the development of the Environmental Leadership Program (ELP). After reviewing many possible options, the Agency has decided to proceed with pilot projects to test the feasibility of a voluntary program to recognize industrial facilities. The pilots will explore ways to encourage facilities to develop innovative audit and compliance programs and to reduce the risk of non-compliance through pollution prevention practices.

The wide variety of public comments on the original ELP proposal (published in the Federal Register on January 15, 1993) clearly indicated an interest in a program to recognize and encourage "environmental excellence." While no true consensus emerged on the best structure or goals for the program, several themes were common to the majority of the comments:

EPA should encourage companies and facilities of all sizes and from all industries to participate in the program.

EPA should focus its program on individual facilities rather than on entire corporations.

Any EPA-developed statement of environmental principles would duplicate existing private-sector efforts and would be difficult to enforce.

In response to these comments, EPA has decided to continue developing a voluntary, facility-based program. The Agency will develop pilot projects with specific industries and states to evaluate the many unresolved issues raised during the comment period. These include a possible multiple-tier structure to encourage broad participation, determining the role of compliance, self-reporting of violations, public accountability, the role of incentives in encouraging companies to exceed minimum requirements, and how pollution prevention practices can help facilities reduce or avoid the risk of non-compliance.

EPA Deputy Administrator Bob Sussman and Steve Herman, the Assistant Administrator for the Office of Enforcement and Compliance Assurance (OECA) have been asked to coordinate this effort. The Agency will provide more information on the process for selecting pilot participants and on the development of test projects in the early spring of 1994. The Office of Compliance within OECA will be responsible for this process. Please call Mike Schiavo at (202) 260-2824 for more information.

Also in response to the comments, the Agency has concluded that it will not issue its own guidelines for corporate environmental principles, but rather work cooperatively with the many other organizations that have developed corporate and industry-wide codes of environmental conduct. The Office of Pollution Prevention and Toxics will take responsibility for representing the Agency in this area, and for ensuring the involvement of other EPA offices where appropriate. Please call David Kling at (202) 260-3557 for more information. EPA thanks all of those who have expressed an interest in the ELP concept {pg 4067} and looks forward to making this program an exciting and effective approach to pollution prevention and compliance.

Dated: January 14, 1994.

Carol M. Browner,

Administrator.

INTERNAL DATA: FR Doc. 94-1953; Filed 1-27-94; 8:45 am; BILLING CODE 6560-50-P

Appendix

Environmental Laedership Program:
Extension of Deadline for Pilot Project Proposals

AGENCY: Environmental Protection Agency (EPA).

ACTION: Notice of extension of deadline for submission of Environmental Leadership Program pilot project proposals.

SUMMARY: This notice extends the deadline for the submission of Environmental Leadership (ELP) pilot project proposals by 30 days. The new deadline is Wednesday, September 21, 1994.

ADDRESSES: Applicants should mail three (3) copies of their proposal and all required documentation to: U.S. Environmental Protection Agency (1102), Attn: Ira R. Feldman, ELP Pilot Project Director, 401 M Street, SW, Washington, DC 20460. Applicants may submit their proposals directly to EPA after discussions with their State environmental agency, or to their State agency for forwarding to EPA.

FOR FURTHER INFORMATION: For additional information about the ELP pilot project effort, see the June 21, 1994 Federal Register notice entitled "Environmental Leadership Program: Request for Pilot Project Proposals" (59 F.R. 32062).

SUPPLEMENTARY INFORMATION: For the convenience of interested parties, EPA REgion and State contacts for ELP pilot project proposals are listed below.

EPA Region Contacts

Region 1
Joel Blumstein, Phone (617) 565-3693.

Region 2
Gary Nurkin, Phone (212) 264-5341.

Region 3
Bill Reilly, Phone (215) 597-9302.

Region 4
Shelia Hollimon, Phone (404) 347-3555, extension 6776.

Region 5
Jeff Bratko, Phone (312) 886-6816.

Region 6
John Hepola, Phone (214) 665-7220.

Region 7
Jim Callier, Phone (913) 551-7646.

Region 8
Mike Risner, Phone (303) 294-7583.

Region 9
Fred Leif, Phone (415) 744-1017.

Region 10
Barbara Lither, Phone (206) 553-1191.

State Contacts

(The following are the State partners that were listed in the June 21, 1994 Federal Register.)

Alaska. David Wigglesworth, Pollution Prevention Office, Alaska Department of Environmental Conservation, 3601 C Street, Suite 1334, Anchorage, AK 99503, Phone (907) 273-4303.

Arizona. Beverly Westgaard, Arizona Department of Environmental Quality, 3033 N Central Ave., Pheonix, AZ 85012, Phone (602) 207-4249.

Massachusetts. Debra Gallagher, Massachusetts Department of Environmental Protection, One Winter Street, Boston, MA 02108, Phone (617) 292-5572.

New York. Frank Bifera, Division of Environmental Enforcement, New York Department of Environmental Conservation, 50 Wolf Road, Albany 12233, Phone (518) 457-2286.

North Carolina. Linda Bray Rimer, Assistant Secretary for Environmental Protection, North Carolina Department of Environment, Health, & Natural Resources, 3825 Barnett Drive, P.O. Box 27687, Raleigh, NC 27611-7687, Phone (919) 715-4140.

Washington. John Williams, Agency Enforcement Officer, Washington Department of Ecology, P.O. Box 47703, Olympia, WA 98504-7703, Phone (206) 407-6968.

Additional State Contacts

(The following States have designated contact people for the ELP pilot projects subsequent to the publication of the June 21, 1994 Federal Register notice.)

Alabama. Dan Cooper, Alabama Department of Environmental Management, P.O. Box 301463, Montgomery, AL 36130-1463, Phone (205) 260-2779.

California. Jim Morgester, California Air Resources Board, 2020 L Street, P.O. Box 2815, Sacramento, CA 95812, Phone (916) 322-6022.

Louisiana. Gary Johnson, Louisiana Department of Environmental Quality, P.O. Box 82263, Baton Rouge, LA 70884-2263, Phone (504) 765-0739.

Maryland. Liz Taddeo, Maryland Department of the Environment, 2500 Broening Highway, Baltimore, MD 21224, (410) 631-3144.

Michigan. Paul Zugger, Michigan Department of Natural Resources, P.O. Box 30028, Lansing, MI 48909, Phone (517) 373-1449.

New Jersey. John Spinello, New Jersey Department of Environmental Protection, 401 East State Street, CN422, Trenton, NJ 08625, Phone (609) 984-3588.

Ohio. Bill Narotski, Ohio EPA, Office of Pollution Prevention, P.O. Box 163669, Columbus, OH 43216-3669, Phone (614) 644-3173.

Pennsylvania. Meredith Hill, Pennsylvania Department of Environmental Resources, Box 8472, Harrisburg, PA 17105-8472, Phone (717) 787-7382.

South Carolina. Neal Hunter, South Carolina Department of Health and Environmental Control, 2600 Bull Street, Columbia, SC 29201, Phone (803) 734-5254.

Virginia. Rich Jefferson, Virginia Department of Natural Resources, Box 1745, Richmond, VA 23212, Phone (804) 786-0044.

Wisconsin. Tom Eggert, Wisconsin Department of Natural Resources, 101 South Webster Street, Box 7921, Madison, WI 53707, Phone (608) 267-9700.

Steven A. Herman
Assistant Administrator
Office of Enforcement and Compliance Assurance

Index

Total cost assessment, full cost accounting and, described, 115

Total Quality Environmental Management (TQEM):
auditing evaluation, 249-250
competition and, 108
Eco-label and Audit Scheme, 76
implementation of, 121-135
customer/stakeholder satisfaction, 133-134
environmental results, 133
generally, 121-122
guidelines for, 122-128
human resources development, 131-132
information and analysis, 129-130
leadership and, 128-129
quality assurance, 132-133
strategic planning, 131
information technology and, 273-280. See also Information technology
management system audits and, 14, 23, 31, 51
measurement data classification, 137-146. See also Measurement data classification
root cause analysis and, 176. See also Root cause analysis
site assessment, 199-210. See also Site assessment
voluntary standards for, 93-104. See also Voluntary standards

Toxic Release Inventory, quality metrics and, 155

Toxic Substances Control Act (TSCA), 257

Training:
auditing improvement strategy, 244
auditor qualifications, 189-190

management system audits, 35

Treadway Commission. See National Commission on Fraudulent Financial Reporting (Treadway Commission)

Treaty of Rome (1957), 69

Trend analysis, automated tools, 286

Underwood, Richard, 275-287

Union Carbide, 77, 225-232
audit process, 228-231
Audit Timeliness Index, 227-228
follow-up, 231-232
overview of, 225-226
preparation, 226
protocols, 226-227

United Kingdom, 67

United Nations Cleaner Production Program, Eco-label and Audit Scheme, 75

U.S. Department of Justice:
enforcement policies of, 31, 34, 80
guidelines of, 23

U.S. Environmental Protection Agency (EPA, US). See also Environmental Leadership Program (ELP, EPA, US)
benchmarking, 166
compliance cost estimates of, 107
Comprehensive Environmental Response, Compensation, and Liability Act (CERCLA), 260-262
cost accounting systems and, 115
enforcement policies of, 31
environmental auditing and, 80
Environmental Auditing Roundtable standards, 264
Environmental Excellence program, 23